STRENGTH COACH
A CALL TO SERVE

JEFF CONNORS, MS, MSCC

EDITED BY BETHANY BRADSHER

Cover photo by Theo Parker.
Cover and interior design by Stephanie Whitlock Dicken.
Photo on page 63 is courtesy of ECU News Bureau.
Photos on page 89, 134, 136, 138, 141, 145, 147, 148, 150,
152, 154, 157, 219 are courtesy of ECU Media Relations.
Photos on page 93, 140,143, 153 are courtesy of UNC Media Relations.
Photos on pages 159, 161 are courtesy of ECU Alumni Association.

Scripture references throughout the book come from www.biblegateway.com.
All rights reserved worldwide.

DEDICATION

When an individual makes a decision to enter the world of coaching, he locks himself and everyone around him into an unpredictable rollercoaster ride of twists and turns and ups and downs. Wives and children have to be prepared to leave friends, schools, job and sometimes what they had considered to be a happy, healthy, comfortable environment.

A coach understands that the people who were once considered his strongest supporters—and even friends—could become his biggest critics and sources of energy toward change. It's a lot tougher for women and small children to experience that realization. They're just trying to be happy. They come to the games to cheer for your team, they interact with the other coaches' families and they innocently view the celebration of a win as something perpetual. Kids aren't built for a preparedness toward the consequences of possible failure. They don't think in these terms. It's hard for them to even understand at times the way you might react to losing a game. They just want you to be happy, too.

I've had a very fortunate career, and I never chose the quest to maintain a constant network of contacts in case I had to field new job offers every January. That being said, I still somehow ended up with a three-hour commute to see my family for four years. That situation was the result of an attempt to protect them from the upcoming storm of change. In retrospect, it was not the best plan.

This book is dedicated to my wife, Michele, my son Beau and my daughter Kaitlin. My initial intention in writing this book was to simply provide them with a record of my career, which ended up being their life experiences. I want them to understand more about what I saw, how I thought and why at times I was no doubt tough to live with. I want them to remember the successes and to know that those were their accomplishments, because they were always a part of the team. They have been my rock and source of security through times of uncertainty. My most treasured memories are their happy smiles and laughter in celebrating the good times.

INTRODUCTION

Everyone has a highway to travel in life, and mine has seldom been without obstacles to negotiate.

When you reflect on some of the turns you could have easily chosen that would have sent you over a cliff, you know that God has had His hand on you. That being said, I think you have to reciprocate the good fortune by bringing something deliberate into your daily walk that enriches someone else's life.

I went through several decades of life's experiences in a state of cluelessness toward what I was called to do. Most of the time I just thought about how many ways I could selfishly enjoy my time. Serving others was probably not in the forefront of my thoughts. I would rather have thought about how I might compete with people and find a way to let them know I was willing to go to any extent to elevate my personal status. I got tied up in the fact I needed to improve my income, no matter how many hours I had to be away from my family. The only person I was truly serving was myself. After all, how many of us genuinely believe that giving is the key to receiving? Luke 6:38 says, "Give and you will be given to. Good measure pressed down, shaken together, running over, will be put into your lap. For with the measure you use, it will be measured back to you." This is not an extremely confusing passage. It indicates that you will receive significantly above what you were willing to give.

Every time you stand in front of a group of young athletes, you need to think about the words that you are about to speak. Your platform is much larger than it feels. If you have earned the respect of your players, chances are they will listen to your voice. Your words will resonate even deeper as they sense that you speak truthfully and you see yourself as the means to their goals. Proverbs 20:5 speaks to the responsibility of the coach to the player: "The purposes of a man's heart are deep waters, but a man of understanding draws them out."

The "heart" of a young athlete in 2013 is deep water indeed. What you see on the surface is many times not even close to the inner turmoil hidden within the substance of the soul. You can reference fatherlessness, poverty, exposure to drugs and alcohol, mental health or the influence of peers. The bottom line is that most young athletes have a list of insecurities well concealed beneath a huge stature and a tough demeanor.

As a coach you must be a master of recognizing and bringing to the forefront the intricacies regarding one's potential. You will never have a chance of accomplishing that if you don't develop excellent communication skills. Not only that, but you must deal with them in sound doctrine and lifelong principles with lasting impressions. You must become a man of accomplished understanding. I Peter 4:10 says, "As each has received a gift, use it to serve one another, as good stewards of God's varied grace."

A master coach should possess the following qualities:

1. Caring
2. Guidance with integrity and skillfulness
3. Ability to provide clarity
4. Ability to relate principles of truth
5. Refusal to use players as a means to his ends
6. An uplifting mentality
7. The attitude of a servant
8. Commitment to pouring his experiences into his players

When these characteristics are in place, the athlete is obligated to return a level of trust and respect. He sees the coach as a master in his field. The relationship is free from bitterness, animosity, deception and negativity. Communication must be constant and truthful. The athlete needs to know where he stands so he has a plan of development and a sense of peace and direction.

One of the primary areas of concern with athletes is playing time. Whether the individual is limited or possibly in some respect undiscovered, he had expectations for himself when he entered the program. You might have a number of scholarship players in your program who work hard and do everything right, but for some reason they haven't seen the field on game day. Sometimes a player gets a stamp on his forehead that is never erased. I've seen some young men through my career who were in the wrong position, or were backing up a great player, or were on the wrong side of the ball. Finally, after a long sequence of events, they got to see the field for part of their senior season and then somehow ended up playing in the NFL.

Somewhere through the recruiting process, someone evaluated that individual as being potentially a good-enough athlete to contribute to the future of the program. If the individual hasn't received playing time, and has no discipline issues, the coaches have the obligation to go the extra mile to recognize the sometimes-hidden potential that exists within that player.

From another perspective, the responsibility you hold as a strength and conditioning coach reaches vastly beyond an effective training program. You have an opportunity to impact the self-discipline level of every athlete in the room. The best way to serve them is to hold their feet to the fire and refuse to let go. There will be a certain number of athletes from every recruiting class who will not make it unless you raise their ability to make the right choices and somehow define the value of strength of character.

Service is not always pretty. It might be disguised as harshness or excessive demands. When you discover that you are called to serve others, particularly young men who happen to be collegiate football players, you will be challenged. The challenge will be in establishing a significant level of rapport. If your athletes believe that you have a genuine goal of serving their best interests, you will have a chance to impact them at the highest level. Remember the words of Shirley Chisholm: "Service is the rent we pay for the privilege of living on this earth."

CONTENTS

CHAPTER ONE

COAL MINES AND BILLY BALL

My hometown of Brownsville, Pennsylvania is nestled in the heart of coal country, along the Monongahela River. Mining was in my bloodlines; both of my grandfathers—one a full-blooded Irishman and one a German who only learned English when he enrolled in school—toiled in the mines and passed along a heritage of hard work and toughness.

My Irish grandfather, Martin Connors Sr., passed away when he was just 57, too early for me to really get to know him. But my father and his brothers were living examples of what he stood for— they loved their family, poured their heart into everything they did, fought for their beliefs at the drop of a hat and shared an appreciation for a cold beer.

Life in a company town, in the neighborhood known as "The Patch," was simple but fulfilling for my father and his family. The mining company owned your house, and any food or supplies you purchased from the company store came directly out of your check. Employees like my grandfather could pocket whatever was left, but it wasn't much. For a mining family to make it through the Pennsylvania winter, a vegetable garden and an efficient kitchen canning operation were necessities.

The Patch, which was little more than a few rows of identical company-owned houses, had only one class of people. They all worked hard and struggled to make ends meet, sharing joys, sorrows, challenges and opportunities. Some byproducts of that lifestyle were the value of strong friendships (helping your neighbor was essential for survival) and the priority of athletics as a diversion from the serious pursuit of toiling in the mine. The intensity of surviving the long days underground transferred to the athletic fields, amplifying the competitiveness in The Patch beyond that of a typical sports community.

There was no specific training regimen in that town, but fitness and nutrition were valued there nonetheless. With no air conditioning or television, the kids spent all of their time playing outside, and doing manual labor like shoveling snow and carrying burlap sacks full of coal made for some strong boys. It wasn't uncommon for young athletes from The Patch to lift a railroad tie or pick up a car by its bumper; they were freakish. A local Boy Scout leader, Cokie Gemas, was known for instilling strong character and toughness in that group of boys. Gemas would encourage the boys to fight it out—wearing 16-ounce boxing gloves—when they had a conflict.

Wild Billy

My dad, William Connors, was the single-most competitive individual I have ever known. He grew up in the life-or-death mentality of the mining culture, and when he became a high school football coach, he brought that ethos with him to the gridiron. He is evidence of the theory that sports in western Pennsylvania stands as a microcosm of life and a dramatization of the immigrant experience.

Even though life was a daily struggle in The Patch, my father's memories of his childhood there were happy. No one locked their doors, and it was no big deal to walk into someone else's house like you were family. The people there even had a name for the way they drew strength from community—they called it "Patch love."

They played together on the town baseball team and spaded a garden together if one family had a need. When the work was done, they celebrated by swimming across the Monongahela.

My grandfathers were both only twelve years old when they started working in the mines, and the things they saw and experienced are hard to fathom. Grandfather Connors was a boss in the mine, which meant that he had to cross a picket line whenever there was a strike. The miners and the unions were serious about strikes; if the strikers caught you driving to the mine to cross the picket line they would mob you and try to turn your car over. My grandfather was forced to sneak there through the thick Pennsylvania woods, and if his family didn't see him after three days they would find a way to deliver him food. The stress of his day-to-day working conditions wore him down, and his family later said that he seemed like an old man in his early '50s. He died of Bright's Disease at fifty-seven, leaving three sons and three daughters who have carried on his mental toughness and perseverance.

My mother's father, Albert Clair, worked in the coal mines for fifty-five years, starting out driving a mule and only taking a "break" to serve in the Army during World War I. As a machine gunner, he fought against the Germans of his homeland, and later told us stories of the strategic battles the Americans fought in an effort to bring down Hitler and his forces.

It would be tough to choose which of my grandfather's experiences was more dangerous and challenging—war or the coal mines. Every time he dropped underground to mine coal, his life was at risk. He had to face not only daily peril but also the black lung assassin that was killing him slowly. I have no idea how he lived to the age of ninety-two. He once had two-and-a-half fingers cut off in a mining accident, and the treatment was to put his hand in a bucket of alcohol. The mine bosses used to respond to the death of a worker by sending that shift home, but soon miners were dying on the job so frequently that the company couldn't afford to let them have the day off. At least in war, you have a weapon.

One of my grandfather's favorite things to do was to sit on his back porch and listen to Pittsburgh Pirates baseball games on the radio. He would sit and listen to his team with a jaw full of Mail Pouch chewing tobacco and a Crisco can to spit in, in a state of full concentration for every pitch. It was striking to me how much pleasure he would get from those radio broadcasts. I still remember names like Roberto Clemente, Willie Stargell and Bill Mazeroski.

As his history of personal survival proves, my grandfather was a man who believed that life was about winning, and I am inspired to this day by his strength, his courage and his iron will. I think about him whenever I feel like I'm having a bad day. Once when he was 80, he refused to let me help him spade his 75 X 100 foot garden. He lived most of his life covered in coal dust, was mustard gassed during his service to his country in France, had to kill men overseas and risked his life everyday in an effort to feed his family. No one remembers hearing him complain.

My parents were married very young, when they were only 19 and 20. My father was offered college athletic scholarships, but he turned them down so that he could get a job to support his family. He drove a bread truck for a while, but it wasn't long before he realized he needed an education, and Salem College in West Virginia was more than happy to help him rekindle his athletic career at the age of 24. He set every football passing record and most of the baseball hitting records at Salem, was named an all-time collegiate athlete in West Virginia over 50 years—for both baseball and football—and was selected to multiple halls of fame. I remember going to Salem when I was four and five years old to watch my dad play quarterback for the Tigers. He was my hero back then, but few people on that field would believe that I would someday play quarterback and defensive back there fifteen years down the road. Some of Dad's former professors taught me too, and some of his former teammates became my coaches.

My dad was such an accomplished baseball player that the Pirates drafted him and sent him down to Georgia to play in their farm league, but that didn't last very long. He missed home, and he wasn't making enough in the minor leagues to feed his family. He hurried back to western Pennsylvania and became a high school football coach at Beth Center High School in Fredericktown. It was the job he was destined to do.

As a coach, my father was as accomplished as he had been as a player. He won numerous conference championships and the Western Pennsylvania Interscholastic Athletic League titles in both 2A and 4A. But more important than the trophies was the relentless way my dad shaped his players into young men of character. He had a passion for finding kids who were life's underdogs and molding them into successful high school football players who refused to lose. He was always looking for tough kids who would hustle and weren't afraid to hit. If you had those qualities and had two legs, he would find a role for you on his team.

One hot day in 1966, when I was ten years old, my dad loaded a football, a softball, some bats, a kickball and a croquet set into the trunk of his Chevy Corvair (The Corvair's trunk was in the front and its engine was in the back—it was unusual but it made it a great car for driving in the snow). I got in the car with Dad and all of the sporting equipment, and we drove up a steep, long hill to Marianna, Pennsylvania, a nearby coal mining community where most of the African-American miners and their families lived. My dad had decided to start a summer recreation program in Marianna, and it probably goes without saying that most white men weren't initiating programs like that in black communities in the mid-sixties.

When we rolled up over the hill that first day, there were five or six kids waiting, and my dad took that small group through a whole morning of competitive, creative and uplifting activities. Every time we went back, the crowd was bigger, and he made every one of them feel important. My father had an amazing gift with young people. He knew how to push their buttons and make them work past the limits they thought they had. I was a witness as he helped these kids realize their potential and gain self-esteem. Providing self-worth was his specialty, and extreme discipline was the main ingredient in the process. He genuinely loved them, and they felt it. On every ride home from Marianna, he would talk about those kids until we hit the door of our house. He had an intentional plan for every visit, a strategy for each boy that would build him up, teach him values and allow him to have fun at the same time.

With the hardscrabble coal mining culture as a backdrop, high school athletic programs in western Pennsylvania were characterized by a blue-collar mentality and a "Friday Night Lights"-like devotion to the local team. People took their jobs seriously, because they were thankful to have a job. That generation wasn't too far removed from the Great Depression, so they appreciated a paycheck, a simple meal and the value of discipline. That's what western Pennsylvania was to me—I was always surrounded by disciplined, tough people. Even most of the alcoholics I knew could work you under the table. That environment was normal to me, and it wasn't until I lived in other communities as an adult that I came to appreciate the hard work that defined my childhood. God did me a favor by allowing me to grow up in western Pennsylvania.

Everyone called my dad "Wild Billy" back then, and people like to ask me if I was Wild Billy's boy. I didn't really understand the meaning behind his nickname until I got a little older. In those days, people didn't have much to do for fun through the long winters other than visit the taverns that dotted the highways. My dad's idea of recreation was a friendly fistfight, and opponents were easy to find. Dad was a full-blooded Irishman, competitive to the point of fanaticism, and he was bent on winning. Dad's two brothers were known to throw a few punches themselves; in fact, my late Uncle Martin is still legendary in those parts.

Uncle Martin served in the Navy during World War II, and as the stories go he fought close to 80 times with fellow serviceman and won at least 90 percent of those scuffles. He even won the title of the All-Pacific Boxing Champion during the war. He stood about 5-foot-8, weighed 165 pounds and was tough as nails. He had such a passion for boxing that he even named his sons Rocky and Kayo. In contrast to his father, the mine boss, Martin served on the International Executive Board for the United Mine Workers after he was buried in a mine accident and lived to tell the tale. He became a committed advocate of mine safety, and his stature as a union leader enhanced his affinity for a good brawl and gave him a larger selection of opponents. He was known to choose the largest opponent he could find, and he and Dad traveled together. Their passion for defending their principles took an ugly turn the night a sore loser stabbed Uncle Martin in the chest and my dad in the stomach. They both recovered, but that kind of real violence contributed to the slow decline of friendly fistfights and escalated the transition to current weaponry. No one fights in bars much anymore, but it was a weekly occurrence in western Pennsylvania during that era. It was just part of the culture, and a way of earning local respect. My dad was all about respect.

I was a student of my dad's life principles from a very young age, both on and off the football field. When I was in about the fifth grade I would suit up in full gear for his high school football practices, and they let me participate in full-speed drills. I was fortunate to be around so many people who had such a passion for the game of football, and I learned about principle-centered leadership by example long before anyone wrote about it.

At those practices, it was glaringly apparent that discipline was number one, and probably number two and three as well. We started with high-intensity agility drills, or what was known in those days as calisthenics. Running through forty or fifty tires was one favorite drill; if you didn't pick up your knees you could break an ankle. Monkey rolls were also a favorite of my dad's—they got the players in shape and tested their equilibrium at the same time. "Mat drills" were also in use in western Pennsylvania long before they were given that name, as well as the grass drills made famous by former Packers coach Vince Lombardi. That segment of practice was brutal. Nothing less than full-speed effort was tolerated, and I don't say that lightly. I mean nothing less.

Even from that young age, those long practices taught me that profanity was an effective means of communication. If you were not the occasional object of profane criticism from one of the coaches you didn't feel loved. A couple of years ago, a lady at a dinner told me that she was appalled when she heard a collegiate coach use profanity toward one of his athletes as they were leaving the field. Please, lady! She would have experienced heart failure if she had watched just ten minutes of practice during that era.

Another part of my dad's practices involved drills with appealing names like "nutcracker" and "bucket of blood." They were full-speed contact drills in which you had the chance to be praised or exposed in front of your teammates. If you didn't love to hit, your existence on that team's roster was going to be short-lived. I watched the coaches run a lot of guys off the field because they weren't physical enough or they didn't embrace hard work. However brutal those standards might seem to some today, they produced results and ingrained an incredible level of toughness that became an important tradition for every player who came through that program.

I've been around football for a long time, and I've never seen a group of coaches who cared more about their players than my dad and his staff. As tough as it was for a kid to impress them, they spent hours talking about every single player, even the least athletic kid who might never see playing time. As a coach's son, I sat in meetings in film rooms and bars for countless hours, living on a diet of "pop," potato chips and secondhand smoke. I learned early that the best way to instill self-esteem into young athletes is to find a place to maximize their strengths. My dad always found a place for the kids who gave their best effort.

That was a trait my dad shared with one of my future bosses, collegiate football coach Butch Davis. Even at the Division I level, Butch would work to find a spot for a young man who was relentless about hustling and hitting. When I worked for Butch at North Carolina, we had a walk-on named Pete Mangum who was 5-foot-8 and 185 pounds, but he was incredibly scrappy on special teams. In a game against Florida State, I witnessed him run down on two different kickoffs and knock two different Seminoles out of the wedge and out cold. Seeing Pete battle that day brought back memories of some of the unlikely-looking kids my dad used to recruit out of his Physical Education classes.

Each August, my dad would take his team away to the mountains for training camp, which featured seven days of "three-a-day" practices. I got to come along and stay in the coach's cabin, and those camps were memorable experiences for me. Each of the three daily practices was brutal and as demanding as the one before it; none of them would fit into the "recovery" category. I don't remember many practices that didn't require full pads, and the only available water was in the form of four buckets with four ladles. You were so hot and exhausted that you were happy to drink someone else's sweat, as well as grass and dirt, with your drink of water. That week felt more like a month.

One year, when I was 10 or 11, we went to camp somewhere in West Virginia or Ohio, and some of the coaches went out to one of the local establishments for a drink one night. On their way back to camp, they caught three players hitchhiking back to camp with a supply of beer in tow. For the offenders, that night was like a welcome to hell. One of the coaches had a motorcycle, and when they returned to camp he rode on those three players' heels around the field for a session of extended training. There were other outdoor activities too, but I was too scared to get out of my bunk to investigate. I didn't have to get up to hear the next punishment—an extended period of screaming in the coaches' cabin that undoubtedly woke up the entire camp. The three hitchhikers were then instructed to sleep the rest of the night on the wooden floor with no bedding, and it did get cool at night in those mountains.

The next morning, those guys were paraded in front of the team as an example of what would happen if the rules were taken lightly, and even their innocent teammates caught hell throughout every practice that day. Then they were given to their parents, who had come up that morning to drive them home. When we got back to Fredericktown, those three visited the coaches and asked that they be permitted back on the team. The coaches put it to a vote, and the other players agreed to allow them back, but not without a little more humiliation. They had to dress in full pads, with rib pads and a cup, and crawl through a full team gauntlet in front of their parents.

If this activity had occurred in the year 2013, it would most likely attract and provoke lawsuits, arrests and media coverage. In the mid-1960s in western Pennsylvania, it was normal behavior, and parents witnessed the events with no complaints. The pride and discipline associated with the football program was important to the entire community. The standard had to be maintained, and everyone was on board. It was no surprise when Beth Center High eventually won it all. The WPIAL in western Pennsylvania is tough to win, and that prize only came as a result of tenacious kids, great coaching and a tremendous commitment to excellence. What it took was an extreme, unrelenting, unwavering, unparalleled demonstration of overachievement. That was Wild Billy Connors in a nutshell.

I don't think my dad ever had a savings account. I know his first job paid about $3,000 a year, and we weren't able to buy our first house until I was in the ninth grade. That house cost $24,000, and the interest rate on the mortgage was astronomical. He was constantly giving his players money and letting them borrow his car, and he always made sure I had money when I was in high school. I made some of my own money through hard work—in the steel mill and on the road crew for the Pennsylvania Department of Transportation. My mother worked as a secretary for the steel mill for nearly forty years, and her life was never easy. She worked long hours and traveled through all kinds of inclement weather to get to the mill. Coaches' wives, as a rule, must be tough, resilient women who know how to manage whatever money is available.

The players my father coached will probably never know how much they meant to him. Once he was offered a new coaching and teaching job in a town called Turtle Creek. It paid better and he had decided to accept it; I even remember visiting Turtle Creek with him so that he could set up his new office and get acquainted with the place. We were sad to think of leaving Beth Center, the close-knit community that had been so supportive of my dad and his philosophy.

He had a very talented quarterback at Beth Center named Bobby Keys. Bobby was special because of his exceptional competitiveness and leadership ability, and he was extremely effective as a mobile quarterback before that model became popular. He was a tough tag, the type of back who ran sixty yards to gain twenty.

As we were preparing to leave Beth Center, after Dad had already broken the news to his players, he learned that Bobby Keys was very upset about losing his coach. Bobby's disappointment hit him so hard that he made an about-face and let everyone know that he would be staying right there at Beth Center. I still remember riding in the car with him—choking down some of that secondhand Pall Mall smoke—when he dropped the news that he was staying. That made my day, and I learned an important lesson about the power of relationships in athletics. My dad was willing to give up a better job to keep the heartfelt connection he had developed with that group of players.

That day has come back to me a few times in my own career, especially when I turned down a few job opportunities during my first ten years at East Carolina University. I think Wild Billy's influence was with me when I considered higher salaries and better facilities and came down on the side of the relationships I had built in Pirate Country. When I finally did leave for the University of North Carolina in 2001, I got physically sick driving to Chapel Hill and experienced a steady stream of water flowing out of my brain and down my face. Earlier that day, Antwane Yelverton, one of our ECU players, had jumped in my truck to suggest that he was coming with me. You don't expect something like that to hurt so badly, but it did. When you pour your soul into people, maybe without even realizing it yourself, you can get emotionally blindsided by saying goodbye. No one has a party for you when you leave a program; it's a cold-blooded process and thick skin is required. You can get hammered whether you decide to stay or leave, and making the right call is a matter of instinct and timing.

Stronger Every Day

No coach develops a methodology or leadership in a vacuum. Your upbringing and the people who influenced you along the way are always going to have an underlying impact on your thoughts and actions today. My personal experience—as a member of a family and a community that were considered the world's underdogs—was unique. Every day was a battle for survival in a mining community, and because of that, I've never been able to tolerate athletes who have a lukewarm commitment to their sport. Training will expose people, and that in itself is reason to train hard. Football is a hard game for hard people, and the intensity has skyrocketed with bigger, faster and more explosive athletes. Teams might not grind it out on the ground like they did in my dad's day, but the collisions are still brutal.

My heritage is important to me, and because of my upbringing, I have always loved the concept of tradition. On a sports team, tradition brings people together and provides them with a passion to strive toward a common goal. When I played for my dad's team at Beth Center, we had a tradition that we would never speak a word or make a sound on the bus traveling to a game. If you won, you could talk on the way home, but if you lost it was dead silence again. My dad and his staff worked to make our high school experience special, even if parts of it were brutally hard. You always remember the tough things in your life with more clarity than the easy times, and the struggles take on more significance in the long run. I've had former players approach me years after they graduated and ask me a question like, "Do you remember when you crushed us with those shuttles on July 27 at 2 p.m. in 1994?"

I usually don't remember, but I do vividly recall when I had to run a mile and a half on my reporting date to Salem College in 1976. I also have a clear recollection of all three times I got my "bell rung," now known as a concussion.

When I was in high school, the prevailing wisdom was that speed training wasn't vital because you either had speed or you didn't. In those years I started to believe that since speed is all about power, it can be developed through weight lifting and maximum effort speed training. Motor learning and drills always came easy to me, but I was slowly learning about the concept of speed development, and we tried to punish ourselves on my high school's cinder track. It was similar to sand training, except it hurt a lot more when you fell. It was initially like trial and error—coaches were just starting to have conversations about effective speed training methods, and some of our early attempts were pretty unwise.

I remember reading one article about the benefits of downhill sprinting and nearly killing myself trying to sprint down a steep hill. My friend Ted Bozick and I also once tried to get faster by tying ourselves to my Volkswagen while the other guy was driving it 10 mph. That wasn't too smart either. I ended up playing defensive back in college, so I became even more obsessed with getting faster. My summer traditions included running uphill sprints and jumping rope in Army boots. I used to run twenty twenties uphill and jump intervals that totaled forty minutes, every day. I know it made me quicker and faster, and the rope jumping boosted my conditioning significantly. It was during those college years, by experimenting with my own body, when I became one hundred percent sold on the benefits of training. I never got beat deep as a defensive back in college, and I didn't possess natural speed. I have been persistent about studying movement ever since.

Birth of a Calling

During my first collegiate job, establishing a strength and conditioning program at Bucknell University in 1988, I had the chance to meet Ronnie Jones, who was then the strength and conditioning coach for the Philadelphia Eagles. One day I called Ronnie and asked him if I could come visit him, and he agreed. When I arrived, he told me he had a meeting with head coach Buddy Ryan first and that I should make myself at home. I proceeded to go through his office as politely and covertly as I could and read everything I could get my hands on. When he came back and we started talking, he was somewhat amused at my level of interest in what the Eagles were doing (probably because I was assaulting his desk drawers.) I had chosen that day to visit for a specific reason—I knew that Kevin McNair was coming in from California to work with the Eagles on speed drills.

Kevin was one of the first true gurus of football speed. He ran track at Stanford with Charlie Francis (who coached Olympian Ben Johnson), and he was adamant about the philosophies he taught his athletes. From the time he arrived in Philadelphia, he jerked a knot in the players, demanding their full attention as he explained his methods in detail. Under his instruction, you always learned what you were supposed to do and why you were supposed to do it. He was the first coach I encountered who separated acceleration mechanics from maximum velocity training. He was definitely ahead of his time in many respects.

Inspired by McNair's methods, Ronnie and I conducted a few small speed clinics of our own, and I was hooked. As I applied McNair's terminology and drills, I literally saw kids get better within forty minutes. His system still has tremendous value today—especially in the areas of postural integrity, hip position and any other aspect of acceleration mechanics. McNair developed the first speed system specific to football.

Another major influence for me—and an obvious one considering the region I grew up in—was the success of the Pittsburgh Steelers. How to describe the level of devotion shown by Steelers fans? Well, my best friend from high school has all six Super Bowl ring designs tattooed on his back. Loyal doesn't even begin to describe it. I used to love to drive down to Latrobe, Pennsylvania to watch the Steelers' training camp workouts. One of the first things I ever saw the players do for conditioning was to run 300s around the field and calculate heart rate after each one. That was the seed of my belief that 300 yards is an excellent measure of anaerobic conditioning.

Of course, the specificity of the game of football is always an interesting topic of discussion when it comes to the optimum method of anaerobic conditioning. I have numerous thought patterns on this topic. Some may be somewhat cynical and some are indisputable.

First, I think that anyone who played defensive back at the collegiate level like myself would have to agree that there is certainly a conditioning challenge beyond training short sprints. During the course of a football game, you might see an out and up, followed by a post, followed by forcing on a perimeter play, followed by a seam route, etc. This happened out of a huddle in the '80s. Now, with no huddle offensive schemes, you just line up on a jog back. Bottom line? You better have had a combination of training the first two energy systems to survive. This applies to both offensive and defensive players. When a receiver gets to the fourth quarter and he is running his fifth skinny post, he needs some gas in the tank. In the same way, as a defensive back, you have action coming at you at a feverish pace.

Putting it into practice

Lets take a look at some of today's conditioning options. Probably the option that makes the most sense would be high-tempo, position-specific training. The problem is that it is still difficult to mimic an entire football game, particularly with linemen. They expend tremendous energy straining against other human beings. Another consideration is the fact that we don't wear pads in the off-season. In addition, the NCAA doesn't allow us to use sleds, other human beings for resistance, or football formations. You have to be creative just to set up a pursuit drill.

Other options might be repeated sprint work in various doses, or traditional protocols, which over a period of specific weeks, prepare you for a specific test. Some coaches like to run 300-yard shuttles in 50, 60 or 25-yard increments. Times and rest intervals are manipulated over time to develop an adaptation. Another popular conditioning test is repeated repetitions at 110 yards. I like Dr. William Kraemer's "Power Unit"—two 300's, followed by ten 40's, four 80's, ten 20's and then two more 300's. I also have used my friend Pete Martinelli's test that he perfected during his tenure at Oklahoma. This was a 200, plus 300, plus 400, plus 500, plus 600. I thought that this was a great test for our skill group. Again, times and rest intervals were manipulated.

An old piece of research from "Exercise and Sports Medicine" magazine still has a great deal of value today. It states that because football doesn't allow for sufficient rest periods to restore intramuscular PCr to trained muscles, football athletes rely heavily on the glycolic system. The researchers studied the pre-practice lactate values of Division III players and found that they started in normal ranges and then more than doubled during games, rose only slightly after unit position drills and exceeded the game-day levels after conditioning drills. They concluded, "Although not excessively high, the game of football does demand a significant source of energy from anaerobic glycolysis, and only conditioning drills appear to prepare the player for such game demands."

This passage indicates that unit and team practice do not prepare football players for the physiological demands of the game, and only the conditioning drills and "in-season" weight workouts maintain physiological fitness for the game. The battle between unit coaches for time and the conditioning demands of the player continues to be an issue.

Some coaches believe that they can get the conditioning result they need from practice tempo. This mentality has trickled down from the NFL. Coaches won't say it, but another factor here is that you can avoid confrontation with NFL players by eliminating conditioning, thereby making your job a little more comfortable. Who needs to run a gasser? Right? When Butch Davis came to UNC, he told me that he would never condition the team in-season. He also said I would never be fired for our performance in the fourth quarter and that practice tempo would be the conditioning stimulus from August to November. That made my job easy, even though practice was run at a traditional tempo in my opinion. The only part of practice with a tempo that really seemed to push the players was our pursuit drill at the beginning. We lost some close games that I would like to play again armed with a week of some old-school post-practice conditioning, but we will never know if that would have changed the result.

Run my Football Team

In contrast to the NFL trickle-down philosophy there are coaches who believe their team benefits from running year-round. I worked for two coaches at East Carolina in the 1990s—Bill Lewis for less than a year and Steve Logan for nine. Both were fanatical about conditioning, and my role was to support them as an extension of that approach. I made sure I fought the conditioning battle every day. We ran all the time, all year round. It made perfect sense to me, because football is a running game. We did speed work five days a week, through the winter, regardless of the weather conditions. We also had what people refer to as "winter conditioning" at 6 a.m. during the cold months, led by the entire coaching staff. The players would rotate through twelve to fifteen stations of grueling drills with very little rest, plus we lifted weights on those days as well. That wasn't an unusual activity; it was normal behavior.

My team's regimen during those early ECU years leads to a couple of vital questions: Why did that routine become normal behavior? Why did those intense workouts have lasting significance? For answers, I like to turn to the lessons contained within the practice of military organizations. In the military, officers use conditioning for fitness, mental toughness, to expose the weak and promote the strong. Just look at the tests a man has to endure to become a Navy SEAL. It's straight survival under duress. During SEAL testing, nobody is out there questioning the specificity of holding a log over your head for an undetermined amount of time. When, during the course of a mission, will a Navy SEAL ever have to hold a log over his head? Most likely, never. What's the point? To expose those who lack the determination and will to press on when lives are at stake.

So, should we expose weak-minded athletes the way they do in the military? Most people in athletic performance training today would say no. I really believe that coaches have reached a point of carefully negotiating degrees of discomfort rather than holding someone's feet to the fire. Certainly, we must consider those with legitimate medical issues like sickle cell anemia or heart conditions. The fact that athletes occasionally die as a result of training is a very serious matter, and it's unacceptable. Given these issues, it has become reasonable for the NCAA to standardize conditioning. What is not reasonable is to fire strength and conditioning coaches because teams lose in the fourth quarter of football games. Why is it acceptable for a man to lose his source of income and his professional integrity due to NCAA changes in the way training is conducted? Every strength coach I know would be emotionally devastated if a young athlete went down. Is it fair, then, to put them in a double bind situation where others' lives or their careers are at risk? Probably not.

Getting back to the military comparison, a key byproduct of boot camp mentality is the discipline that athletes develop in that culture. There's something to be said for consequences. Conditioning can serve as a meaningful consequence for some people, but not for everyone. During my time with Steve Logan, we just ran the hell out of everybody all the time. That's the simple truth. As a result, we won a ton of games in the fourth quarter and had a very high level of team discipline. If an athlete didn't like to run, he probably was not going to make it to graduation as a member of the football team.

I've worked for other coaches who negotiated their discipline issues and coddled their premier players. I'm here to tell you that soft-pedaling your team discipline program is a plan of failure. Conditioning is a valuable tool if you establish its importance up front. "Winter conditioning" is also a valuable tool to re-educate an undisciplined team, as long as you don't lose focus and push things too far. Whatever you do has to be supported and handed down by the head coach. When we had some players missing class at ECU, Logan got the entire team up every day for two straight weeks to run at 5:30 a.m. Missing class became obsolete.

At this point, I will go ahead and reference some history. I punished people at 4 a.m., yes, 4 a.m. I made players crawl and roll in the mud to the gate so my 6 a.m. group could see the carnage. My staff and I once broke down some doors in the dorm to get to some slackers. The rest intervals I used were probably not within the appropriate guidelines at times. I once took a player five miles outside of Greenville and made him run back. I could go on.

I do not engage in such activities in my current position, nor did I engage in them on the grounds of the University of North Carolina. When I arrived in Chapel Hill, the athletic administrators put limits on me very quickly. On my second day, the trainer approached me and told me that they did not believe in physical punishment. This was shocking to me, because I had heard a vicious rumor that the strength coach for former UNC head coach Mack Brown had led an activity called the "dog pound." Who would start such a rumor? Surely they wouldn't tie John Bunting's hands from the get-go by limiting his ability to discipline his team if there were any truth to it.

During the Logan era from 1992-2002 we beat South Carolina five times, N.C. State three times, West Virginia twice, Miami twice, Virginia Tech twice, Pitt twice, Syracuse twice, Texas Tech in the Gallery.com Furniture Bowl and Stanford in the Liberty Bowl. Coach Logan became the winningest coach in ECU history, and he was recently inducted into the school's athletic hall of fame. Do you still wonder whether discipline and conditioning matter? It wasn't like we were favored to win any of those games.

Prior to Logan, I worked for one year with Bill Lewis, who was at the helm at ECU from 1989 to 1992. Like Logan, Lewis was adamant about conditioning. In 1991 we lived the dream season, going 11-1, defeating N.C. State in the Peach Bowl and ending the season ranked ninth in the country. Lewis was named the National Coach of the Year.

From time to time I run into a player from that era, and they all want to talk about the same thing—the 300s. These men, some of them 15 or 20 years removed from their playing days, still remember the specific year, date and temperature on the day they finally made ten 300s under the required time. Why did the 300s matter so much? Every man is proud when he overcomes adversity, particularly if that man made sacrifices that paid dividends. We started running the

300s at ECU in 1991. We would normally fun three or four reps and build it up to six. Rest intervals in those days were one minute, but somewhere along the way we cut it down to thirty seconds. Thirty seconds rest is tough; it'll light you up. At some point the players asked me if they could increase it to eight reps. It wasn't my idea, but I obliged. So the skill players were running eight, the combo players seven and the linemen six. The times were adapted for each group.

In 1996 we had a freshman named Kevin Monroe who came in and made eight 300s with thirty seconds rest in under 55 seconds for each. He did it the first time he tried, which was unheard of. The next day the players asked me if they could bump up the challenge to ten reps for skill players, eight for combo and seven for linemen. I was not about to argue with an attempt to get better, even if I wasn't exactly sure it was humanly possible. Those upperclassmen were driven by Kevin's accomplishment; they didn't want any freshman to be able to pass the conditioning test on the first try. The bottom line? Those players made ten reps. They made ten every single summer, and they knew that no one else in the country—or maybe in the history of football—was in that kind of shape.

The upperclassmen during that era would not tolerate failure. If someone struggled, they became engulfed by a pack of barking seniors who would not tolerate mental weakness. That kind of unity—forged in the fire of grueling summer workouts and one more 300—was special. At that time, we really didn't know how special it was. A group of players was turning into a team, and young men were becoming full-grown men. They were going to take those lessons to the field and later into their lives. I have heard too many athletes tell their success stories to believe otherwise. The experts can debate specificity, energy systems and whatever else they can dream up to dispute the value of confrontation. I just have a treasure of memories of a bunch of tough kids who were hungry and seeking a challenge.

The Power of Discipline and Spirit

The Marine Corps Drill Instructors' creed accurately reflects the flavor of the player/coach relationship:

> "These recruits are entrusted to my care.
> I will train them to the best of my ability.
> I will develop them into smartly disciplined,
> physically fit, basically trained Marines,
> thoroughly indoctrinated, in love
> of the Corps and the country.
> I will demand of them, and demonstrate
> by my own example, the highest standards
> of personal conduct, morality, and professional
> skill."

For further flavor of the Marine Corps' philosophy that I embrace, consider the speech the drill instructors give when they first encounter their recruits:

> Eyeballs—my name is Staff Sergeant _____:
> our mission is to train you to become United States
> Marines. A Marine is characterized by one who
> possesses the highest of military virtues.
> He obeys orders, respects his seniors and strives
> constantly to be the very best at everything he does.
> Discipline and spirit are the hallmarks of the Marines.
> Each of you can become a Marine if you develop
> discipline and spirit. We will give every effort to train
> you even after some of you have given up on yourselves.
> Starting now, you will treat me and all other Marines
> with the highest of respect, for we have earned our
> place as Marines and will accept nothing less from you.

We will treat you as we do our fellow Marines.
We believe in fairness, firmness, dignity, and
compassion. At no time will you be physically
or verbally abused by any Marine or recruit.
If someone should abuse or mistreat you,
I expect you to report immediately to me
or one of my drill instructors.
Further, if you feel that I've mistreated you
I expect you to report it to your commander.
Starting now my drill instructors and I will be
with you every day, everywhere that you go.
Now, I've told you what my drill instructors
and I will do for you.
From you we demand the following:
"You will give 100% of yourself at all times.
Obey all orders quickly and
willingly without question.
Treat all Marines and recruits
with courtesy and respect.
At no time will you physically or verbally
abuse another Marine or recruit.
Be completely honest in everything you do.
A Marine never lies, cheats, or compromises.
Respect the rights and properties of others.
A Marine never steals.
You must work hard to strengthen your body.
Be proud of yourself and the uniform that you wear.
Try your best to learn the things that you are taught.
Above all else, you will never quit and you will
never give up. For we offer you the opportunity
to earn the title of United States Marine."

If discipline and spirit are the driving forces behind the fiercest war-fighting machine of all time, we might want to give some consideration to these qualities as we develop athletes. Every single Marine recruit hears the above presentation verbatim, so it must be incredibly important.

Many of today's athletes step through the door with a sense of entitlement and an individualistic demeanor. It becomes clear within a short period of time that these attitudes will be detrimental to team chemistry. Like any successful organization, it is vital on a sports team that everyone is unified in their thinking and their attitudes. A team must be fueled by the power of agreement. It needs a common work ethic and a common set of goals, and anything that erodes that unity must be erased.

Spirit has been defined as, "the vital principle or animating force believed to be within human beings." It is also defined as, "The predominant mood of an occasion or period." In athletics, spirit combined with belief can be a very powerful combination. I have a clipping of the 1991 Peach Bowl season at East Carolina on my wall. It is a picture of Luke Fisher catching the winning touchdown pass against N.C. State in Fulton County Stadium. At the bottom of picture are the words, "We Believe," the phrase our fans chanted throughout that magical season. That three-syllable chant was an awesome sound that sparked a fourth-quarter rally in Atlanta that day—a rally that gave the Pirates the victory and still shines as the ultimate moment in many Pirate fans' memories. With every victory through that season, the players' spirit of confidence grew until they truly believed that they could beat anybody. In the book, "An Enemy Called Average," John Mason describes the union of passion and believing as a conviction. This is the ultimate condition of confidence.

We recruit athletes with the expectation that they will excel at the collegiate level, but when they arrive they also need some guidance regarding their spirit. They will inevitably face challenges and some level of discouragement, and they will discover that they will have to push themselves far beyond what they envisioned when they signed that letter of intent. No one can persevere through the suffering of intense training and the setbacks of an athletic career without a love for the game and a hunger for the sweet taste of victory. A successful athlete must have the perspective to know that someday—years after their prime—they will reflect on how they handled the opportunity that was given to them through athletics. Those with great spirit can never find enough time in the day to make themselves better. It's a choice that comes down to a denial or acceptance of maximum commitment.

Spirit is the intangible quality that sets the East Carolina fan base apart from many other university communities. It's the thing that brings coaches like me back and the environment that energizes every athlete to excel. It's the unforgettable feeling of disembarking from your plane and walking into an airport so full of chanting fans that you have to wade through, slapping high fives all the way to baggage claim. It's a vision of thirty miles of road from Kinston to Greenville lined with people upon our return from the airport after the 1991 Peach Bowl victory.

The Peach Bowl was special, but in my mind no game in the history of college football can surpass the atmosphere of the 1999 East Carolina-Miami game that was played in Raleigh. That game was the finale of about nine days of insanity. We left Greenville eight days before the game on a bus bound for Columbia, S.C. for a date with the Gamecocks, who were coached then by the legendary Lou Holtz. As we drove away from eastern North Carolina, a hurricane called Floyd was coming in, and we timed our trip to miss the storm. Floyd made landfall just weeks after another hurricane named Dennis, and the cumulative rainfall of the two storms led to the biggest flooding catastrophe in the history of eastern North Carolina. Schools were closed for weeks, hundreds of people had to be rescued from their rooftops by helicopter and, nearly 15 years later some are still trying to regain what the floodwaters took away.

Of course, we had set our sights on the Gamecocks and could not possibly fathom the destruction that was befalling our city. Many of our Pirate players—those who lived in apartments near the historically high Tar River—would never see their apartments or many of their prized possessions again. We tried our best to keep up with the news of Floyd's aftermath, but we still took the field at Williams-Brice Stadium focused on the job we had come south to do. East Carolina owned the Gamecocks in the nineties, defeating them five of the eight times the two teams met, and this game wouldn't be any different. Coach Logan managed to hang a "L" on Lou Holtz as his Pirates prevailed 21-3. Having worked with Steve for many years, it was particularly rewarding to see him shake hands with Coach Holtz following the victory. He had poured his heart and soul into the program to a level that only those closest to him could appreciate.

With that victory in the books, we faced a new and unique challenge. Due to the disastrous conditions in Greenville, there was no way we could return there to prepare for one of the biggest games on our docket—Miami. The Hurricanes (the irony of that wasn't lost on anybody) were scheduled to come to Greenville on Sept. 25 to present another challenge to the upstart Pirates, but it became clear that Dowdy-Ficklen Stadium and the Greenville community would not be hosting a football game.

Even though they had just tasted defeat at ECU's hands, the University of South Carolina community graciously offered to let us stay in Columbia to live and practice. We found hotel rooms, worked in time on the Gamecocks practice field whenever we could and lifted weights at a local Gold's Gym. One of our biggest challenges was a severe shortage of underwear and socks, and the players couldn't help but worry about their homes and their friends back at ECU. Through it all, we just kept chopping wood.

To add to the unusual events of that week, our rival 70 miles to the west, N.C. State, offered their stadium for our matchup with Miami. Despite all that we had been through that week—or more likely because of it—when Butch Davis and his Hurricanes rolled into Raleigh that weekend, we were ready to prove our mettle and to give the residents of eastern North Carolina something to celebrate in the midst of crisis. The atmosphere of that game was unlike any I've ever experienced. The Pirate fans who had braved the flooded roads to make the trip seemed to fill that stadium to capacity two hours before kickoff. Something electric was in the air. There was a sense of emotion so thick that it was almost unsettling. There had been two consecutive hurricanes that took life and property away from the Pirate Nation, and our intention for that three-hour period was to get at least one win from the Hurricanes that we had before us.

Things didn't look promising early when we fell behind by three touchdowns. Miami was loaded with talent and looking for payback from the 31-6 loss we handed them at their stadium three years earlier. Their roster included well-known players like Santana Moss, Mike Rumph, Ed Reed, Clinton Portis, Dan Morgan, Nate Webster, Ken Dorsey, Reggie Wayne, Daniel Franks and others. Despite our early setback, the fans behind the bench were on fire, and they gave our players a wake-up call with their unwavering encouragement.

The second half of that game would be a testament to the perseverance and strength of pure will. We always had confidence in our conditioning and in the exceptional coaching abilities of

Steve Logan. What transpired after halftime was an incredible momentum swing that resulted in a singularly memorable Pirate victory. Propelled by David Garrard's 328 passing yards and Pernell Griffin's 17 tackles, we defeated Miami 27-23 that day, and in the week that followed, East Carolina climbed to No. 16 in the national polls. It was amazing to see those Carter-Finley Stadium goalposts come down. The whole experience of defeating two consecutive major programs in the face of unparalleled hardship was truly special, and it was a lasting lesson in the strength of brotherhood.

The resolve of those young men did not go unnoticed. ESPN chose the Pirates as the recipient of the 1999 Disney National Spirit Award, given at the ESPYS. That was a proud moment for the Pirate Nation. It was a perfect award for a group of players who demonstrated a high level of courage, enthusiasm and selfless regard for their teammates, their coaches and their fan base. Every coach aspires to lead a team through such great moments, and that experience was one of the best. It was spiritual.

As a coach, you take any experience and knowledge you have gained into your job and hope it helps make you more effective. I never aspired to follow in my father's footsteps and become a high school football coach because of poverty-level wages, demanding school boards and crazy parents. But I could never shake the hundreds of hours I spent around athletics and training, and I seemed destined to bring the shades and influences of "Wild Billy" into my own career. Twenty-five years into my journey as a strength and conditioning coach, I am immensely thankful for my father's footprint on my life. Wild Billy was not only talented, he was right. Watching his refusal to compromise discipline and spirit through the first nineteen years of my life had a permanent impact on my soul. Even when he had a few too many beers and repeated the same statement one thousand times, those lessons turned out to be rooted in wisdom. Playing quarterback for him through high school taught me to accept nothing less than perfection. I will never forget the day I ran a "dive" play at least twenty times in a row during practice until it was perfect. Once when I went the wrong way on a play during a game and scored a touchdown, I thought my father was going to twist the facemask off of my helmet. I had scored six, but I had deviated from the program, and Billy expected the highest levels of both discipline and excellence. My cousins have a saying when they are on the precipice of a bar fight. They say that, "the Billy comes out." Like my dad, they expect to win.

My experiences have provided me with specific perspectives that mold my coaching methodology. These perspectives—which are central to everything I do as a coach—will be presented at the conclusion of several chapters, and they will culminate in an overall training program that is reliant not only on the application of sets and reps, but on the life and experiences behind those exercises.

Foundational Perspectives

1. Be a great role model to the athletes you coach. Lead from the front. Demonstrate toughness, but be humble. Athletes respect your experiences but need to feel your presence. Lift them up whenever possible.

2. Treat every athlete the same, even if the people you work for do not. It might cost you a job, but never your integrity. You must confront even subtle forms of insubordination, quickly and effectively.

3. If you want results, demand perfection, or at least the closest thing to it. As a coach, you will only achieve what you insist upon achieving. If there is no confrontation, there is no coaching.

4. Attitude and mentality are daily quests. You must find ways to mold and improve team chemistry. You are with the athletes year-round. Sometime you might have to scream. Most of the time you just have to be smart.

5. Make things competitive whenever possible. We use the concept of testing teams and awards. They must take pride in winning.

6. Conditioning is a mentality. Conditioning is discipline. Conditioning standards establish a sense of authority and a standard of membership. They precede mental toughness. Military organizations use standards of tolerance for a reason. Don't succumb to the soft mentality that has infected our youth. Keep it safe, but keep it tough and provide the meaning behind your methods.

7. Invest your soul. You will be rewarded if you care about young people. It's the right thing to do. If you are called, and you will discover if you are called, you must respond.

8. Listen to the voices. As a young athlete I tried to listen, and as a young coach I tried to listen. It paid off. Now as a seasoned coach I still listen, but I can now discern true intelligence from self-promotion and effective techniques from a collection of words.

9. Ordinary people achieve extraordinary things every day. Never forget that, and never let your athletes forget it. You are probably an ordinary coach. Do something extraordinary. Find a way.

10. It doesn't matter what you have going on in your life, show up with energy and enthusiasm. Be approachable. Look athletes in the eye and convey a positive spirit. They have problems too. You might be able to make them forget theirs, even for just a while.

CHAPTER TWO

WILD, WONDERFUL WEST VIRGINIA

I showed up on the Salem College campus in Salem, West Virginia in August of 1976. I was not quite 5-foot-10 and I weighed 172 pounds. I had played quarterback and outside linebacker in high school, but to play in college I would have to get bigger and stronger. It made sense for me to take a redshirt year so that I could develop physically, and with that goal in mind, I worked my way up to 195 pounds and started putting out some very respectable numbers in the weight room. I earned a starting role on the team after my redshirt season, and I thoroughly enjoyed my collegiate athletic career.

Salem was a truly unique place, and that small college has been part of more prominent peoples' athletic journeys than you would think. Terry Bowden and Rich Rodriguez were both head coaches there, and Jimbo Fisher is a former Salem player. Unfortunately, football at Salem didn't last long after I graduated. In the late '80s, my father was selected to the Salem Athletic Hall of Fame, and soon afterward, a Japanese university bought the school—now known as Salem International University—and eliminated the football program. Many old-time football fans in West Virginia still have fond memories of afternoons spent in Catalano Stadium watching Tiger teams that were perennially competitive.

Many viewed Salem as a haven for renegades whom—for whatever reason—couldn't cut it in a Division I program. Admission standards seemed to be nonexistent for athletes; I don't even think that felonies placed you on the exclusion list. One winter, one of our linebackers went home for Christmas and was arrested for robbing three gas stations with two of his friends. He was consequently given four to twenty years in the federal penitentiary in Ohio. Somehow, after one year inside, he returned to the Salem football team. I might be wrong, but I would bet that a redshirt year in the federal pen has never been repeated anywhere. Other wonders I witnessed during my years at Salem included the skinning of a deer in the shower of the men's dorm, a fullback shooting at his car from his dorm room window after a few drinks, an offensive lineman burglarizing the business office (he was sent to the U.S. Army after that incident) and one of our linebackers staging a fall from a sixth-floor window tied to a rope. Those boys weren't "all there."

That renegade spirit was new to me when I hit the Salem campus. I was used to things being highly disciplined, and I didn't want to run five miles with a motorcycle at my heels—which was a memorable consequence of the beer caper I witnessed as a child. I was looking forward to three-a-day practices, and I was determined to do everything right. The first test of our fitness was a 1.5-mile run. I think only three guys outran me that day (strength coaches now know that the 1.5-mile run has little relevance for football). The fullback who liked to use his car for target practice was 6-foot-4 and 235 pounds, and he ran like a quarter horse. He was impressive, but I never even knew his first name. His nickname was "Evil".

The night we showed up for camp, with a full slate of practice the next day, I was exposed to some eye-opening realities of college life. I never drank much in high school; I really didn't enjoy beer and I had a low tolerance. I also couldn't fathom going out somewhere during camp. Based on my experiences in high school, I assumed that we would be locked down in the dorm and that a curfew violation would lead to expulsion or worse.

That night some of the upperclassmen approached me and informed me that they had liked my effort in the running test and that I would be joining them that evening. I had been planning to be asleep by 8 p.m., so when they came to get me to go out at about 9 p.m. I was somewhat apprehensive. If I managed to get in trouble during my first night at football camp, I was thinking, my family would disown me and the only resolution might be Hari-Kari. They drove me a few miles down the road to a questionable establishment known as The Tiger's Paw. My experience with strip clubs was about as extensive as my record with alcohol consumption, but I figured that in the hierarchy of such clubs The Tiger's Paw had to be somewhere near the bottom. There was an abundance of adipose tissue and a deficiency of tooth enamel.

I was beside myself; here we were about to start camp, and the defending WVIAC conference champions were hammering down beers at a strip club. Even worse, it seemed to be perfectly normal behavior for them. We left The Tiger's Paw at 11:30 p.m., and I was certain that I would be caught and then put on a bus and shipped home to Pennsylvania. I walked to my room as quickly and quietly as I could, praying that I wouldn't see a coach. I made it, but morning came very quickly. I jumped out of bed and took a hot shower to make sure I was awake, and as I was returning to my room, I passed a tall, beautiful blonde in the hallway. I tried not to act surprised, and I said 'hello' like she was supposed to be there. I didn't ask questions. Maybe she was the hall monitor.

My first practice with Salem was intense, high-tempo and extremely organized. I noticed that the upperclassmen who had accompanied me to The Tiger's Paw the previous night were working harder than just about anyone else. They were also vocal leaders on the field. Evidently, these guys were just wide-open 24/7. That was the day I was educated in the concept of party hard-play hard. Those guys might have had too much to drink the night before, but they never skipped a beat out there. I was somewhat amazed, but also impressed with their leadership.

Our third practice that day was pure conditioning. It seemed like we ran more than a hundred sprints. NCAA rules governing practice length or frequency didn't exist in those days, and I think that our three-a-day schedule lasted for a full two weeks. That wasn't unusual in 1976; it was typical practice for a college football team. Every single coach was a grinder, and there was no place to hide. As the days progressed, team numbers dwindled, and the bus station in Salem, W.Va. stayed busy.

Even if some of the newcomers were buying their ticket home, the upperclassmen were clearly enjoying the preparation. Practice was tough but loose, particularly on defense. Our defensive coordinator, Larry Blackstone, was a slightly potbellied balding guy with thick, black-rimmed glasses. The players respected Coach Blackstone, but it was an unusual type of respect. Our free safety, who we called Stas and wore No. 76, liked to run up behind Blackstone and leapfrog over his head at random times during practice, sending the whole team into hysterics. He was everyone's favorite coach, and his 52 slant-and-angle defense had carried the team to the 1975 national championship game.

Blackstone left Salem after my freshman year and went to West Virginia Wesleyan for one season, after which he returned to Salem to become our head coach. We preferred our relationship with him when he was defensive coordinator, because we could affectionately antagonize him more in that role. It wouldn't look right for twenty players to grab footballs and simultaneously throw them at the head coach in the middle of practice. There was never a dull moment in practice when Blackstone was our coordinator, and we would go to any extent to make him happy.

Playing under him was a very unique experience, and we forged a relationship that still endures thirty-five years later. Even though I worked my way into a starting position, I felt like I had to outwork everyone to maintain that status. I loved the weight room. I also really enjoyed full contact, because I learned its value through my whole childhood. One day I did ninety dips and Blackstone—who doubled as our strength coach—thought it was great. He liked me because I would hit hard and work hard, two things that came easy for me.

During that first season, when I was redshirted, I became the scout team quarterback. Our defense was basically full speed on our scout team every day in practice, so I got hit frequently and got into more than a few fights. Our defense didn't see a problem with late hits or with hitting a teammate in the back, but I did. I probably had a slightly losing record with our defensive linemen, but that was OK since I had a 100-pound disadvantage. Even if I didn't get to compete during games, I loved that redshirt season, and I was proud of our team when we finished the season 10-1. We played our home games at night in Catalano Stadium, and the little town of Salem loved us. I remember some unbelievable victory celebrations that year.

There was a guy in that small town known as Pee Wee, and he ran an establishment on campus called "The Joint." He loved the football team, and we ruled that place. You could get a draft beer for a quarter and a cheeseburger for forty-five cents and play pinball until you were nearly blind with flashes of accumulated points. That was back in the time when people liked to dance, and nobody was concerned with getting shot. We could justify our nights on the town because we thought that the West Virginia draft beer would help us put on weight for football. So we tried to drink as much as possible. Thanks to Pee Wee, I acquired a taste for beer, and I developed a little more tolerance.

One night that fall, Pee Wee hosted a party for the football team. For $5, you and your date could drink all the beer and eat all the deer steak you wanted. It was a pretty good deal, but unfortunately, I lost my date after about an hour. I wasn't as bad off as one of our offensive lineman, who kept lining up into a three-point stance and plowing into a wooden beam. He was losing that battle. Eventually, I tried to leave with some degree of self-worth intact, but two of our senior linemen picked me up by the arms and carried me back inside, a unique expression of leadership.

One of the keys to my positive experience at Salem was the unforgettable relationship with teammates and coaches. The experiences that bonded us—the sweat and blood, the parties, the adversity, the insane way we trained—stuck in my head like glue and helped make me into the coach I am. Another result of battling in the trenches with those guys was the elimination of racial prejudice. We never really thought about skin color much at Salem; we only thought about the fact that we were there to win.

One of the teammates I became close to was a guy from Florida named Clifford Wells. Cliff was as fast as lightning, and he looked like he was chiseled out of stone. I used to go down to Florida with Cliff for spring break and stay with his large family. Cliff was adopted and his parents, Mamma Sally and Clarence, kept twenty-plus foster children of every skin color you can imagine. Clarence cooked for all the kids and for us, and we hung out in the front yard playing games with them. Life in that home was amazing to see. Seeing their love and sacrifice was a great lesson in humility and human kindness for me, and I stayed in touch with Mamma Sally long after I graduated.

Salem Strong

I have made athletic conditioning my life's work, and I scratch my head sometimes when I look back on the way we trained at Salem.

During our pregame routine our lineman did something called "bull in the ring," where they would take on their teammates at full speed on the fifty-yard line without helmets on. It was a display of our toughness, and those Tigers squads were widely known for being strong and physical.

Our weight room consisted only of a large, progressive resistance machine, known as a "universal" machine, and a squat machine that someone had built for Blackstone. He was really proud of that thing. Every time I watch "A Christmas Story" and see that father in the movie with his leg lamp, I think of Blackstone and that precious squat machine. I think the smallest amount you could load on it was about 350 pounds. We cycled through stations like deadlifts, upright rows, pull-ups, dips, power cleans and an exercise known at the "Billy Cannon." (I never met Billy Cannon, but I grew to hate that guy.) I know now that power cleans should never be part of a circuit; my back hurt for four years from doing ten reps of power cleans with iron weights on a concrete floor.

We had twenty-four exercises in our circuit in that little Salem weight room, thirty seconds on and thirty seconds off for two rounds. Some days you did agilities before lifting and some days after. Agilities lasted for forty-five minutes. I remember a particularly intense rope-jumping routine—ten sets of three minutes with thirty seconds rest between each one. Try that some time. It's a lot of rope jumping. During the summer before my senior year, I did it every day wearing army boots. Some guys on our team would throw up every Monday when they returned to training after a weekend spent in a drunken stupor. Despite my early experience at training camp, I didn't know too many players who drank on weekdays during the season.

One of my favorite coaches at Salem was Bill Stewart, who coached there from 1977-'78. He later became the head coach at West Virginia before dying of a heart attack in 2012 at age 59. He was very young and enthusiastic when I crossed paths with him, and he was a good man. One time I had a misunderstanding with some fraternity guys and I got into a little scuffle in the cafeteria. My punishment was to meet Coach Stewart at 5 a.m. to go through our circuit, and believe it or not I looked forward to seeing him every day at the crack of dawn with that dip in his mouth. He always made me feel important while he was kicking my ass. I wish I could have told him how much he influenced me back then before we lost him.

We routinely went through that circuit from Monday through Thursday, but if Blackstone saw you walking to class on a Friday he might grab you and make you do dips, bench press or power cleans. You would hear a voice, "Hey, Connors, come on and give me two sets of power cleans," or "Let me see how much more I can bench than you today." Bench pressing was the only thing Blackstone could do. He couldn't even swim, and he was terrified of water. We tried to push him into the school swimming pool many times. When Blackstone could find us on a Friday, we were training total body five days a week. It was tough and it violated every rule of recovery, but we did get strong. Of course, everyone knows that steroids were readily available during that era. Most of the guys I played with had no idea about the reality of the side effects, but we were fortunate that our coach sold the value of hard work as the alternative.

During my first season of eligibility at Salem, I was competing for the starting quarterback spot with a 6-foot-4, 225-pound teammate more suited for a straight drop-back offense. I didn't open the season as the starter, but I started seven games and ended the season with the top job. Coach Blackstone was at West Virginia Wesleyan that year, and we beat his team on a tipped slant pass that I threw on the last play of the game. I don't think Blackstone ever forgave me, because when he returned to Salem he moved me to a position then known as strong corner, and I started at that spot for the rest of my career.

The light comes on

I became very passionate about speed development during those years as a defensive back. We never saw anyone use fewer than two backs in an offensive scheme back then, because everyone ran the ball, which made things a little simpler for defensive backs. We played a lot of zone, and I can definitely say that I never got beat in a game. Blackstone was clear—he said that if I ever got beat deep I should just head to the sideline. I was determined to improve my speed, and I succeeded by trying everything I thought would work. I ran up and down hills, tied myself to a car (again), stretched relentlessly, studied tons of film and read everything that had been published about speed training in 1978. Sometimes the things that saved me were quick feet and good motor learning.

Coaches didn't preach about improving speed in those days; speed was considered something you either had or you didn't, and the only purpose of sprints was to keep you in shape. But I started to believe otherwise as I saw results from all of my labors. There were rumors the Dallas Cowboys' efforts to make their players faster, but it all seemed somewhat covert. I didn't really have any guidance in my speed training, and I was lucky I didn't injure myself. The hills I trained on were very steep, especially for downhill work. It was a miracle I didn't have any stress fractures from racing down them. We were clueless about proper running mechanics, and we were game for any rumored speed drill that might be effective.

Kevin McNair, who I mentioned previously, was definitely the first guy on the scene to teach a system of acceleration for football. His key concepts included force application, arm stroke, hip position and total body coaching cues. McNair's system centered on an ingenious method of establishing posture, which then allows the athlete to correct other problems as well. He focused on acceleration mechanics rather than top-end mechanics or maximum velocity training, and his teaching cues are still effective today. Following are some of the most relevant applications from McNair's instruction:

1. Attack the ground and accentuate backside force.
2. Arm stroke is a rotation from the shoulder.
   Never run elbow to fingertip.
3. Keep the forearm facing the navel and place
   your hand in a loose thumb on forefinger position.
4. Extend the femur to overcome inertia.
5. Get the hand through the hip to optimize force
   application in the opposite leg.
6. Keep your head level. Where the eyes go the head goes,
   and where the head goes the body goes.
7. Punch the knee forward to a focal point.
8. Rotate violently from the shoulder joint.
   The bigger the man, the more violent the rotation.
9. Accentuate horizontal components.
   Front side arm swing should be sternum level.
   We don't want to run Heaven to Hell.
10. Three-point stance involves a down arm, free arm,
    flat back, eyes focused three feet ahead of stance
    and the legs in optimal power angles. A huge arm split
    is necessary, and the down arm should scrape back.
11. Put holes in the ground.
12. Work tall and open by the sixth to eighth step.

Those were just some of the revolutionary coaching cues that Mc-Nair hammered into the minds of athletes and coaches, since he had been a sprinter with the great coach Charlie Francis at Stanford, and he was very passionate about his beliefs. The world of strength and conditioning is very fortunate that he came along and multiplied our body of knowledge about acceleration training. He progressed my profession considerably with his assertion that speed can in fact be improved.

When I was coaching at Bucknell, I worked with a number of athletes who would not be classified as "fast twitch." After visiting the Eagles and being exposed to McNair's philosophy, I implemented his fundamental program and saw quick results. We adopted the approach of developing speed by involving the whole body, and we focused on attacking the ground through acceleration. Improved posture also became a priority, and our players benefited significantly from those seemingly small adjustments. Loren Seagrave, a well-known speed training expert, always talked about body position dictating muscle recruitment, and we found that to be true as we improved our efficiency of movement and, consequently, our athleticism.

Chasing bad guys

Through every aspect of my career, running fast has been vital, and I have long pondered the most effective way to train for greater speed. However, my need for speed hasn't always been linked to football. I went to the Police Academy in Palm Beach County in 1981, shortly after graduating from Salem, and when I finished the academy I was assigned to work the streets of Delray Beach, Florida.

I had received a double degree in physical education and criminal justice, but I graduated in the middle of a recession and hit dead ends in my early job search. Finally, the door opened for police work. I was assigned to a steady midnight shift. Desperation for a paycheck can force you into some unexpected situations. I never expected to become a police officer. I wasn't certain I wanted to be a coach either, but chasing down felons was definitely not part of the future I envisioned.

The academy was an interesting experience—endless videos of blood, guts, violence and death. They made sure to fill you in on all of the various ways to lose your life as a result of stupidity. I attended one week of driving school, one week on the shooting range and one week of self-defense. For eight hours a day we took notes on what we learned, and then we had to type up every word and organize them into a master manual. As a result of all that specialized education, in 1981 I was hired for an annual salary of $10,000.

For the first thirty days we had a training partner, and mine was an excellent cop we called "Pop" for his efficiency with rookie officers like myself. During that training period, we had several calls to burglaries in progress, and I was shocked to see the dark side of a city at night. It was definitely an eye opener. I pulled out my gun much more often than I had anticipated, not to shoot anyone but to prevent others from shooting me during dicey situations. Those frightening situations occurred frequently.

During the zoo that was the midnight shift, Pop and I arrested a lot of local felons, most of whom Pop already knew well. We had to handle some DUI incidents, and in those days we punished the drunk driver by taking his keys and letting him sleep off the alcohol. Later we returned, made sure he was sober and allowed him to drive home. Even if some people got off easier than they would today, we were occasionally forced to make arrests.

One night a lady attacked me with her high-heeled shoe so she had to go to jail. Another time we brought in a guy and left his friend with his car, and his friend decided it would be a good idea to drive the car over the grass and right up to the police department's front door. The secretary called me downstairs, and I found a guy who was 6-foot-6, drunk and belligerent. He was a good candidate for a double leg takedown, and when I executed that move, the secretary was highly amused. We didn't have tasers back then, and you couldn't exactly shoot a guy in that situation. We did have long hollow metal batons and another restraining tool known as a "sap." The sap was lead covered in leather, and you could seriously injure a person with either that or the baton. My week of hand-to-hand training was basically useless, so I just went back to my high school wrestling experience, and that was mostly effective, especially since drunk people have slow reaction times.

Pop and I had a disturbance call, very late, and we went by and asked them to turn the music down. We left and soon had another call to the same house, and this time we went around to the backyard to see what was going on. We found eight naked people in the hot tub—two men and six women. A girl jumped right out of the hot tub naked, walked over to the stereo, turned the music down and then invited us to stay. We weren't sure whether to arrest her or to accept the unexpected invitation, but we decided to leave that party alone.

After a month of on-the-job training with Pop, I was on my own to work a beat. A week or so after I went solo, I was called to a burglary in progress at a local elementary school. I had been assigned to zone eight—known as a high crime area that offered cops a steady supply of memorable experiences. I wasn't aware of it when the call came in, but this situation would give me the opportunity to showcase all of that extra speed training I worked on to keep my starting cornerback job at Salem.

When I got to the school, I screeched up with my lights on and quickly learned that the culprit was still inside the building and had given himself away when he activated the silent alarm. Detectives had already surrounded the place, so I anchored myself outside a cafeteria window. I looked inside, and almost right away I saw the burglar, making a sandwich. I quietly radioed, "Give me 10-33 traffic," which meant I was broadcasting to the police forces of Delray Beach, Boynton Beach and Boca Raton. I gave my fellow officers play-by-play of his snack until he finally finished the sandwich and started to exit the school. One of the detectives informed me that he was coming out the door I was guarding, and I pulled my weapon. Game day.

As the culprit walked by me unaware, I put the gun to his head and instructed him to freeze. He looked straight down the barrel of my .38 revolver, turned his head and took off. I was shocked. Evidently, he was unaware of the Florida provision that allows a cop to shoot a "fleeing felon," or he didn't expect me to choose that option. I was running with my gun, thinking that putting a bullet into a guy for stealing a chicken salad sandwich probably wasn't justified. As I ran, I longed for my football cleats. He was in running shoes and I was wearing some kind of a boot and was laden down with equipment —flashlight, radio, baton and sap—which I lost a little bit at a time during the chase.

We crashed through some backyards, and after about seventy-five yards, he got stuck in a fence. He turned toward me, and convinced that he might be a threat, I hit him in the face with my gun. When he went down, I grabbed him by the throat and held on until my backup force arrived, which didn't take very long. When we searched him, we discovered that he had been packing a .357 Magnum but had tossed it when the chase started. It's not a good feeling to realize that you are risking your life for $10,000 a year, but I believed then and now that someone had to sacrifice their safety to protect the community. I was gaining a new appreciation for law enforcement, and after that night, I become the unofficial "chaser" on our force—not a job I was really looking for.

Once I realized that I would be participating in regular footraces with criminals, I returned to a running program in the hopes that I could stay in the kind of shape that would allow me to catch young burglars in running shoes. Twice a week I ran 400s and 800s, and twice a week I ran what might now be referred to as tempo 40s or tempo walkbacks. This routine gave me more confidence when I entered dicey situations like the one I encountered one night at Pompey Park.

Pompey Park attracted troubled juveniles and drug activity, and crowds gathered there for regular dances every weekend. While the kids were practicing their dance moves, I was testing my speed training. One night I was chasing a girl when I slipped in the sand, and when I got up my target was gone. I hated to let her get away, because we had a significant warrant on her for serious crimes. The next night, I saw her on the street at about 3 a.m., and I ran her down and pinned her to the outside of a building. Female suspects were known to carry knives, so any time you had a warrant on a woman you had to be make sure she couldn't reach into her pocket. I could feel a crowd starting to gather around me, which is never a good thing, so I keyed my pocket microphone to send the K-9 unit. My backup arrived within two minutes, which still seemed like an eternity.

Speaking of K-9, we had a dog on the force back then who would certainly make an impression. His name was "Swamp," and he was so vicious that he chewed up the dashboard of the K-9 vehicle. Whenever the unit would arrive, with Swamp head butting the windows, people would scatter pretty quickly.

Domestic calls were always tricky. One night when I was on beach patrol, it looked like a slow night until a young lady flagged me down and told me that the guy she was with refused to take her home. When I said that I was going to give her a ride, he grabbed her by the wrist and she became hysterical and screamed at me to get him off of her and arrest him. I asked her if she was going to press charges, and she said "yes." So I pulled him off of the girl and had to throw him down in the sand and physically restrain him. Somewhere in the midst of the chaos I called my sergeant for backup, and when he arrived I was still battling the guy. Sergeant Shea arrived and pinned him down, placing his baton over the guy's neck like it was a routine occurrence.

At this point the girl changed her tone, and suddenly she was screaming that we were hurting her boyfriend and she was against us.

We still had to take him down to the station and book him, but when all was said and done she didn't press any charges, after all that. When love is involved, even law enforcement isn't cut and dried.

During my time on the Delray Beach force, our chief decided to install a fitness facility on the top floor of police headquarters. I had recently won a Florida State Police Olympics Powerlifting event, so the chief took me off the road and named me the director of the fitness center. It was a good gig because I could train both myself and my fellow officers throughout the day. I also enjoyed the rare chance to work regular business hours, but that normality was only temporary. Soon I was called back to the steady midnight policing shift. Eventually I was offered a new opportunity in Tennessee as the manager of a fitness center, and that ended my weekly criminal chases once and for all. But I learned that anyone who chases criminals must be in great shape, and my speed obsession in college contributed greatly to my success as a cop. Despite the popular portrayal of police officers, donuts and a sedentary lifestyle will never prepare them for sudden full-speed activity with no warm-up.

It wouldn't seem right for me to tell my police stories without mentioning my final night as a cop. I received a call at 3:30 a.m. from a facility called South County Mental Health, informing me that a female had escaped and was knocking on random doors throughout a neighborhood. We got frequent calls to track down runners from South County, and those pursuits were always adventures. On one occasion an escapee popped out of a dumpster like a jack-in-the-box and nearly sent me into cardiac arrest.

I figured there wasn't much going on in the middle of the night so this girl—who I pictured as a disheveled wild child—would be easy to locate. As I patrolled one street, I noticed a very nice-looking young lady who appeared to be standing near a driveway. She was well-dressed, and I assumed she might be the complainant. I assumed wrong. The well-dressed young lady attacked me, and she had very sharp, long fingernails. Somehow, she locked her legs around one of my legs in an effort to scratch my face. I grabbed her hair and pulled her head toward the ground to protect my eyeballs, all while she screamed at the top of her lungs for help. She was waking up the entire neighborhood with her screams, begging people to call the police because I was a murderer from Miami.

This was not a good scene. Someone within earshot must have believed her cries for help, because soon my entire shift of cops pulled up to the house and witnessed me limping down the street with a mentally disturbed woman glued to my leg. I'm glad I could provide everyone with a good laugh before I left the department. It only took three of them to pry her off of me. Fantastic finale.

Play fast

My life experiences are full of chapters that have influenced my ideas, beliefs and training methods. Within that journey is a ten-year period marked by my determined quest to define the keys to speed training and pinpoint the conditioning tactics that would give athletes an extra step.

Playing corner at Salem was a lesson in, "run fast or don't play." Long touchdown passes will expose slow defenders very quickly. I never got beat deep because I was absolutely terrified of losing my starting role, and I knew when to turn and run. I did give up some short and intermediate passes, but no touchdowns. I ran so many uphill and downhill sprints on my own time that I couldn't possibly count them, but I do recall the time I tore my hamstring running down a steep hill. Elastikon, an incredibly strong supportive wrap like a super Ace bandage, saved my senior season after that injury.

On the police force, most criminals in running shoes could outrun me for about eighty yards, but got tired because of too many Black and Milds. My tempo speed endurance training certainly helped me to stay on top of the chase game, even if chasing someone in full gear is harder than most of the conditioning workouts I endured on the football field. Those "real-life" sprints taught me my top speed under duress, aided by a significant dose of adrenaline. As a strength coach with a passion for speed development, I'm grateful that I have more than a few miles of sprint and sprint/tempo work under my own belt, and that's not even mentioning the fact that my own father had me running 400s on a cinder track through high school. That memory alone makes me think of shin splints.

Even in today's world of high-level performance training, many experts are still not totally convinced that speed can be developed. The question will rage on, but one thing is certain: unless you train hard and consistently, progress in speed training will never come. You must train speed to gain speed, train the appropriate muscle groups, work to become more elastic and work to improve your flexibility.

I have seen athletes gain speed through a sound training program in just a few months. I had the opportunity to train defensive end Julius Peppers, a freakishly gifted fast-twitch athlete, during my tenure at North Carolina. I got him after his final season in basketball. After about two and a half months, he ran a 4.55 at 285 pounds. Peppers was a classic example of my conviction that a high-level fast-twitch athlete will respond to aggressive and intentional training. If a young man walks in the door with a 36-inch vertical jump, he is much more likely to respond to the training than a teammate who can't jump high to start with.

NFL scouts often ask about the players' attributes that are specific to football, and I tell them that two of the most important are hip rotary power and linear speed. My interaction with hundreds of scouts and my beliefs about power output led me to devise my own power quotient for assessing an athlete initially and predicting his potential for developing power. For this formula, I use five values of vertical jump, plus three values of broad jump, plus one value of power clean, then I divide that by the forty-yard time. I really like this quotient because it puts slightly more emphasis on vertical power, while still providing a measure of horizontal power with the broad jump and 40-yard components.

I have been able to use this number to establish valuable standards relative to different position groups, and I can name 25 NFL players who scored near the top of the scale in their collegiate career, which has further legitimized the value of the measurement. Bruce Carter, who played collegiately for us at UNC and was drafted by the Cowboys in 2011, is a perfect poster child for my power quotient. His initial measurement as a freshman was between 185 and 190, but coming out of college he recorded a vertical jump of 40.5 inches, a broad jump of 10 feet, 8 inches, a 405-pound power clean and a 4.38-second 40. Those numbers gave him a final quotient of 227.5, the best I've ever seen. Improving power output is our primary objective.

During my early years, I connected myself with Loren Seagrave, and also brought in my early mentor Kevin McNair. The result of adopting both of these men's philosophies was an interesting mix of teaching cues and drills for my Pirate athletes. Anyone who has studied speed has seen the early tapes produced by Loren Seagrave and Kevin O'Donnell. They were very popular in establishing a set of motor learning drills, effective body position, and methods of developing power. We jumped all over that information as a method of teaching coordination and athleticism. My goal was to develop football players who ran like track athletes, and we taught the same system to all of the position groups. The results were definitely noticeable. We had improved arm stroke, an awareness toward force application through acceleration, foot plant under the hip or behind center of mass to overcome inertia, and better posture and hip position. We were able to improve speed over an athlete's collegiate career in the forty-yard dash by an average of .17 to .20 seconds. This occurred more readily in those athletes that came through the door with fast twitch indicators.

Using Seagrave's lower body drills as a tool, we discovered that his exercises were effective in activating speed-specific muscle groups. His drills emphasize top-end mechanics, or what we now refer to as maximum velocity. Max velocity training has great value in teaching athletes a proper running technique using a "tall hips" position. Football players are typically plagued by tight hip flexors and an anterior pelvic tilt, and adjusting their running posture can lessen these problems. From a young age, they have been taught to assume a low position with power angles at the ankle, knee and hip joints, which is great for football but problematic for sprinting. I've seen football players who run a full forty yards in that low position, as if they are fearful of being tackled every step of the way. Instead of running low all the way down the field, I like to see them open up their hips fully between twelve and fifteen yards.

Several considerations come into play when attempting to design a speed program that is tailored specifically to football. Football is a game of acceleration, deceleration and reacceleration. It is not played out of a three-point speed stance, and very seldom does any player run in a straight line for more than 25 or 30 yards. Max velocity training is effective for teaching basic running mechanics, but it can be counterproductive for optimizing acceleration. The maximization of force from a static position does not mix well with cyclical movement. An athlete who is accelerating must get his foot back to the ground, which increases the ground time. As Seagrave points out, "Human beings do not possess jet propulsion." If your foot is in the air, it is obviously not applying force, so we want to cover more ground with each step. Our ultimate goal is to obtain stride separation at the proper angle (feet close to the ground in a dorsiflexed position).

Because football is often played in an upright position, the athlete has more of a vertical projection with each foot strike through acceleration. Strength in the glutes, hamstrings and quadriceps femoris is crucial to the initial phase, since a football player needs to be able to accelerate repeatedly over a short distance. An inside linebacker might accelerate or re-accelerate as many as 160 to 200 times a game, and those bursts of speed require specific preparation that has little to do with running the forty. One key is identifying methods for strengthening the muscle groups related to acceleration, especially since a linebacker must be sudden in movement and explosive through resistance. Our goal is maintain the highest quality of movement through four quarters of football, and the program aimed toward that goal must include precise emphases on strength, multi-jumps, linear speed and position specifics.

Corrective strategies

After more than twenty-five years of studying the need for football players to optimize linear movement, I have been able to design specific, effective, corrective strategies that have resulted in faster athletes. Any progress we make in speed training must be adaptable to the game of football; one size certainly does not fit all sports. The following outline details various issues that can inhibit effectiveness on the field and the methods I have pinpointed for correcting them:

I. **POSTURAL INTEGRITY**
   Problem
   - Anterior Pelvic Tilt
   - Swing leg bock
   - Casting/braking
   - Optimal leg recovery
   - Hamstrings injury

Resolution
- Active speed cueing
- Hip drills (Mann Run, Pose Chop Series, Scissors March)
- Variations—overhead resistance, hip level resistance

II. STRIDE LENGTH
Problem
- Stride Separation
- Level of Flexibility

Resolution
- Wall posture sequence
- Elevated target swing
- Elevated scissors drills
- Fly in speed bounding
- Stick Drill
- Reverse Bandit Loop Lunge

III. FORCE APPLICATION
Problem
- Strength to Overcome Inertia
- Upper Body Mechanics

Resolution—Dynamic Strength Movements
- Straight leg bound
- Pull through
- Low lunge
- Acceleration march
- Stadium progression:
  - A March
  - Lunge
  - Sprint
  - 3 Count Chop
- Arm rotation drills

IV. ACCELERATION MECHANICS
Problems
- Short stride
- Cyclical action (spinning)
- Air time

Resolution
- Multi-starts
- Sprint Bound
- Contrast Sprint Bound/Sprint

V. COME TO BALANCE SEQUENCE
Problems
- Deceleration with control
- False step
- Efficient transition mechanics

Resolution
- Multi-pattern specificity
- Reactive sequences
- Inside-out / Open field tag drills
     + Tackling technique—Shield
     Defense/Special Teams
- Sprint Bound Index
- Blending

Again, the chief problem with a football players' mechanics is the anterior pelvic tilt, which is the result of inflexibility and postural awareness. The tightness in the hip flexors, a common issue, prevents an athlete from firing his glutes. If he can't fire the glutes, he becomes quad dominant, which makes him more susceptible to a hamstring injury. Through those frequent accelerations on the football field, the glutes need to be the primary working muscle group. Another issue with the anterior pelvic tilt position is that it causes the athlete to block the thigh, referred to as "swing leg block." This means that the thigh has less distance to accelerate back to the ground, which inhibits force application. When the thigh blocks, momentum carries the lower leg forward, and as a result the foot hits the ground in front of the hip in a breaking force. Now the player has to pull his body over his foot, which is slow and counterproductive to acceleration.

When the hips are in that improper position, an athlete does not have the hip flexors on pre-stretch, and consequently the leg is slower to recover. It is impossible to fully optimize force down and back with the hips improperly positioned, and an athlete is at risk for a hamstrings injury if he repeatedly overstrides. Another issue in overstriding is that it causes the hip to drop, which causes slack in the muscle and consequently impacts elastic response.

The resolution to this hip positioning issue is absolutely crucial if an athlete is going to perform at the top of his game. When I brought Kevin McNair to ECU to teach our team proper posture and mechanics before the 1991 season, I videotaped the session, and the recording is a simplified work of art. McNair did an incredible job of conveying the "why" of each cue to his audience, and the athletes were immediately sold on each coaching point, because they felt the difference as they ran.

When we teach acceleration mechanics to athletes, there is a fine line between the time needed to apply force and the risk of overextending to the point of plantar flexion in the ankle joint. The feet are kept close to the ground, and we want to maximize "split," so we gain ground rapidly. This is also where the proper application of the "stick drill" comes in, in which an athlete uses three feet on the initial step and nine-inch increments on the next five steps. We use both a two-point falling start and a three-point start, and the objective in both is to gain ground on each step through applied force, without overstriding. Using this pattern, we measure the distance behind or in front of the distance of the sixth step, and we also time the six steps.

Next, we take that number and divide it by the time squared, then multiply it by two. This is our acceleration quotient. The acceleration pattern an athlete learns through this drill helps him stay in extension to propel effectively over the next stick or piece of tape. McNair liked to use the swimmer analogy; you must push back to go forward. We are seeking to correct excessive airtime, cyclical movement and short choppy steps through acceleration.

Jeff Howser, a former hurdler who is now the assistant strength and conditioning coach at Duke University, gave me a system of advanced drills specifically geared toward acceleration. I had become very weary of the old wall drill and pushing a car or a sled, and I was grateful for new ideas. Seagrave always emphasized that speed bounding had very specific application to acceleration, and Howser introduced me to the sprint/bound index, which is related to both lengthening the stride and turning over foot strikes. I've always referred to this technique as blending. I like to take our players with high speed bounding ability and put them through a drill of projecting themselves over four-inch hurdles for a total of eight strides, moving each stride up between 8'6" and 10'. We perform these reps with a fifteen-meter fly-in approach, which helps develop stride separation and teaches the athletes that inadequate force makes the drill impossible. Football athletes generally cannot "open up," a common trait that we must keep in mind as we seek to increase the movement capacity of a team.

I group our acceleration training into three areas: stationary acceleration, acceleration strength and acceleration power. Howser places his sprinters in a counterbalanced position so that they can feel a sense of angle from head to contact foot, and the stationary drills progress from marches to runs. These are very effective in grooving a piston-like motor learning pattern with proper joint angles. Acceleration strength, or functional strengthening, can involve a variety of modalities, such as heavy sled march, wooden sled push, stadium lunges and marches and lunges with the "run rocket." We also power walk and perform exercises in the sand pit to target specific muscle groups.

Acceleration power movements include contrast sprint/bound from a two-point or three-point speed stance. These various forms of bounding can be executed with multiple forms of resistance, such as a gradual hill, weighted sleds, the "run rocket," sand pit or stadium steps. The contrast concept has provided us with significant visible improvement in improved stride separation through increased backside force. Alternate bounding is a very effective method for improving an athlete's stride length and specific power.

Another way to teach proper hip position is through various drills with an overhead object. Keeping a dowel, medicine ball or Olympic bar behind the ears forces the hips to stay in an upright position. We use three specific drills to accomplish this objective—pose chops, Mann run and scissors march. These drills emphasize a vertical stack position, which is crucial when an athlete is "at speed." Anytime he flexes forward at the waist, the line of projection of his center of mass will be ahead of his foot strike. There are two ways he must compensate when this occurs. The first is to extend the lower leg and brake so that gravity doesn't land him on his face. The second is to adjust force application away from horizontal thrust to a vertical projection to remain upright. Neither of these reactions facilitates speed.

When planning a weekly four-day program, we first put in two max effort speed days that emphasize acceleration mechanics along with upper body lifting. These days are then alternated with two platform and lower body/tempo running days. The max effort days will result in some level of neural fatigue, and they generally include a dynamic warm-up, postural running, neural drills, vertical stack drills, bounding and full speed sprinting. They conclude with functional strengthening. In our total program, the emphasis is placed on movement, and we frequently run before lifting. The optimal schedule on a max effort speed day targets the upper body. This classic four-day split approach, with two max effort speed days and two tempo days, is a very effective protocol for the summer phase of conditioning.

Tempo running is tall running at a sub-maximal level. In the winter cycle, we run tempo forty-yard sprints and reiterate proper form. During the summer months, we might work 110s, 100-meter walk-backs on the track where we run 100 meters and walk back 50 meters, and also what we refer to as speed makers. Speed makers consist of 80 meters at 85 percent of maximum speed and the last 20 meters at 90 percent with maximum relaxation. Our favorite approach to tempo running is a technique that I developed at UNC as a method of conditioning with thoughtful running. It is a rhythmic form of running with a partner, consisting of three consecutive 20-meter zones. One of the partners designates tempo through the first zone, and when they hit the second zone the second man begins to press, with the partner mimicking the same tempo. The athletes are only one yard apart, and as the partners reach the final zone they press each other at ninety percent of maximum speed to remain hip to hip.

We are running with maximum velocity mechanics on tempo days. However, we will never provide cyclical cues. Those cues come back to haunt you on pure acceleration days. Acceleration is very specific piston-like movement that remains constant through every drill. I like to keep the cues consistent.

My favorite training schedule in the off-season winter phase is a three-day total body program in which four of the eight hours are devoted to achieving mobility, linear speed, foot quickness and change of direction. Monday, Wednesday and Friday include twenty minutes of linear work and twenty minutes of training other movement attributes. Tuesday and Thursday are directed toward contrast speed bounding and contrast sprinting, with thirty minutes of position specifics. Various days finish with a functional strength progression depending on fatigue levels.

Another method of developing strength, especially in the all-important hip flexors, is a stadium progression, preferably with a weighted vest. Our stadium has about eighty steps, and we A-march, lunge, sprint and three-count chop, in that order, for three to four rounds. This regimen will absolutely cook the hip flexors, a neglected muscle group, and it has a tremendous conditioning component.

My experience is that collegiate athletes have little to no knowledge of acceleration principles, and they also have numerous mobility issues related to weakness and inflexibility. It takes tremendous work and deliberate coaching to help an athlete become increasingly faster and more athletic through his collegiate career. Much like learning the primary multi-joint movements to develop strength and power, speed training is a process. Olympic lifts, basic pressing movements, kettlebell work and speed mechanics must be coached with the expectation of perfection.

Unfortunately, the NCAA has provided the athlete with eight weeks of discretionary time. This prevents the intense coaching of speed and movement. During these eight weeks, the strength and conditioning coach can be in the weight room for safety purposes only, when they could be operating in a much more beneficial role. I am fully convinced that there is no understanding what positive, deliberate coaching can produce during this period. Becoming a more productive athlete is not about a voluntary strength program with no accompanying mobility or speed training. Coaching should be year round and purposeful, as well as comprehensive. Greatness is not produced in intervals, a truth we learned with crystal clarity in 1978 in the no-man's land of Salem, West Virginia.

Foundational Perspectives

1. Football players have a set of unique problems that are commonly observed in relationship to posture and flexibility.

2. Football is a game of acceleration. Acceleration requires strength. It is possible that a player may have to accelerate, decelerate, and re-accelerate over 200 times during the course of a game. Strength training must be specific.

3. Coaching cues must be simple and specific to acceleration.

4. Developing speed requires a relentless, frequent, and fundamentally sound approach.

5. Improper hip position is related to a number of significant issues that impact the progress of the athlete. The hips must be positioned correctly and strengthened correctly to optimize speed.

6. The winter training phase should be directed toward maximizing the fluidity, mobility and overall movement capacity of the team. Football is a running game.

7. The pre-season phase must be adjusted to facilitate speed/endurance and achieve a higher level of work capacity. Max effort speed training remains necessary two days a week.

8. To stay on the cutting edge of speed training, coaches need to be aware of ongoing research and developments. Continuous education is critical.

9. Athletes need to be aware of the distinct possibility of underachieving as they neglect movement training during the NCAA discretionary periods.

10. Video is a tremendous and effective tool in providing feedback to the athlete. With proper assessment and coaching, an effective system of corrective strategies can improve performance.

CHAPTER THREE
THE COLOR PURPLE

In 1991, out of somewhere in left field, I received a phone call from a man named Bill Lewis, a coach who got my name from his offensive coordinator Steve Logan. Logan got my name from Ronnie Jones, who was the strength coach for Buddy Ryan at the Philadelphia Eagles and who had mentored me when I arrived at Bucknell. Ronnie told Steve, who then told Bill, that he thought I could bring something to the table at East Carolina University, where Lewis was trying to build a winning football program. Sometimes God works in very mysterious ways. Lewis had another recommendation ahead of me on his list, but he disqualified that guy because he didn't have a master's degree. I'm eternally thankful for that coach's lack of motivation to go further in school, because it changed my life. It's crazy: Sometimes you can be heading down a road to a place you've never been to start a career you never anticipated.

Three years before that random phone call, I had quit the high school coaching and teaching job that I took after leaving the police force and moved from Florida to Lewisburg, Pennsylvania to assist with the wrestling program and start a strength and conditioning program at Bucknell University. My wife Michele was pregnant at the time, and we moved into a dorm on the Bucknell campus because my job also entailed serving as a resident manager when I wasn't busy as a master's degree student, assistant wrestling coach, part-time high school teacher and founder of the Bucknell Bison strength and conditioning program. Joe Susan was doubling as strength coach and offensive line coach when I arrived, and I was the first coach at Bucknell to hold the strength and conditioning post exclusively. I had my first lessons in the high price of entering the college coaching world, which included multiple job titles, fourteen-hour days and of course a life of poverty.

When I was at Bucknell, I continued my habit of promoting overachievement in myself and others—a trend that had followed me through high school and college, as a high school wrestling coach and now in coaching and recruiting at the collegiate level. I was starting to feel like living this way—having to constantly grind and outwork people to stay at the top of my game—was my inescapable destiny. But I didn't realize those earlier activities were a mere warm-up for what was to come.

In North Palm Beach, Florida, I took over the wrestling program at an exclusive 1A private high school where I had originally been hired to teach history and coach football. In addition, I wound up coaching eleven wrestlers, most of whom were in the ninth or tenth grade. We lost every single match that first season. We were young, and most of our competition came from 3A and 4A schools, so it was a tough challenge.

After that season, I took a new approach. I recruited twenty-five football players to come out for wrestling, then located a bus and took them to Clemson for summer wrestling camp. The tide turned, and the next three seasons ended with winning records. We didn't have a gym in which to practice, so we had to roll up a big one-piece wrestling mat, put it on a truck and transport it to another school for practice every day, then roll it up and bring it back afterwards. That took commitment. Over a three-year period, our little school defeated quite a few 4A programs, including a one-point victory over Boca Raton High that demonstrated our team's heart and guts. We also had wins against larger local schools like Jupiter High and Palm Beach Gardens High. All of my little rich kids benefitted from something money can't buy—a rare journey that you can only take when you learn to believe in your own mental toughness and preparation.

When I took over that team, I hadn't wrestled since high school. I wrestled with my athletes every day to re-acquaint myself with the sport, and that helped bring our team together. The conditioning regimen I put them through was brutal, but those young men surprised me. Before I arrived there, I had assumed that fortunate sons had a limited level of toughness. Not so. Those kids had their own unique list of frustrations, and in many ways they weren't much different from the kids who came out of tough neighborhoods.

Those kids understood the principles of success, because all of their parents were highly educated. But that doesn't mean they escaped loneliness, broken families, low self-esteem or the abundance of temptations that come from prosperity. Some of them would never reach the success level of their parents, which was a stressor itself. One of the students there, the son of a famous golfer, looked just like his dad. It was no surprise that Gary had quite a golf swing himself, but it would have been tough to come close to his father's accomplishments. But Gary was a tremendous young man with a good heart and plenty of self-confidence. He also gave me his lunch every day because he preferred to leave campus and go eat at the Ocean Club with his friends. That bag lunch, with four sandwiches inside, was a tremendous supplement to my $15,000 a year income. Some of my wrestlers would stop by my apartment occasionally, and they couldn't believe that the only thing I had was a bed. I think it was good for them to see the way I lived.

While I was coaching there, I organized a wrestling clinic one year and became acquainted with Bob Ferraro, the head wrestling coach at Bucknell. Long story short, that's how I ended up at Bucknell. Bob would eventually form the National High School Coaches Association, which now hosts a number of national events annually. I juggled a multitude of responsibilities for three years, but during that time I was proud of the fact that we produced four Division I All-America selections and helped football coach Lou Maranzana and his staff achieve their first winning season in twenty years. Things were heading in the right direction, and just when Bucknell was about to take some of hats off of my head and improve my financial picture, the Pirates rang my phone. At that time, I was also finishing my high school principals' certification, so I had to make a pivotal decision. It was definitely the right one.

On the morning of my first day at ECU, I walked into the weight room at 4 a.m. I hadn't been able to sleep, and I was chomping at the bit to get in there and start grinding. One of the first players to enter the room was Robert Jones, who later would be a first-round draft pick of the Dallas Cowboys. Robert was with some other players who definitely looked the part of tough college football players, and they all seemed eager to get started. I liked the subtle climate of confidence that I sensed with these guys; they liked to lift weights and they were very upbeat. I sensed leadership and chemistry in that group, qualities that are innate on some teams and are almost always indicators of success. Evidently, Bill Lewis and his staff had the Pirates thinking the right way. East Carolina has a reputation as a hotbed training ground for coaches who experience considerable future success, and the assistants Lewis had brought in were no exception. Steve Logan and Jeff Jagodzinski would both become head collegiate coaches and NFL coaches, Mike Cassidy would coach in college programs all over the country, Bob Slowick would coach in the NFL and Dave Huxtable would become a defensive coordinator at a number of major programs. Lewis's staff was no joke. Of course, Bill Lewis would soon leave to take the head coaching job at Georgia Tech, bringing Huxtable, Cassidy and the others along. Bad move for everyone who made that transfer to Atlanta, because Lewis's tenure was short-lived.

The first football player who failed to show up for a workout on my watch at ECU was Dion Johnson, and I knew right away that I needed to set a precedent. I went straight to his dorm room, where another player named David Daniels answered the door. David was a great kid who benched about 500 pounds. Later during camp, I would jump in to break up a fight he was involved in and discovered that I could barely move the guy. David broke into hysterics when he saw me standing at his door; he knew I wasn't there for him. I scooped up Dion, took him straight to the field and we completed every minute of the entire two-hour workout. Message delivered.

During my time at ECU, these little house calls became common practice. The players knew that if they didn't show up, we would roll over to the dorm. If you compromise accountability as a coach, consider yourself dead. For a period of time, our standard punishment sessions for no-shows began at 4 a.m. and culminated with rolling and then crawling in mud to the gate. Those were great days, because we were instilling discipline and establishing a standard that would not be compromised. Lewis and Logan always had my back; they wanted what I wanted.

The players were terrified of the possibility of going to see Coach Lewis because they had failed to toe the line. He only weighed about 160 pounds soaking wet, but they still did not want any part of that meeting. Even the assistant coaches were intimidated by Lewis. Our staff meetings were rigid, businesslike and extremely quiet, and no one except the head guy expressed an opinion. Everyone was speculating that if Lewis had a successful season in 1991 he would be ascending rapidly within the business, and no one wanted to do or say anything that would interfere with future coattail prospects. That speculation was dead-on. Lewis would be voted National Coach-of-the-Year after ECU finished the season 11-1 and with a No. 9 national ranking. That ranking was an injustice to the Pirates, especially since the one loss to Illinois was the result of an illegal celebration call—probably the first game to ever be lost to that penalty.

One look at the roster from that year shows that we were going to be losing some key players after that milestone season, standouts like Robert Jones, Jeff Blake, Dion Johnson, Ken Burnette, Zaim Cunmulaj, Clayton Driver, John Jett, Luke Fisher, Keith Arnold, Greg Gardill and Chris Hall. Bill Lewis, as the intelligent and perceptive man that he was, undoubtedly sensed that it was time to make his exit. He recognized the "time factor" that his successor Steve Logan would himself make reference to later, as his stay in Greenville was nearing its end. I'm sure that the prospect of a higher salary also came into play, but Bill might have been surprised at what ECU might have done to convince him to stay. Logan's "time factor" for a coach was simple: the longer you stay, the larger your crowd of critics becomes and the more they like to talk about the need for change. Like a spouse who has forgotten that initial infatuation phase and is bored with unchanging habits and a predictable personality, they basically get tired of you. Even though you pay the bills, they just can't help themselves. You are old news.

I have seen this theory proved out time and time again with highly visible coaches. They hear the public criticisms and take them personally (which of course they are). Their response is either to withdraw from the fan base or to develop a degree of disdain for the critics. When your children or your wife come to you and tell you that there is a thread of trash directed at you on some fringe message board, you fantasize about a number of ways you would love to react, and none of them are good.

A look back at that special 1991 season at East Carolina yields several important lessons. One takeaway is the value of momentum and the total sales approach of Lewis toward players, staff and fans. He converted every ounce of success and momentum as fuel for the upcoming game, and he was a master of getting between your ears with something powerful and motivational. I absolutely loved watching the guy work. I'm not sure he ever came close to reaching the peak of his abilities during his time at Georgia Tech, because it's tough to instill the grind when you don't have early success to build upon. In 1991, the Pirate squad was ripe. They knew they should have won that season opener at Illinois, and they got hungry.

Logan gave a masterful performance as the offensive coordinator that ultimately catapulted him into the driver's seat. The combination of his coaching expertise and a willing, talented quarterback named Jeff Blake yielded unforgettable results during the course of each game. Blake would absorb Logan's coaching and go out there and make some incredible plays. He should have sent Steve a bonus check when he signed his first NFL contract. Just a joke.

Any form of success with today's athletes should be used to fuel the fire for more success. Sometimes players think they are great when they are merely good because they stumbled into a few close victories and started to believe in themselves, but that confidence can lead to unbelievable things. I think our 1991 team was well-conditioned, but Lewis sold our fourth-quarter success to the players like it was a new suit, and they bought it eagerly. As a team, I'm not sure we were superior to our opponents in that area, but the combination of physical preparation, confidence and attitude kept us winning. The stadium full of fans chanting "We Believe," was just icing.

That ECU team learned to fight together down to the last whistle. Lewis kept gluing additional components to a rolling object, and it just gained more momentum. Our last regular season game was played in Cincinnati. We were a 9-1 team hunting for a tenth win, and before the game, Lewis broke out about one hundred dimes and passed them out to represent the tenth win of the season. By the time he finished talking about those dimes, we were thinking that they should be displayed on someone's mantle or put in a safe somewhere. We had to win that game to put up two digits in the win column, and we did it. It was great. Incidentally, I ended up throwing my dime off the Emerald Isle Bridge on my way to the beach a month later, after Lewis kidnapped himself.

After we accepted a Peach Bowl bid, Lewis announced to the team that we would have the biggest celebration and parade the town of Greenville had ever seen if we could defeat N.C. State in Atlanta. It became a magical, famous comeback win—perhaps matching that 1999 Miami win as the most legendary victory in Pirate history—and it resulted in a No. 9 preseason ranking for the returning team. Unfortunately, Bill was a no-show at that victory celebration. He accepted the Georgia Tech job and stayed in Atlanta, sending a letter to be read aloud in his absence. The victory party was replaced with an empty feeling of betrayal. Enter Steve Logan.

The Logan era at ECU can be characterized as one rich in over-achievement, exceptional coaching and a progressive educational process that was rooted in his genuine spiritual commitment. Every coach is known for certain strengths and weaknesses, even if many of those perceptions are fabricated by people who didn't actually know the coach. Anyone who really knew Logan knew that his faith was unwavering and it guided him in everything he did. He was one of the most morally sound people I have ever known, and he wanted the very best experience for anyone who played under him.

His intelligence, along with his uncanny ability to guide teams to score points, were vital components in ECU's success during that time, and we were all fortunate to be the beneficiaries. Like Lewis before him, he also made some incredible hires. His staff included Larry Coyer, who would become an NFL defensive coordinator, Paul Jette, a national name among defensive coaches, Tim Rose, who was legendary for his defensive coaching style, Chuck Pagano, who went on to be an NFL assistant, coordinator and head coach and two future Division I head coaches—Doug Martin and Todd Berry. Jim Fleming would also be a head coach and defensive coordinator, Bob Babich would coach for years in the NFL, Ruffin McNeill would return as the head coach at ECU, Pat Flaherty would coach in the NFL, Chris Thurmond worked in several top programs and Steve Shankweiler had later stints at ECU and became known as an offensive line guru.

I always considered it an honor to work around such great people. They each brought something unique to the table. Through my interaction with dozens of coaches, I was proud to learn that Wild Billy was still the only coach I have ever met that did not, under any circumstances, compromise his beliefs. He never even let a kid breathe wrong, including me, and we all benefited from his high level of discipline. We were football soldiers. Outside of Billy, I've met very few coaches who didn't make a decision that trumped a principle when a paycheck got in the way. The problem is that my Dad could have coached any college team in the country had he been willing to compromise things that might have appeared extreme to others. He never would.

Most places present scenarios like these. The strength coach has to maintain accountability even when special privilege has been shown to an athlete. The trainer has to rehabilitate a player who is a no-show for treatment and doctor's appointments. The equipment manager has to keep the team in fresh clothes that were never turned in. And let's not forget the academic advisor, who must keep players eligible even when they don't show up for study hall or class.

Collegiate athletics is a carnival of unexpected challenges perpetuated by whatever level of tolerance you want to justify as the standard. Logan's standard made him successful. He knew how to make players feel incredibly stupid for idiotic behavior. He also did a great job of purging people from the team when their destructive addictions threatened to bring us down. I believe that hardline treatment of problem players was crucial to keeping our ship afloat. He had the wins to keep that boundary in place and still dodge the criticism.

Logan also had some great young men in his program who stepped unflinchingly into leadership roles. The overachievement dynamic was powerful in that group. Logan's teams learned to work and keep grinding through the tough times, particularly in the early years. After going 5-6 and 2-9 in the two seasons following Lewis's departure, the Pirates saw a turning point with their victory over Southern Miss early in Logan's third season. The Logan at the team hotel prior to the game was much different than the guy you saw in postgame interviews later that day. He was extremely confident after the game, because I think he realized that he really was a head coach on the way up, and that his guys believed in his leadership. That's a heavy burden, but it's an enormous part of the battle.

Somehow, through the constant background noise that was me running my mouth about respect, the power of the mind, mental toughness and God knows what else, Logan asked me if I was interested in doing some pregame speaking. I think Junior Smith and Damon Wilson had mentioned the idea to him after they survived a twenty-minute rant I gave about people not respecting our program as they should. I was not going to say no, even though I had some reservations. My main concern was that the assistant coaches might think, "Who the hell does the strength coach think he is?"

The first time I addressed the team before a game was in 1994, and we were preparing to play Temple. I jumped up and started to talk about being an underdog, and I pulled out some stories about the importance of winning and liking your life as a winner. I think I talked about the standard that we needed to establish, what our identity should be, blah, blah, blah. I think I was screaming and getting a little wild, but I didn't care. After I finished, I thought, 'There it is, they won't want anymore of that western Pennsylvania craziness, but at least I got it out of my system." Then Chuck Pagano got in my face and said, "That was really good, Connors. That's what we need." I always thought Chuck was a really special coach, so that meant a lot to me. He never minced words. We went on to win the game, which was great, because I would hate to pour out my soul and lose.

From that first speech grew an expectation from the players that I would invent something memorable every week, and that was a tough standard. I had been reading a lot of material about principle-centered leadership and the Biblical origin of those principles, and as a team we were also talking a lot about what it meant to have heart. As we identified a principle that would be important in the coming week, we found the scripture that was related to that principle, and that process guided my preparation for the weekly talks. Doug Martin, the offensive coordinator, also had a weekly message, and he worked our theme into his words as well. I'm not sure how godly my presentation was at times, but I spoke about universal principles that would hold true throughout the players' lives, and it's hard to argue with those.

That first year of pregame talks included a series of principles that we developed and named "Principles of the Heart." These principles were expressed with the purpose of correction and education, to progressively build character. The idea was that the cumulative effect of developing character would build better men and also result in more victories on the football field. About five years after we started this program, I picked up a book by Tom Osborne called "Faith in the Game." Surprisingly, the University of Nebraska had used an approach that was very similar to ours at ECU. The resemblance was so striking that I wondered briefly if they had found out what we were doing in Greenville and copied it. Probably not, though. Like the rest of the world outside of Greenville, they probably though we were "Eastern" Carolina and didn't give us much thought. As if the great Tom Osborne needed to investigate and copy the success of ECU.

We didn't know if those methods would work, but I can pronounce that year as one of my most gratifying as a coach. We can always say this: in 1994 we changed people. We developed confidence and team chemistry. We helped young men grow spiritually. We elevated their mental toughness. Most importantly, we taught them to sell out for each other. That was how you demonstrated that you deserved to wear the purple and gold. Some of the concepts we preached included tenacity, focus, leadership, like-mindedness, overcoming discouragement, the power of believing, commitment, the tremendous importance of consistent effort and the uniqueness of being an East Carolina Pirate. Every time we won another game, team unity increased and they believed in those principles more deeply. With his direct style of communicating objectives and his uncanny way of forcing players to think logically about what they could achieve, Coach Logan had a great impact on them. He could perfectly cue his quick wit to make a point or cause people to think. It was always both insightful and entertaining.

After about fifteen or twenty pregame presentations, I felt like I had to start getting creative. We were running out of key principles.

At some point during the 1995 season, after a game riddled with mental mistakes and responsibility malfunctions, a friend of mine told me the story of the dog soldier, which led me to research the elite warriors of the Cheyenne Indian Tribe. A warrior would dismount his horse, drive a stake into the ground and tie a rope around his waist and to the stake. When his enemy approached, he had to come inside the circle to fight the dog soldier, who was determined to battle to the death.

As I read about the dog soldier, I knew exactly how that concept would apply to the players who would soon be sitting before me in search of motivation. Football is a game of territory; every player has a specific assignment on each play. Defensive players usually have a piece of turf to defend, whether it's a gap, a flat, a third or a half. On offense or defense, your task is to win your territory or your assignment. If you don't defend your turf, we don't win. When they put that proverbial stake in the ground, we expected them to get the job done.

That story was a huge hit, and it has become one of my favorite analogies through the years. Our players came to expect that they—and the players around them—could and would win their personal battle on every play. Logan, a Cherokee Indian himself, liked the concept as well. We put a huge picture of a dog soldier in the locker room as a reminder. We also had dog soldier bandanas made to give out as awards. I believe that football players must understand the importance of their personal assignment on every play, and they must execute that assignment as if there is no one there to help them. If eleven people make that commitment, things start to click. The result is more physical effort and fewer mental mistakes. The combination of collective pride and focused responsibility on those around you has tremendous power, and we proved it in 1995.

That team was comprised of a special group of athletes with a unique commitment to the task and tremendous coachability. I am thankful for the experience of coaching that group, because it certainly doesn't come around every year. Each team has a different chemistry, but what this team did for Logan was solidify the foundation of expectation we had started to build. After a 3-3 start, they ran the table, capping it off with a Liberty Bowl defeat of Stanford. I will never understand this, but those players never received bowl rings, despite defeating a PAC-10 program and capturing a Liberty Bowl Championship. Sometimes college athletics is a puzzle. If I could win the lottery, they would all have rings—at least before they turn fifty. It isn't easy being a Pirate.

As the '90s went on and I continued to be on point for the pregame rituals, I gradually became more creative. Through the Veterans Administration, I met a wheelchair-bound guy who had served in Vietnam. He told me that he had once been forced to pull out his weapon and take out somebody in a Saigon alley. He was in a situation where he had no choice. I weighed the idea of bringing him in as a guest speaker for that week's pregame principle, which was, "Sometimes you just gotta do what you gotta do." I ran the idea past Logan, and even if he thought I was a touch unstable he gave me the okay. Later, as we were planning the production, he said, "When you get done, I'm going to smash the damn VCR on the floor" because he wanted to drive the point home. I said, "Hell, yes!"

I had to drive a special adaptive van to pick the guy up and take him to the team hotel in Williamston, which at the time was reflective of where the football budget stood. We started down the road with some idle conversation, and about fifteen minutes into the trip he lit up a joint. I almost drove the van into a ditch. I said, "Whoa, my man, I can't afford to get arrested. This would not be a good story!" He said that he only needed a little "roach" to get his mind straight, and I'm thinking, "What in the world have I gotten myself into? I'm going to pull up to the hotel, bust open the sliding door and a cloud of smoke straight out of the Vietnam jungle is going to serve as the red carpet for my wounded warrior." I said, "Dude, we're going to wind these windows down, and you're going to toss that mess out the window ASAP. You need to understand that we get rid of people for that type of stuff." He complied and my blood pressure—which is borderline anyway—began to return to normal.

When we were before the team, I gave the introduction and defined the theme for the week. My Vietnam vet was ready and I was nervous. He started to deliver a compelling story about survival in a hostile environment, and he related it to situations in life and athletics. He was articulate and had everyone's ear. When he got to the incident where he had to kill or be killed, the room was absolutely silent. He did a great job conveying the exact message the team needed to hear. I got up and said a few words, and then Steve got up and threw the VCR on the floor to finalize the message. I don't think that VCR actually broke, but he brought it all together perfectly. Everyone was jacked. I don't know what that dude was smoking, but it worked.

That night turned into the green light for me to do my thing for the pregame presentation. As soon as I could define a theme, I would begin to research the possibilities. I have a master's degree in education, and I have always believed that people learn at a much higher level when they are engaged. I started to think out of the box every week, and it took off from there.

One night I was in a video store and I saw this crazy-looking video about fights. Some of the fights featured in the film were prison fights, but it also included something about a football game, so I took it home and watched it. The football game depicted some street guys who were playing tackle football in a field and trying to knock the living hell out of each other. Also on the tape was the actual footage of a gangster being "jumped in." It was extreme, but it emphasized a point.

Every time we played West Virginia it was an extremely physical battle, and anyone who has ever played the Mountaineers knows that the climate isn't exactly friendly. I thought the footage from the video I discovered would be perfect preparation for the down-in-the-dirt, smash-mouth game we were anticipating when the Pirates met WVU at Charlotte's Ericsson Stadium. The way we had run 300s that summer bore some subtle similarities to being "jumped in," and some of our guys might have preferred a few punches in the head to those 300s. The similarity came in the fact that you had to pay a steep price if you wanted to be accepted and respected. Once you made your times in the 300s, you coached those who hadn't. If you got within two reps of making the mark, those who had succeeded before you would literally drag you around the field and toss you across the line. After you went through the pain of those reps and demonstrated the mental toughness and character of an East Carolina Pirate, you were accepted and you knew you were part of a brotherhood.

There was no doubt in anybody's mind what that video represented. It was just a much different type of brotherhood and a different price to be paid. Our video people mixed in some clips of the tackle football game in the video with footage of our previous West Virginia games, including times when Mountaineer fans threw objects at our players. It was a meaningful message, and our players responded by playing an incredibly physical game. Quarterback David Garrard ran over one of their linebackers and scored. Jeff Kerr put the quarterback out of the game. We were the more physical team that day, and the scoreboard showed it as we defeated the Mountaineers 30-23.

Since the parallels between football and the military are undeniable, I always found military experiences that related well with our chosen topics. Remaining focused and disciplined under duress is important in every football game, since turnovers and mistakes are equated with failure. Certainly, another loss on your record can't realistically be compared to the possibility of losing your life, but all consequences of being outmatched on the field are painful. When the word got out that we liked to use military references, Pirates in various branches of the military volunteered their services. Some guys from the Army helped us set up a presentation that definitely got everyone's attention, and when I say everyone I mean several of the Greenville neighborhoods that surrounded the Holiday Inn Express.

The plan was to gather our team in a meeting room, let them settle in and then begin the presentation with a loud blast right outside the conference room. No one knew then what would be happening around the world in the next decade; we would never consider a demonstration like that today. I don't know what that device was called the soldiers set off, but it rocked that hotel. I thought the place was coming down. It was quite an opening for the officers, who addressed the team about a level of preparation and readiness that allows for adaptation to any situation. They emphasized a fully comprehensive training method, so exhaustive that it would make game day somewhat routine. It was a great message, because it reiterated the importance of tough practices and tough physical and mental preparedness. It gave everyone something to think about, with special emphasis on getting your mind right in the locker room before taking the field. I absolutely despise a loose locker room. It almost makes me sick to my stomach. Suffice it to say, I grew up in a very different era where pregame preparations were serious business. When all was said and done, we played hard that week, and that message certainly had a lasting impact and gave us something solid on which to build.

My son earned a black belt in Tae Kwon Do when he was twelve, so I became familiar with some of the martial arts instructors around town. I always thought that the discipline of martial arts could benefit anyone, especially an adolescent. One of the key areas of concern when training athletes, particularly in 2013, is making sure they focus. Our society has distributed medication with little restraint to anyone who can't concentrate, which is interesting to me because when today's youth are working with a computer or a video game their depth of knowledge and concentration seems to be at an exceptional level. According to Clifford Nass, a professor of communication at Stanford, "The neural circuits devoted to skimming, scanning and multitasking are expanding and strengthening, while those used for reading and thinking deeply with sustained concentration are weakening and eroding." That may or may not be a positive trend for the future of athletics. Many experts in human behavior would contend that we are genetically more suited for one task at a time, like the air traffic controller who is responsible for landing one plane at a time while maintaining a wide field of awareness.

One of my martial arts connections in Greenville, Bill McDonald, is a tenth degree black belt who had earned all of his belts in Japan. Greenville wasn't a very large place, but it yielded some tremendous resources. I asked Bill if he would work on hand techniques and flexibility with our players, and he was eager to help. Some of our players visited his gym frequently, and Bill quickly made them a believer in his skill. He wasn't a very heavy guy, but he did damage when he faced a few of those football players. With the right instructor, this type of training can be quite beneficial for football players. At UNC, I brought in sensei Mike Storms and his "combat football" experts in to work with our players, and I thought they benefitted from the specific application to upper body striking technique. I really like the way that martial arts teaches the athlete to focus.

We were scheduled to play Cincinnati at home one year in in-clement weather, which sometimes levels the playing field. I wanted to make sure the team was prepared for a physical game, because the Bearcats weren't afraid to hit you. In an effort to get their attention, I called McDonald and asked him if he knew anyone who would be willing to fight in our locker room. He had two fighters he could send, and when these two guys showed up in the locker room before pre-game warm-up, one was missing some teeth and both looked like they had experienced multiple concussions. They were eager to beat the hell out of each other and this was a boxing match, not Kung Fu. We decided we had time for about three rounds, and it was on. These guys knew how to scrap, and they were getting in some good shots.

Logan walked in about halfway through the first round, and the look on his face was classic. He was probably wondering if this pregame routine thing had gone totally over the edge. When the fight was over, the locker room was pretty quiet, and I wasn't sure if the message had been delivered. The players seemed incredulous. We played a very physical football game and came away with a victory, and the players from that team still talk about that fight to this day. It was certainly memorable. Evidently, Cincinnati coach Rick Minter was smearing mud on the faces of some of his players before the game. When Logan heard about that, he said, "Hell, that's nothing. We had a middleweight Golden Gloves fight in our locker room while we got dressed." I'm just glad we won.

Master Byung Lee is something of a Tae Kwon Do legend in Greenville. Every time I took my son there it looked like organized chaos, but the parents of his students were absolutely sold on this man. Every class from five years old on up appeared to be at maximum capacity. One day I got the opportunity to talk with Master Lee about his background, and I told him about some of the unique things we were doing with the football team. The wheels started turning, and when I suggested that he might come in and speak to the team he jumped at the chance. This man was all about hard work, persistence and toughness. He was proud and powerful, but also extremely humble. Of course, I discussed our ongoing theme of teaching athletes to focus with minimal mental mistakes, and he was all about it.

Within three minutes after being introduced to the team, the 5-foot-6 Master Lee jumped up and kicked the ceiling. Not a chair, not a wall—the damn ceiling. Now that certainly got the team's attention. It wouldn't have mattered if he had read from the dictionary at that point; they would have listened closely. Everything he said had a similar theme—paying a price for success. He said that ordinary people could do extraordinary things with commitment and years of hard work, and he represented a real-life example of "deliberate practice." It was another great message from another unique individual. I was using the village to raise the family.

Probably my favorite pregame speech ever came from a young man who was working as a bag boy in a local grocery store. This young man was mentally challenged and was probably considered to have grade-school aptitude and capabilities. He had absolutely no anxiety about addressing the football team, and he was very deliberate about what he wanted to say. He was excited to tell everyone about his responsibilities and how each and every one of them was extremely important and needed to be carried out with perfection.

He was very detailed about the way you stocked the shelves, placed groceries in a bag, placed the bags in the cart and politely took care of the customer. Doing all of those things correctly was important to him, because they showed how he represented himself and the store. This guy was incredibly appreciative just to have a job and to have an outlet for his enthusiasm. He was very impressive to listen to, because he expressed an attitude that you just had to love. It illustrated that happiness in life is connected with passion, and our players ate it up.

Before another game, I went through the Veteran's Administration again and somehow found another Vietnam vet from Ayden, near Greenville. I was not going to give this guy a ride under any circumstances; I had learned my lesson. We were staying in a hotel somewhere in Kinston, and this guy showed up looking like one of the hotel maintenance staff, just your everyday average guy. You never know who might be a hero in this world.

When he started telling his story, you could hear a pin drop in that room. He remembered every step, every shot and every detail about being on a hill with his unit. He battled for an extended period of time, taking several bullets and watching friends die. I can't fathom how the guy survived, but I understood clearly that this man had the courage of a gladiator. He had no fear. I was surprised that he was willing to share the details of such intense memories with us, but everyone in the room learned something that night. Here was another humble man who walked down the street every day as an unknown hero. Those players needed to understand that they had been afforded the luxury of playing football while other men their age sacrificed all of their rights for freedom.

Another interesting military experience came in Columbia, South Carolina, on the day before one of our games against the Gamecocks. I had connected with some of the drill instructors at nearby Fort Jackson, and somehow they sent me the DI who was in charge of all the other DIs. He showed up right before I gave an introduction to another movie that our video guy Tom Doyle and I had put together. Tom was great to work with—he's the only video guy I've ever met who would stay up all night with you making a motivational movie in the video room. I think we had clips from twenty-six different movies in the film we showed that day in Columbia, including more than a few from the movie Tombstone. Clips from that movie would also help UNC beat Clemson in 2001.

I don't remember exactly what I was talking about that day, but it had to do with earning respect and discovering the meaning of a killer instinct. Our definition of killer instinct just meant taking care of your business at a very high level, and our players really did understand that. They had no problem with sacrifice; they knew it was necessary. After my rant we showed the movie, and during the movie I talked to the drill instructor briefly, concluding that he seemed like the real deal. The movie ended, and I couldn't find him anymore. I searched for him for about ten minutes.

Finally, I had to find Coach Logan and break the news that I had lost a soldier—and a very important one at that. We were perplexed, to say the least. We cooked up a quick finale to the pregame routine and went on to hang fifty-six points on the Gamecocks for a victory. A few days later, someone told me that the drill instructor got choked up and felt that he didn't know what to say to the team. I never really believed that, but it was an inside joke for a while. I thought I might have offended him somehow, but I can't imagine how. I would love to see him someday and learn the truth. Hey, we won!

Any time we mention the influence that the U.S. military has had on athletics, we would be remiss if we didn't include the late Colonel Charlie A. Beckwith. Colonel Beckwith trained the anti-terrorist Delta team known as "Charlie's Angels," and Reverend Stephen Harrison of Wilson once gave a great account of that Delta force for our ECU team that provided some perspective about commitment. Of course, a high level of physical tolerance is always the measuring stick for true commitment.

Each man on Charlie's Angels was asked to perform a series of individual, timed, land navigation exercises in the mountains. The length of each march increased daily, starting with six miles and capping at forty miles. Each man began with fifty pounds of equipment, with the weight gradually increasing to seventy. When the candidate reached the last exercise—a forty-mile trek with seventy pounds of equipment—he was already physically exhausted. The point of the exercise, however, was not to measure the physical capabilities of the candidate. It was designed to assess the strength of the mind.

There was one more unique twist to the Delta Force training regimen. The soldiers were not told where they were going or how long it would take to get there. They would start each march with a map and their first rendezvous point, knowing that they had to successfully complete the march within a time limit. At each successive rendezvous point, the candidates were handed a map to the next stop, never knowing when it was going to end or if they were moving fast enough. At no point during the exercise were they encouraged or discouraged, harassed or advised. The motivation had to come from within.

Their grueling final exercise had to be accomplished at two miles per hour, or twenty hours total. From a physical standpoint, if the candidate was moving at the right speed when the twelfth hour of the exercise came, he was almost completely exhausted. The final eight hours had to be completed with heart and commitment. As they approached the end of each segment, they would pray that it was the last, only to be met by the blank eyes of their superiors handing them the next map. Needless to say, many men quit. Others rested too long or slowed to a pace that kept them from meeting the time requirement. Very few had the sense of purpose and the will to finish.

The parallel of this process to East Carolina football through the '90s has to do with the value of consistently taking players toward a higher level of physical preparation. No one had to walk forty miles, but the final result was a highly-prepared eleven men sent out to take the field. The objective—at a level nowhere near the intensity of the

Delta Force—was to expose those who had a lower level of mental toughness and commitment.

The reason teams initiated practices like "winter conditioning" and "mat drills" had nothing to do with football specificity. Florida State became the model for other programs in this respect because of the Seminoles' great success in the Bobby Bowden era. Since then, there has been much debate about the value of those routines when Saturday afternoon rolls around, and factors like the increased awareness of sickle cell trait, threat of heat exhaustion or cardiac arrest and the lack of education for safe supplementation have changed the landscape.

Our focus, during those ECU years, was on overachievement and finding ways to maximize overall performance. I wanted the players to know that I was willing to go to any length to convince them to maximize their effort and refine their way of thinking. I enabled them to raise the bar. Through it all, we kept things safe, because we kept the exercises progressive and we had a great sports medicine staff. Mike Hanley was the type of athletic trainer who would personally be on the field for every group and punitive session, whatever the time of day. He was aggressive with rehabilitation, but he was always very professional. Our players never viewed the training room as a safe haven; Hanley expected them to be tough, and that consistency was crucial to our success.

I thought it would be great to incorporate some former players into the pregame schedule, so I called guys like former quarterback Leander Green to come speak. Leander provided a deeper perspective on Pirate tradition, which was great unifying information for my team. We also brought in former ECU head coach Pat Dye, which was a great honor. Every word that came out of Coach Dye's mouth was perfect, and it hit home because he was old school. He came from the tradition of kicking ass and taking names, and he had developed a proven formula that got it done. Of course, after hearing from Coach Dye, we won again. I don't think we had a choice.

I hatched many other unusual pregame schemes, but those are probably the most memorable (at least among those we can talk about). I just wanted to be a soldier in Logan's army, and he was unbelievably encouraging to me as I sought new and innovative ways to get our message across. He valued me as a team member and allowed me the boldness to disagree at times and get a fair hearing. Steve's leadership style was right in line with the gurus who write books about open lines of communication and collaborative decision making.

Zig Ziglar said, "Cooperation is not getting the other fellow to do what you want. Rather, it means getting him to want to do what you want. My loyalty to Logan was based on his confidence in me, which was expressed in the autonomy he gave me in my position. Another Ziglar quote is, "True cooperation generally depends on certain feelings that have been established over a period of time. It's the responsibility and opportunity of the leader to understand and develop those deeper feelings and then work with them, rather than against them." Those are good words.

Logan frequently used vision and a preemptive approach when communicating with his players. He recognized that many situations are predictable, and if you head them off at the pass you can prevent poor performance or other problems. For example, he would outline the entire season at the preseason meeting in August, dividing the schedule into mini-seasons to allow the players to focus on short-term goals. During game week, we began on Sunday with an assessment of the upcoming opponent, placing emphasis on strengths and weaknesses as he tried to map out exactly what each position group would need to do to win the game. That principle worked in non-football ways as well. Before we gave the team any time off, whether it was a day or a week, Steve confronted the players with all of the ways they could get stupid and embarrass themselves and the team. He was always thinking ahead, which was incredibly wise when you consider the number of issues that can smack a coach right in the back of the head.

Logan coped with the stress of the head coaching job by seeking some level of peaceful solitude. He often read and meditated early in the morning in the confines of his office, and he loved to break away to the beach with his wife. One knock on Logan was that he was sensitive to criticism, but I really haven't ever met a coach who wasn't. I think they have to know to present a front and let the negative comments bounce off, but it stays with them nonetheless. I like what Emerson wrote: "It is easy in the world to live after the world's opinion; it is easy in solitude to live after our own; but the great man is he who in the midst of a crowd keeps with perfect sweetness the independence of solitude." To me, that described Logan. He always appeared to be thinking about something deep, even when he was having a conversation about the weather. People wondered why he often separated himself from the team and squatted down to watch the game with his odd demeanor. Most likely, he was trying to facilitate deep thought and optimize the power of his intelligence in the heat of the moment. That was the nature of the man.

People want to be coaches because of the atmosphere on game days. The excitement of being on the court or the field—of transferring the hard work and preparation to the reality of victory—is an experience that can't be duplicated. When you have coached a team to victory, everybody loves you and life is as good as it gets. You want to savor every moment, because you never know what the next week or year has in store. Our time at ECU in the '90s was unbelievable, and no one can ever take that away. Steve Logan made it happen, and I'm grateful that I could be an extension of his approach and hopefully one of the aids in his success.

One of the reasons I embraced military analogies to motivate our teams was the need for structure on a successful team. One of my favorite books is the Warfighting Skills Manual of the United States Marine Corps. I go completely off the chain when I read some of the statements in this book, because it is so on the money. Some examples:

1. "Military discipline is the state of order and obedience among military personnel resulting from training."

Training is the key word here. This is what we do. We train people. If we want order and obedience, we must train in a manner that demands these important components in the process. Pretty simple.

2. In the Marine Corps, we do not refer to regulations, punishment or a state of subservience. What we teach is exact executing of orders resulting from an intelligent, willing 'obedience.'"

Athletes will need to know why we train like we train, and they must give 100% effort. To view training as punishment is an excuse, ignorance, or possibly the wrong type of training. Basically, you need to eliminate lazy athletes and stupid coaches.

3. "Discipline is necessary to secure orderly action which alone can triumph over seemingly impossible conditions of battle. The individual must be able to recognize and face fear, because fear is the enemy of discipline."

I don't think I could find a statement that would be more perfect to justify the reason for the success of a team who were underdogs in so many situations. If our team was plagued with anxiety and a lack of confidence, it would have been very difficult to execute against superior opponents. Our discipline was superior, and that always gave us a chance.

4. "It is too late to learn discipline on the battlefield. It must be learned in training."

This is another beautiful statement that validates the importance of preparation. It also infers that the innermost part of the mind is trainable. A disciplined mind is focused, confident, and coachable. It would be great to see an alliance between the NCAA and the Marine Corps. Just another thought.

These principles helped us accomplish something special. Each game was memorable, because there was a pattern of comprehensive preparation that worked. We learned how to get the most out of what we had. We had inner strength, like-mindedness, discipline, and spirit. If you can combine those elements with some degree of talent, you always have a shot at victory. My first year at East Carolina culminated with a Peach Bowl victory over N.C. State. My last game during my first tenure there ended with a Galleryfurniture.com Bowl victory over Texas Tech. It was a great ten years and an amazing learning experience.

Bill Lewis kicked off a decade of distinction in the history of East Carolina football, and Steve Logan took the baton to finish out the '90s and beyond with the highest standards imaginable. Let me reiterate that he became ECU's all-time winningest coach, and he was recently selected for induction into the ECU Athletics Hall of Fame. Happy endings in the exit process of collegiate head football coaches are virtually non-existent. Whether a coach leaves for a better job or is asked to step down because of lost favor with influential people, those scenarios always occur with some form of public criticism. Even if a coach retires favorably, some people will say he should have retired sooner.

Steve Logan left his post at East Carolina in 2002, but the body of his work at ECU stands for itself. I can't speak for Coach Logan, but I think this Ben Franklin quote is relevant here: "We must not, in the course of public life, expect immediate approbation and immediate grateful knowledge of our services. But let us persevere through abuse and even injury. The internal satisfaction of good conscience is always present, and time will do us justice in the minds of the people, even those at present the most prejudiced against us."

Foundational Principles

1. Collegiate coaching is a "dues paying business." The most effective method of advancement is a relentless work ethic combined with a willingness to meet people who can facilitate your strengths.

2. Strength and conditioning coaches have the opportunity to gain insight about the inner qualities of a team from the sheer time spent among the players. The chemistry of a team is a great predictor.

3. Momentum is very important. If a team can capture a few significant victories early in the season, it is vital to strategize on taking advantage of the momentum and positive spirit perpetuated from winning.

4. There is a tremendous level of power in collective overachievement. Average athletes who are willing to grind on and off the field can find a level of confidence that becomes a tsunami of desire. The key word is collective.

5. Military principles are very specific because they develop men and save lives. We are in the business of developing men, and we hope to save lives by providing them with principles that perpetuate success.

6. Some head coaches have become instant millionaires, which often changes people. Steve Logan was unique in that he was in his office every day throughout the summer. Every player knew he was there.

7. There are some very powerful resources throughout a football community who are willing to step up if you just ask. Greenville, North Carolina is a place saturated with those who are willing. Former players can be great mentors and resources for current players. Young people desperately need role models.

8. If you ever experience a team that becomes a like-minded, true brotherhood, you will know you have been a part of something very special. Like-mindedness yields unity of purpose. It must be built from the ground up. Sometimes problem people have to be eliminated to maintain it.

9. The most successful teams do not tolerate negative talk about a team member or the team. You will eventually think what you speak. Each member of the team must think the same about everything related to the team in a perfect world.

10. As a coach, you must be the right voice. Wrong voices can poison the water fast. Even if your program is hanging on by its last string, be the right voice.

CHAPTER FOUR
TAR HEEL TIME

When you're an East Carolina Pirate, one thing is drilled into your head: Never wear Carolina blue or make any kind of positive comment about Chapel Hill. Even though I spent ten years in that anti-UNC climate, I never knew much about the Tar Heels. I had watched them play on TV when I was growing up, and I remember thinking their uniforms looked cool. I never imagined, as I was helping build a winner at nearby ECU, that I would someday accept a position there. A move like that would surely result in the loss of all of my friends in Greenville—as well as excommunication from my fellow coaches. Out of all of the schools in the NCAA, only N.C. State might be more damaging to my professional life.

The ECU Pirates were rolling in 2000. Quarterback David Garrard was coming into his own, Keith Stokes was special on kick returns, and we had talent and depth across the board. Our team leaders were both talented and vocal—guys like Leonard Henry, Vonta Leach, Brian Rimpf and Devone Claybrooks from that roster have all played or are still playing in the NFL. The season ended with a 9-3 record and a victory over Texas Tech in the Galleryfurniture.com Bowl in Houston. The program appeared to be on solid footing, but somewhere along the line the athletic director Mike Hamrick and the head football coach Steve Logan began to see things differently. Such tension is not unusual in college sports, but when people sense the discord they start to talk, and soon those close to the program are forming opinions and allying themselves with one faction or the other.

Crazy things started to happen. During one home game, an airplane flew over the stadium pulling a sign that said, "Fire Hamrick." Of course, this may have sparked unnecessary turmoil within the Pirate Nation. I have no clue what prompted this inharmonious climate, but it escalated quickly, and soon players became aware of it as well. It might have been a slight distraction, but not enough to prevent the Pirates from dominating Texas Tech in the bowl game. They did, however, become disheartened when—for the second time in five years—they didn't receive bowl rings for their victory. My thoughts were starting to project to instability down the road in Greenville, and when your professional future is at stake that's never a good road to travel.

I was close to Logan and felt a very strong allegiance to him, and I have joked in the years since that I once thought Mike Hamrick was trying to kill me because of that loyalty. He included me in a group that would go on a whitewater rafting trip in West Virginia as a charity auction prize. I had no idea what class six rapids were before that day, but I found out pretty quick. Hamrick and his family were true blue West Virginians; I think his brother was in charge of everything outdoors in the state and his Dad was like country-strong Jed Clampett. The pregame talk for the rafting trip was classic: "The water is uncommonly high and cold, and people have died here. If you fall out during the 'put in,' expect to be underwater for a long time. Do exactly what the guide says, or you will be thrown into the mercy of the rock configuration." Matt Maloney, a fundraiser for ECU athletics, was so spooked that he put his wet suit on backwards. I paddled my brains out that day, and I proved to be extremely coachable on class six rapids.

Another time, I was invited to West Virginia for some trout fishing with the Hamrick clan and former Green Bay Packer George Koonce. We walked down a mountain to a stream; it was a beautiful setting. At some point, George walked away to relieve himself in the woods, but he wasn't gone long. He came running back yelling, "Bear! Bear!" and the Hamricks hardly raised an eyebrow. They said, "No worries, lots of black bears here. They're just hungry and looking for food. They are protected, and they shouldn't be harmed." Somehow, that didn't calm my nerves at all. After dinner we put our food up in a tree and retired to two tents. It was darker than dark. In the wee hours of the night, George, Mike Hamrick and I were awakened by a loud yell— something about a bear. George was the only one there with a gun, and I quickly requested that he unholster his small revolver and be ready to shoot.

It turns out that Mike's brother, who was the Commissioner of Wildlife or something similar, was rudely awakened by Mr. Black Bear, who tore a hole in his tent to get to a loaf of bread. Mike's brother punched the bear in the nose, and the bear took off. Now, I have never heard of anyone punching a bear in the nose and living to tell the tale, but I was an auditory witness. The bear didn't clear out completely; he perched himself up on a nearby hill and eyeballed us. Morning came slowly. Finally, when the sun rose, we decided to go ahead and conquer the mountain. Mike's dad established a kick-ass pace up that seemingly endless mountain, and I kept my head on a swivel. Again, I was coachable, and again I survived.

At some point during that tempestuous period, Steve Logan called me into his office and discussed pursuing opportunities elsewhere. I was confused, because he really seemed to be rattled by the tension and the politics, and I could not understand why we would leave when outwardly things were going so well. Still, he seemed serious about the idea. Hamrick had always given me the impression that I would keep some kind of job at ECU even if Steve left, but there was no guarantee it would be the same job. That kind of uncertainly wasn't my cup of tea. I could never step away from football, and I really didn't want to coach with anyone else. I was very comfortable with Steve, and we shared the same philosophy.

Meanwhile, in Chapel Hill, head coach John Bunting was struggling to find a strength coach since his buddy Dana LeDuc had turned down the offer. Two of my coaching acquaintances from earlier ECU days, Dave Huxtable and Jim Webster, had landed in Chapel Hill and mentioned my name to Bunting. They contacted me and indicated that I would have a very good shot at the job if I wanted it. At that point I really started to get a sick feeling in my stomach; suddenly leaving had become a real possibility, and even though Steve treated me like a brother all of the underlying turbulence was making him behave out of character. When he came into the weight room before we left for the bowl game and talked to me again about leaving, I knew it was time for me to go. There was no room for sentiment or emotion. I had to make sure my family was secure.

After the Galleryfurniture.com Bowl win, we got back to Greenville at about 7 p.m. I interviewed in Chapel Hill until about 11 p.m., accepted the position, and was in the Virgin Islands on a sailboat the next afternoon. The warm breeze and the clear blue of the water helped me to keep my sanity through that process. Some people find excitement and intrigue in change, but it makes me nauseous because I hate to leave relationships. I take friendships very seriously, and I had to leave a bunch of young men into whom I had poured every ounce of myself. I had to tell myself over and over that it was the nature of the coaching profession.

I definitely had some misgivings, but when I arrived at UNC I felt like I had just made it to the mountaintop. The football facility was plush, and the new staff was introduced in the Dean Smith Center at the halftime of a basketball game. The media was all over us. It was honeymoon time, and if you couldn't keep it in perspective you might end up with a serious humility deficit. Allowing your head to swell can make you complacent because you, of course, have all the answers. Fortunately, I wasn't that stupid. I knew this was going to be a grind, because I had already been through the roster and the write-ups from the previous year.

The offensive line was average at best. Quarterback Ronald Curry and defensive end Julius Peppers were incredible talents, but they were also playing on the basketball team. The defense would be very solid, but you could see major holes would start appearing in the lineup soon when talents like Peppers, Ryan Sims, Quincy Monk, David Thornton, Merceda Perry, Joey Evans and Anthony Perkins said goodbye to Chapel Hill. Defensive coordinator Jon Tenuta must have known what was coming too, because as the 2001 season came to a close he had a phone glued to his ear searching for his next destination. The defense played well that year in our 16-10 Peach Bowl victory over Auburn, which didn't hurt his marketability, and before long he was settled at Georgia Tech.

My first year at Carolina was enjoyable and rewarding. The players worked hard and responded to the strength and conditioning program, and we had some good results. We beat Florida State 41-7, won the Peach Bowl and saw some players drafted that spring. Our pro day looked like a Who's Who of NFL coaches.

The summer before my first season in Chapel Hill, I was introduced to the UNC Big Hitters Golf Tournament at Pine Needles in Pinehurst, North Carolina. This event, funded by the football boosters and run by the Rams Club, included three days of golf and social events. Two highlights were the fundraising auction, which was conducted at the apex of the golfers' insobriety and the awards ceremonies for the superball events. The tournament was a lot of fun, and it featured a rock star cast of accomplished UNC boosters who also happened to be great people.

In addition to those committed boosters, Coach Bunting had the support of his former teammates, who were hardnosed old-school type guys willing to do whatever it took to help him build a winner. Those two groups of people combined for an exceptional network of support, even if other pieces of the puzzle also had to fit into place to yield success. It was a formula that worked well for Mack Brown, and after Bunting Butch Davis would also maximize it skillfully.

The Big Hitters Tournament helped raise camp money for the staff, which is a key bonus benefit that helps keep good coaches around. It was clear that those Tar Heel fans wearing collared shirts—featuring a logo of a football and a golf club—and checking in golf bags were serious about making something significant happen over that three-day weekend. It was an impressive gesture of football-specific influence and support that magnified the demand for quick success.

Following the Peach Bowl win over Auburn in 2002, it was time for that January jump-ship fever that is such a common affliction throughout college football. The money keeps getting more lucrative, the grass is always greener and coaches just can't help themselves. Jon Tenuta's departure for Georgia Tech didn't help the outbreak that year; we lost a number of key players on defense along with their coordinator. We wouldn't see another group with that much combined talent until several years later. Our out-of-conference schedule would remain extremely challenging, adding to the barriers on the program's horizon.

Over time, UNC observers would question the continuing problems within our defense. It was very simple to me—the defense lacked talent, depth and toughness. A defensive tackle who bench pressed close to 500 pounds and had a 30-plus vertical jump came into my office one day and told me he was playing football because his parents wanted him to, but he said it wasn't his passion. The rest of the defensive front was less talented and showed less physical potential than the players I had coached at ECU. I had coached high-upside guys like Rod Coleman, Norris McCleary, Devone Claybrooks and Mbayo Ahmadu at ECU, and I thought UNC would have those type of players stockpiled. That was one of the reasons I took the job, because I was under the impression I wouldn't have to invent people like we had to do in Greenville. In order to establish some sense of depth across the board at ECU, we always needed a supply of overachievers.

Chopping wood in Chapel Hill

After you have been in this business a while, you usually know what you have to work with after two or three days of observation. In 2002, as we prepared for our second season, I determined that we were going to be deficient on defense and slim in some other areas as well. At this point I had two choices. I could get on the phone and search for a job or dig in. I saw the storm coming, but I was convinced that it was time to start turning over stones and looking deeper.

In an effort to help improve the landscape at UNC, I felt compelled to stay on the cutting edge of any training methods that were out there. Strength and conditioning is a dynamic profession—it's constantly changing, and no one ever totally masters it. Obviously, talent and work ethic are vital components to success, but the degree to which the remaining potential emerges is dependent on how we spend our training minutes. We want to optimize absolute strength, convert that strength to power and apply that power specifically to the game of football.

At this point, it was my opinion that we had somewhat of a "stiff", non-athletic football team. We went back to the basics and emphasized any training method available to boost our athleticism. We needed to headline such things as the importance of stability to maintain posture. We also emphasized the importance of mobility in the joints to facilitate power through specific ranges of movement. The team we were dealing with was in need of a total overhaul in the area of fluidity, which can be viewed as a byproduct of these other factors.

Through years of working with football players, one of the most important things I have learned is the necessity of spending large amounts of time training position-specific movements. We want to budget enough time to hammer home motor learning skills on a daily basis so that they can become second nature. Movement skill is our primary objective for the hours spent in repetition. We emphasize excellent posture, eye position and arm stroke, so that doing it right becomes automatic. We teach players to come to balance, change direction and transition without compromising their body position. We try to spend whatever time we have working toward these goals.

Vonta Leach, who turned an excellent ECU career into seven seasons and counting in the NFL, couldn't touch his toes on a good day, but he was a fluid athlete. Some people refer to this characteristic as "athleticism." Vonta looked good on the football field, because he was strong, had great posture and played relaxed. He has made the Pro Bowl and is arguably the best blocking fullback in the NFL today. The progress of players like Vonta proves that drilling position-specific movement patterns is similar to wrestlers drilling takedowns. If you execute enough reps, you are guaranteed to improve.

During these years, we began to see very favorable results when we prioritized football-specific movements. To improve acceleration, we worked to increase both force application and stride separation. We continued to emphasize basic methods such as fly-in speed bounds over four-inch mini-hurdles. The hurdles were set between eight and ten feet apart, using a maximum of eight steps. This drill promotes force application and requires the athlete to strain and scissor his legs. Speed bounding combined with the proper back squat, elevated barbell step-up and a number of resisted movement drills involving the posterior chain was and still is an excellent formula for developing speed-specific strength and power and improving range of motion. This was also the time when we started taking a closer look at the power quotient and implementing a higher level of contrast training to improve our results. These are the numbers we came up with:

POWER QUOTIENT STANDARDS
40 time: 5x VJ/ 3x BJ / 1x PC

	Excellent	Good	Fair	Poor	Freak
Offensive Line	>155	145-154	134-144	<134	>165
Defensive Line (TACKLES)	>163	155-162	147-154	<147	>170

	Excellent	Good	Fair	Poor	Freak
Defensive Line (ENDS)	>185	172-184	16-171	<162	>192
Linebackers	>190	177-189	167-176	<167	>200
Tailbacks/ Safeties	>182	170-181	163-169	<163	>190
Wide Receivers/ Corners	>178	168-177	158-167	<158	>185
Fullbacks/ Tight Ends	>180	170-179	162-169	<162	>190
Quarterbacks	>167	157-166	147-156	<147	>175

If you look back at that period of time—between the Peach Bowl in early 2002 and 2003, you could refer to it as the Old Mother Hubbard's cupboard era. Bunting's cupboard wasn't exactly overflowing, but he was picking up some steam and starting to hit some recruiting home runs to remedy the issue. We were also seeing significant progress with physical development. Bunting brought in some really promising receivers like Mike Mason, Adarius Bowman, Brooks Foster and Jesse Holley. He signed Khalif Mitchell, Terry Hunter and Kenny Price out of Hargrove Military Academy to join Kentwan Balmer from Weldon and Hilee Taylor out of Scotland County. Other key players were Chase Page, Shelton Bynum, Jonas Seawright and Tommy Davis.

After they were officially Tar Heels, the problem became, as in many programs, keeping the team intact. Eleven players from that 2004 roster would eventually wind up in the NFL, including Balmer, Foster, Holley, Seawright, Taylor, Jason Brown, Tommy Davis, Madison Hedgecock, Gerald Sensabaugh, Victor Worsley and Wallace Wright. Others, like Bowman, Mitchell, Alden Blizzard, Charlston Gray, Terry Hunter, Mike Mason, Fred Sparkman, "Puff" Thomas and Rashaad Tyndall, exited the UNC program early for various reasons and caused major concerns about our team's depth. I personally believe that at least five of these UNC hopefuls could have been NFL players given the right conditions.

It was clear that Coach Bunting was reeling in some talent and that we were successfully developing their potential after they came to us, or those players wouldn't have made it in the NFL. But we were losing too many players to discipline and academic reasons, and in 2004 and 2005 our out-of-conference matchups included Wisconsin, Utah twice and Louisville twice, which was a double Cardinal nightmare. We managed a home victory against Utah in 2005, but we lost the rest of those. We finished 6-5 in

2004 and made it to the Continental Tire Bowl in Charlotte, but we lost that game to Boston College. In 2005 we lost in overtime to Maryland 33-30, and that close scrape kept us out of a bowl. It was a low point for the UNC program, and a dagger in Coach Bunting's heart.

A coming storm

Players are always keenly aware when their coach is wounded, and by 2005 Bunting was being fired on and his opponents had outflanked him. He had raised a lot of hell with knuckleheads on the team for academic underachievement and other behavioral issues, which was the only right thing to do. When malcontents like those smell blood, they bail, and some realized that they could take a break from the team and wait for a new coach. They were less than 100 percent committed to the team. You could feel the individualism winning out over team unity during the offseason, and it wasn't difficult to predict the coming storm. Bunting's right hand guy had moved into marketing, and many of those around him moved into "CYA" mode.

I was struggling to help right the ship, to find any techniques that might help give these players an edge, but by this time there was a problem between their ears that would need to be remedied. It was a tough time. There was a scramble for a sense of direction, and there were honestly a number of things happening that would make you sick to your stomach. I've seen some pretty unpleasant things happen around the game of football. I've seen my Dad fist fight with school board members. Someone once shot out our neighbor's window in Pennsylvania, thinking it was our house, and our neighbor had a heart attack soon after. I've watched grown men who are supposed to be friends stab each other in the back to deflect blame. Losing brings out the ugly.

Fundraising is absolutely essential to building and keeping a football program, but I've noticed over the years that typically the most powerful boosters never played the game. Some were never involved in any type of athletics. Incidentally, a number of good football coaches never played either, so lack of experience on the gridiron doesn't necessarily translate into lack of understanding. I have had the pleasure of developing genuine friendships with many of these boosters in my time at various schools; they visit our facilities quite a bit because of the large investments they make in them. They are extremely intelligent, innovative and high-achieving individuals—influential in the community, the state and sometimes the nation.

The "Big Hitters" at UNC included people from every walk of life, and some were even former Tar Heel players. I envy and respect those people, and I don't mean to come off the least bit cynical about them. They remind me that I should have spent more time in the library. I should have studied harder. I can't imagine what it's like to have the power to influence a university and control your own destiny. The freedom of financial independence must be incredible. If I was in their position, I could experience things like tailgating, a respectable golf handicap, parking places and a place on the sideline without the urge to choke a player who taps their helmet to come out in the fourth quarter. My wife and children wouldn't have to feel like the whole world was coming to an end because we lost a game.

Even though I am envious of those boosters at times, I wouldn't trade my coaching experiences for anything. And I really have enjoyed getting acquainted with 98 percent of the people who help support our programs. But in every group there are those who have no self-control and feel compelled to belittle coaches or other decision-makers whenever the opportunity presents itself. They enjoy the status of full-time critic while being completely insulated from the devastation of losing a job.

The real problem I have with those criticisms is that I vividly recall the pain of three-a-day practices in high school and college. I can still feel the shock of a headgear right under my chin. I caught some painful shots in the middle of my back, and I distinctly remember a kickoff where I got hit right in the front teeth. Fortunately, I was wearing a mouthpiece, but it still hurt like hell. I remember the exact three plays that led me to see the "stars," as I was no doubt concussed. I can respect someone's opinion in a whole new way if I know that they paid the price. I would settle for them surviving just one day of Wild Billy's three-a-day camp.

When the Tar Heels played at Notre Dame in 2006, one of those "critic types" traveled with the team and stopped me to say, "I want to thank you." Well, I knew what that meant. I knew it was a subtle farewell. This was the same guy who would one day present Butch Davis with a life-sized picture of Butch Davis. Butch was obligated to hang it in the building, but I don't think he was ever very comfortable with it. That picture was the first thing you saw when you exited the elevator on the second floor of the Kenan Football Center. When that booster thanked me that day, the hair stood up on my neck and I had a flashback of the day my dad tried to choke a school board member by his necktie. I just muttered a, "We'll see what happens when the smoke clears," as I quickly removed myself from his presence. I could have stomached it better if I knew the guy ever ran down on a kick-off or took on a double team block. Anyway, life went on that day. We ran past Irish guys playing the bagpipes and caught a glimpse of Touchdown Jesus. During the game, JB picked up a player by the jersey with one arm and threw him about fifteen feet. You could sense the frustration. Besides some Hakeem Nicks plays, that was one of the notable physical efforts of the day. We would later defeat Notre Dame in Chapel Hill, when Butch Davis had taken over, and that was a memorable victory for me.

Following the Virginia game that year, there was a serious meeting between the football staff and athletic director Dick Baddour. He announced that Bunting would finish that season but then he would be finished in Chapel Hill. All of the coaches were informed that they would be given the opportunity to use the phones up in the old press box to search for a new job. What a sad ending. Bunting had a combination of misfortunes over his six seasons, but I am definitely a better man for having been part of his staff. He played in the NFL for fourteen years, and he knew just about everyone in the league. He was a defensive coordinator under Dick Vermeil for the St. Louis Rams in 1999 when they won the Super Bowl. Vermeil is known for his emotion, and JB shares his love for the game.

You never knew who was going to come visit Coach Bunting; I got in the elevator one day and there stood Reggie White. JB was known for his toughness, his loyalty, his integrity and the tenacious way he played the game. He was a Tar Heel born and bred, and he ran with a group of former teammates who were all highly successful, tough people. They had a lot of pride, and they were full of rich stories about their UNC experiences. Their favorite stories always featured former coach Bill Dooley, who evidently brought a brutal approach to the team. They had won more than any other group in school history. I enjoyed listening to those stories and seeing their camaraderie, and I knew it was tough for them to see their brother step down from the program they all loved.

My personal situation at that point was similar to that of everyone else in the building. I might have had an 'assistant athletic director' hung onto my title, but that had no value because I was connected with football. I don't know where it started, but these days strength coaches seem to think that a title like that gives them more security. The truth is, the bottom line for strength coaches hasn't changed: Winning and losing determines everything. You can be a great strength coach tied into a poor football staff, and you will lose your job. It also works the other way. Winning can often protect a subpar strength coach.

No one ever measures or even cares to evaluate what you do. Very few administrators have a clue about the actual quality of work taking place in the weight room. They might ask the trainers if the environment is safe, or they might rely on the opinions of the football staff. I have never heard of an athletic administrator who looked at test results, or how you refused to compromise team discipline, or how you fought tooth and nail to change a player's character, or how much you value education. It's a lot easier just to leave it up to the next head coach, who is also limited in his knowledge of what's happening in the weight room and just wants to bring in his own guy.

During my decade at Carolina, I sat down with the AD to talk shop a grand total of three times. I assume to this day that everything he thought about me as an employee or as a man was second-hand information—reports he heard from the football coach. The NCAA changes have limited the strength coach's ability to develop his own identity within the program. Most people never bother to learn what that distinctive approach is. UNC AD Dick Baddour had one thing to say to me: "It depends on what the new coach wants."

While I was still at ECU in the '90s, I had flown out to California to interview with Butch Davis and Greg Schiano for the strength coach job at the University of Miami. Butch offered me the job, but I turned it down because the pay increase didn't work for me and I still had a great situation at ECU. Chuck Pagano had secured the interview for me, and I appreciated the fact that he thought of me when he started running in "big-name" circles. It was hard to believe that I turned down the offer, but I really needed more money than they were offering. I had lived in South Florida before in a state of both teacher and law enforcement poverty, and I was acquainted with the high cost of living there.

Enter Butch Davis

When I heard that Butch was going to take the UNC job, I was convinced that there was a higher power somewhere that was allowing our paths to cross again. Still, I really didn't think that he would consider hiring me again after I had turned down the Miami offer. My only source of information, during this uncertain time, was Pagano, who was finishing out a grueling season with the Oakland Raiders and was probably tiring of my 5 a.m. phone calls. There was a rumor that he was going to accept the UNC defensive coordinator position under Butch; he couldn't give me any definite answers, but I knew he was in my corner.

Around that time, I received a call from Jeff Jagodzinski, who was about to take the top job at Boston College with Steve Logan as his offensive coordinator. It is absolutely true that God is good all the time, because suddenly I had another good option available. I knew I would be comfortable working with my old ECU buddies, but I also knew it would be very difficult to leave before my son's senior year in high school. I didn't think I could do it.

Butch Davis's arrival in Chapel Hill was like the election of a new president. There were ceremonies, interviews, high-level meetings, remodeling, restructuring, media members in a frenzy and a line of people hoping to get a pass to the third floor to be near the new coach. In the middle of this chaos stood a group of coaches wondering if they still had a job or not. Every week was kind of like American Idol; you didn't know who was next to go down the road. In staff meetings, I tried to sit like a church mouse and take it all in. I've been in a ton of those meetings, but I only ever made it to the conference table at ECU under Lewis and Logan. At Carolina, I was a second-row kind of guy, and I have to honestly say that there were days I really enjoyed the show.

At one of the early meetings, Butch referred to the stress and heartache of his situation with the Cleveland Browns, who let him go in 2004. Not surprisingly, everyone involved took it hard and needed a healing period, but that conversation was ironic to me because of the people sitting in that room who were currently going through the same thing. They had experienced a year of hell, and they still didn't know if they had a job. I was one of those people. We were coming to work every day, but we were a little zombified. I remember in 1993 at ECU defensive coordinator Larry Coyer had a saying for the players: "No fe fe." No false enthusiasm. I kept telling myself, "No fe fe."

I am always looking to learn something from other people, and the experiences of Coach Davis—especially his association with Jimmy Johnson in Dallas—are nothing short of famous. National championships and Super Bowl victories are tough to argue with. If I was going to work for Butch, I would need to be an extension of his beliefs, so I started to write down everything that came out of the man's mouth. One trend I noticed early was some quotes from Zig Ziglar, and those made my ears perk up because I liked to read his books. It just so happened that Zig and Butch were friends. Rock star coaches run in rock star circles.

I had read a book by Ziglar called "Expect the Best," So when Butch mentioned the "Pygmalion Effect," I was right there with him. The research indicated that children's IQ could actually be raised when they were expected to do well, and another study showed that workers performed better when their supervisor was told that they showed special potential. I had coached against Butch Davis twice before when I was an officer in Steve Logan's army, and we had won both times because we hung our hats on the Pygmalion effect concept. If you want to champion an underdog—and sometimes it seemed that underdogs were all we had at ECU—you must strengthen the mind through the self-image. Ziglar said, "Self-image is the key to human behavior. Change the self-image and we change the behavior. Even more, the self-image sets the boundaries of individual accomplishment. Expand the self-image and we expand the possible."

This is great information, particularly for athletes who are willing to rethink themselves and emerge with renewed mindsets. The problem? Every roster also includes some individuals who are overconfident and have a sense of entitlement. But for every one of those, there are the athletes who transfer the training to the field, experience a higher level of success and continue to heighten their effort. They get it.

I was always excited to hear what Butch would say next in those early staff meetings. What I didn't hear him say, during his first few weeks in Chapel Hill, was that I had a job. One night Coach Jagodzinski called to make an official offer for me to come to Boston College. We agreed that he would call Butch the next day to ask permission to bring me up to Boston for an interview; that's proper procedure in the coaching world. When I came in the next morning, Butch called me into his office and asked me if I wanted to go to Boston College. I replied that I didn't want to miss my son's senior football season and I had some anxiety about moving back up north—but I needed a job. He said, "I thought you knew you had a job. We want you to be part of this staff." I said, "That's all I needed to know," and walked out. That exchange was typical Butch; even if he liked you, he would probably prefer that you assumed that rather than knew.

I've read every management book I can get my hands on over the years, and Butch defines that CEO who is known for a structured, high-achievement approach. He is all about production and results, and the road he builds to get there is meticulous, well thought-out and goal-driven. He knows the plan with perfect clarity, and a few others around him also know the inside plan and share that clarity. Others wait to hear what they need to know next, and they try to stay in that "ready" state. Those working around someone like Butch would be smart to bring a bag lunch to work. Some refer to it as being "on call," but I prefer the term, "on alert."

At times I got the impression that Butch was somewhat entertained by watching people jump around the building trying to discern how to gain his approval. Some days you would see him walking through the facility with three people following him taking notes about the furniture or the walls or the floor; they looked like they might trip over each other any second. Coach Davis could also be unbelievably cordial. My wife and I went on some of the best coaches' retreats imaginable that he arranged for the UNC staff, including a few days at an Asheville spa and a trip to the Bahamas that would make any coach's wife happy to be one.

The trips featured golf, boat rides, top-notch dinners and full slates of evening entertainment. When we were traveling together, Butch and his wife treated all of us like royalty. In taking us on those retreats, Butch went a long way toward developing a family-style atmosphere in his staff, and we came home wanting to run through a wall for the guy. I couldn't wait to get back and train the hell out of our football team.

Looking back, I think those trips might have been Butch's way of apologizing ahead of time for the sky-high expectations he was about to place on us. This pressure wasn't new to me, since I grew up with Billy Ball. Once camp started under Butch, it was go time, and no one was safe from the personal onslaught of mind-bending and exaggerated arrows to the heart. When the whistle blows for practice, coaches like Butch often stay in attack mode for the duration. I usually just stayed out of the way and avoided confrontation with Butch; it helped that his knowledge of what I did was somewhat limited. For example, if he wanted a cool down, he would say, "OK, Jeff, P and F." What he was really referring to was proprioceptive neuromuscular facilitation—"PNF." I just said, "Yes sir," and did my thing. He did call me out during my final staff meeting at UNC when he said the facilities director had reported seeing dust under the treadmills. I pled guilty as charged.

The other unforgettable incident indicative of coaching behavior occurred after our loss to Virginia in 2007. We were using a defensive philosophy of rushing three and dropping eight into coverage. The trouble was, our defensive backs were pretty average, we were being double teamed up front, and the Virginia quarterback was very accurate. He picked us apart in the fourth quarter and the Cavaliers tied the game. We didn't make any changes to our defensive scheme, and overtime was a replay of the fourth quarter. We lost the game.

Of course, the locker room was full of frustrated people after the game. I had some of my staff with me, and we all just tried to stay out of the way while the coaches talked to their position groups. All of a sudden, Butch hit me out of nowhere with an uncomplimentary remark about my staff. I was caught off guard, and I could feel my face fill up with blood, but I just walked in another direction. Sometimes your need for a paycheck outweighs your need to respond. I could have forgiven him for what he said, and I did, but he would not have forgiven me if I had said what I was thinking. He later apologized, so I'm glad I kept my mouth shut. A lot of things go down in the pressure cooker of a post-game locker room, and comments made in the heat of frustration require a short memory. Part of Butch Davis's success came because his demands were sometimes over the edge. I grew up with that ambitious intensity, and I'm guilty of it myself. I've also had to come back and apologize to people.

Like I had tried to do for pregame motivation at ECU, Coach Davis liked to bring in outside people to speak to the team. Tony Dungy even made an appearance, and he was every bit as impressive as his reputation. If a collegiate player can't draw inspiration from someone like Dungy, he needs to find another way to spend his time. Successful people tend to emphasize a lot of the same things; it comes down to doing what's right and understanding the natural consequences for stupidity. Davis also brought in a psychologist who related some important Biblical principles and also told some good jokes. It seemed that the "Kum Ba Ya" approach really hit the mark with some of the players, but others didn't take it seriously at all. On any team, you have your group of subtle insubordinates who seem to be going along for the ride, but their body language tells you otherwise. Coach Davis also brought in people from the sports ministry Athletes in Action. I was fortunate to hear some excellent messages from some very inspiring people during my time at Carolina, and I was also honored that Davis occasionally asked me to address the team.

Steve Logan always told the Pirate players that they should never neglect the spiritual part of their lives, and my personal belief is that any worthwhile life principle has its origin in the Bible. Just read Proverbs and the New Testament, and you'll understand that concept pretty quickly. Not every player is grounded in the Christian faith, and even the college kids who call themselves Christians aren't always ready to walk in that belief. I think you have to just keep plugging away with them, throwing out nuggets of righteous living and the value of respecting others in conjunction with what it takes to win football games.

ECU offensive coordinator Doug Martin was a devoted Christian, and he gave regular devotionals to the players that we named "upper room" messages. Some of the players chose to exclude themselves from those gatherings because they had converted to another faith, and we had to respect that choice. Whether it's through memorable pre-game talks, guest speakers, leadership committees, spiritual messages or weekly themes, the need to educate is unceasing within a football program. With all of those techniques, the end goal is to get the very best out of every player, and that objective requires a continuous process of learning and development.

Taking out the garbage

When a coach takes the top job at a major Division I school, he needs to prioritize the quality of his interactive team. That team should include a strong academic advisor, an aggressive trainer, a strength coach who is willing to confront, an adamant nutritionist and capable assistant coaches. This list does not include other important players, like recruiting specialists and administrative assistants, because they don't interact with the team on a daily basis. The most important consideration, once those people are in place, is to define the expectations for players and to clearly outline the consequences for violating any of these people's requirements.

This process is unquestionably the biggest challenge we face in developing a successful football team. Even though coaches go out and try to recruit the finest athletes with the optimum level of character and academic achievement, we still sometimes end up with young men who fail to meet the minimum standards for self-discipline or behavior. So we have to find the right responses to their bad choices. In an ideal world, we would be able to line up the predictables before an athlete steps foot on campus, but of course it seems to get away from us, and when you're in the middle of a discipline issue it just feels like insanity. Incidentally, the strength and conditioning coach is usually smack-dab in the middle of the storm.

I spent more than two decades kicking ass and taking names for a long list of behavior issues that never seem to go away—misguided choices like missing class or study hall, skipping treatment sessions or appointments with the team physician, disrespecting tutors, a variety of off-field incidents, failing drug tests, and the list goes on. Making young men bigger, stronger and faster is easy. Dealing with all of the unnecessary garbage on a daily basis is where the challenge comes in. Of course, if an athlete has no immediate consequence for off-the-field issues, his production on the field under duress will follow suit.

If you want to be successful in this business, you have to take out the garbage every day. If you let it build up, it's going to overrun the house. If you start losing games, the pile of trash seems to multiply, and soon it's going to cover you up and make you smell bad. The worst-case scenario is that you get thrown out with the rest of the garbage, and it looks like your standards were never any better than those of the people you chose to tolerate. You can drive a fancy car and wear an expensive suit, but it won't matter one bit if you get into the mud with people of questionable character. Better to lose games and keep your integrity.

Head coaches in 2013 must be visible year-round, and they absolutely have to confront every difficult issue quickly and thoroughly. That's why they get paid millions of dollars. It might sound burdensome, but they must let the academic people and the trainers do what they do and not expect them to fix the problems. Most of those individuals are intellects, and they aren't built for confrontation and handling disrespect. If the tutors are young females, just expect issues to arise. Trainers are smart people; many of them could have been physicians under the right circumstances. They don't have the mentality of the bouncer down at the local taverns. The head football coach should be like a rabid dog toward any player who even slightly disrespects these people. If they let those attitudes go, they're dead in the water.

Back in the 1990s, you could count on your strength coach to wake players up early and initiate extensive punitive activity. If he couldn't cause extreme discomfort with creative physical punishment, the conventional wisdom was that he should probably be replaced. That's how he got his reputation as a great coach. During that era, head coaches could be relatively comfortable giving the discipline responsibilities to that guy. For whatever reason, you didn't hear much at all about deaths occurring during conditioning or about an athlete buying dangerous supplements that could cause his heart to race. You didn't hear anything about sickle cell anemia, which can cause death during intense exercise conditions. The steroid era had run its course, because the NCAA had initiated testing. You were somewhat aware of the presence of athletes with unforeseen heart issues, and you were careful with severely obese individuals. But in the year 2013, things look very different.

Nobody takes more pride in maintaining discipline than me. I really don't want my head coach to have to deal with those issues, but in this day and age that is the reality. Nothing aggravates me more than the feeling that I've been reduced to doing a job that removes my personal influence and my ability to motivate people at a higher level. My highest goal is to capture a competitive edge during the offseason and to attempt to eliminate discipline issues at the same time. At the end of the day, though, today's landscape has strength coaches like me in the same category as the academic advisor and the trainer. Strength coaches do their jobs and have to count on someone else to bring the wood. We are limited by the growing number of conditioning-related tragedies and NCAA-mandated time off for athletes.

In my opinion, the head coach must not only be readily available for any discipline issues, he must put some heavy-duty expectations on his assistant coaches. The money has become very attractive for assistants and coordinators, so these coaches should feel well compensated for the task of micromanaging every breath a player takes when he sets foot on campus. Assistants should have some influence toward the players who are recruited and signed within their position group. Each coach averages about a dozen players within his position group, and some have as few as five, so accountability should be very tight within those groups.

Sam Pittman was the offensive line coach at UNC under Butch Davis, and the players under him were known for executing well on the field, handling their responsibilities and showing up on time. Pittman brought in five-star players with a great work ethic and a high level of character. They respected authority, went to class and study hall and stayed eligible. As a result, their professors and tutors, the academic advisor, the trainer, and the strength coach were able to do their jobs at the highest level. If I'm the head coach and you can't control your position group or recruit at a high level and you're making a quarter of a million dollars a year, you are going to catch some heat. I feel very comfortable in voicing that opinion, since as strength coaches today we are still on shaky ground when coaching staffs get the axe.

Formula for success

When Butch Davis came in, I thought we were beginning to see significant success with our off-season program. We were breaking records regularly, and we kept progressively improving our power quotients and our forty times. Forty times, of course, are in interesting discussion, because you can't really make claims about improvement unless you test under exact, replicable conditions with everything from surface to footwear staying the same. We hand time, but you should average the times of at least three watches over two reps.

Somewhere around 2005 we changed our UNC winter program to a three-day total body lift with three maximum effort speed workouts and two days of contrast training and position specifics. This came as a result of a favorite theory of mine that includes scientific, trial and error and recipe considerations. My methodology includes three sources of information—my tried-and-true recipes that have worked for years, experimenting with new techniques and emerging scientific research. With training cycles becoming shorter and periodization going by the wayside, we had to find ways to make people strong in six- to eight-week periods. At this point I want to get very specific about our program during this time, because we were seeing records repeatedly crushed under exact testing conditions, and those are the results I live for. I believe that you are only as strong as the weight you can lift and you are only as fast as the times you can post today. You can tell me what you did, or what you will do, but I will believe what I see, and at UNC in the mid-2000s I saw 73 out of 77 all-time records going down repeatedly. End of story.

This off-season approach produced the best results of any program I've experienced as a player or a coach, and it's still achieving excellent results in my current position. The priority in the winter phase should be maximum strength and power, linear speed development, position-specific fluidity and individualized assessment and programming. Within the strength and power considerations are speed, strength and joint-stiffening techniques. Monday is a max effort power clean day with component bench press, barbell step up and push press as the primary exercises. Max effort power clean is defined as a three-repetition maximum with no longer than ten seconds between repetitions. The bar must be racked. Component bench press is sets of three off of two boards, and barbell step up is performed on an elevated box to activate the adductors as well as other primary lower body muscle groups. Supplementary work is directed toward the posterior chain, with a full shoulder prehab sequence. Finish with Turkish get-ups.

Before we move on, let's address some things regarding recovery. One of the buzz phrases in the current training era is "neural fatigue." If you aspire to be seen as Professor Peabody in the strength and conditioning world, you will need to be able to use this phrase correctly, at least twice a day. Sometimes I think we try very hard to find the perfect formula to optimize recovery, and on one hand I think that's wonderful because I'm all about recovery. I do have a slight problem with it, though, because I grew up around wrestling, both as a participant and a coach. Wrestlers are human beings, just like football players, but the amount of stress and abuse that a wrestler endures far exceeds the demands of football practice or games. I have seen wrestlers at the collegiate level wrestle six or seven seven-minute matches in a day to win a tournament, with limited food ingestion the previous week to maintain their weight.

Now, to put this comparison in perspective, consider that wrestling matches are continuous and physically grueling. Go wrestle sometime for one minute, with full effort. You will be a believer. Football, on the other hand, is a three-hour endeavor, but after a four- to six-second play you get a rest. They put you on a "rest" clock until the next snap, but wrestlers don't get the luxury of the "rest" clock. In wrestling, it's called stalling, and people boo you for it.

Let's imagine now that a football player has to play a total of eighty snaps in a game, which is somewhat unheard of with most position groups at the collegiate level because of frequent substitutions. Defensive linemen today have to "two platoon," and so they go full speed for thirty to forty snaps a game. Folks, that's a total of four minutes, if each play goes six seconds. Remember, that's the total maximum effort demand over three hours! I almost get physically ill when I think of a player who can't go full speed, dominate an opponent and help us win for a grand total of four minutes over three hours. I have absolute zero sympathy for people who can't pull that off.

Football players used to go both ways—no subs, no tapping the helmet. They were proud to play as much as possible, and they would have been totally pissed off if someone were sent in to replace them. I have a memory of my last game at Salem College, when we winning in the fourth quarter 32-0 and the coaches kept sending in people to replace me. There was absolutely no way I was coming off that field. It was my last game ever as a player, and they would have had to shoot me and carry me off. Finishing that game was painful, like losing a great friend. My coach was livid. Too bad.

The bottom line here is that you have to train people to give you at least forty, "Dog Soldier," full-speed reps over three hours or you, my friend, are not an effective strength coach. The mentality of defensive linemen will be your biggest challenge, make no mistake about it. It's in the water. I personally take that group, and I am on the hunt for trouble. I'll find it, because they are defensive linemen. You'd better take control and stay focused, because if they sense you're soft they will eat you alive. That's my best advice for a young strength coach. For a classic example of a defensive lineman with the proper mentality, research Tim Krumrie. He was a wrestler and an exceptionally tough and talented football player. I have a tape of him pushing Julius Peppers and Ryan Sims to the brink of quitting during a Pro Day at UNC, and he was sporting boots and jeans. I love that guy. He is the model for defensive linemen. He once played a game with a broken leg, and I would be willing to bet that he never once worried about limiting himself to forty snaps a game. I wish all of my defensive linemen would approach the game like Tim Krumrie, but I don't know if that's possible without a mentality revolution.

Neural fatigue, that favorite catch phrase, could actually be the kissing cousin of strength fatigue, conditioning fatigue, speed fatigue, go-to-class fatigue, go-to-study hall fatigue, get-somewhere-on-time fatigue, and on and on. What we, as strength coaches need, is energy! Don't worry about neural fatigue. Train your athletes hard. If your best people look tired, back off. OK, I'll get off my rant for a moment. Let's define neural fatigue and explore ways to avoid it. Looking at Dr. William Kraemer's work, the first consideration might be excessive eccentric training. We look at the volume of total eccentric loading in our program.

The second factor would be related to the size principle. Motor units are recruited from smallest to largest, depending on the force they produce. Even at the greatest tolerable load, Type II b/x is assisted with Type IIa and I fibers. This is significant because fatigue in low threshold muscle fibers has been observed as having an impact on total neural fatigue. Obviously then, there is a cumulative effect of possible training sequences that might be evaluated. Kraemer, from the University of Connecticut, has been talking about these things for years. This is wonderful information, but I will still go back to the effort level of my hardest workers as the chief indicator.

Let's move to Tuesdays and Thursdays during our winter program. These are days of contrast speed work, featuring three reps of speed bound with fifty pounds of resistance followed by three reps with no resistance. The distance of the bound is fifteen yards. Next, we run three sprints with resistance and then three reps with no resistance. Ultimately, we look to get two rounds of both speed bounding and sprinting with a total of twenty-four reps, but we build into that goal over time. The remaining daily time for Tuesdays and Thursdays is devoted to position specifics, which are carried out at a high tempo for conditioning and training benefits.

Wednesday is our maximum-effort bench press day. On this day, we hit a three-rep maximum after an extensive warm-up. We are looking to strain through weight and hit a new maximum every week, but we can only advance if we are patient and achieve our reps with proper form. The other primary exercises on Wednesdays are box squat with tendo unit, and the speed on those dictates the weight. We are looking for .6 mps. If you hit above that number, you add weight, and we perform a total of six sets with two reps per set. It's all about how fast you can move the bar out of a static position. We take the stretch reflex out of the movement. Complex training would include adding some form of jump, and my favorite are horizontal hurdle jumps. To maximize these, we want to drive the feet to the floor, take out the muscle slack and pop off the ground over the next hurdle. The goal is to stiffen the ligaments and tendons in the joint to improve the elastic response and enhance explosive movement.

We want an explosive hip rotary movement in every workout, so we will include a hang snatch on this day as well. I really like to incorporate some form of snatch in our total program. You can't catch a bar over your head without fast hips. The beauty of this exercise is that players with inflexible wrists that inhibit their ability to maintain a proper power clean rack position can quickly transition into an exercise that they can execute perfectly. Onlookers who have never seen a snatch before are often shocked by how dangerous it looks, but the bottom line is that most male athletes who want to execute an explosive hip rotary movement will consistently have trouble with the power clean rack position. Female athletes, by the way, can normally rack a clean beautifully, because they are naturally more flexible. Our supplementary work on Wednesdays is directed toward heavy pulling and grip work with more emphasis again on hamstrings and glutes. I like the get-up sit-up on this day, because it's another abdominal exercise with progressively increasing resistance. We have also seen good results on this day by adding band tension to the bar for box squats—I recently had an athlete execute doubles and hit .6 mps with 405 pounds. That's moving big weight fast, which reflects the objective.

Friday is a max effort back squat day. We cycle from five to four to three reps over a nine-week period. (Of course, one or two of those early weeks may be discretionary.) This is a little different than what we do with power clean and bench press. We use triples with those two exercises through the entire training cycle period. I like a little more volume with the back squat. It gives me more opportunities to assault people for not being low enough.

Also on Friday, we will power clean using what we call "cluster singles" and block clean using tendo units on opposite weeks. The final primary exercise on Friday is the push jerk. For the sake of time, we combine posterior shoulder work with this exercise. We also hit kettlebell swings between sets of bench press, and we incorporate med ball core work as well.

Using variation and component exercises in conjunction with the basic foundational exercises has proven to be a very effective fundamental approach for our collegiate athletes. What sets our approach apart from other programs is our commitment to staying with the same variation and component movements through the entire cycle, once we specifically identify those exercises. Younger athletes with fewer training years in primary exercises need more time to adapt. They can also handle more volume and have the ability to recover quickly. Because of this resiliency, they can train the same muscle groups more frequently than those with higher training years. We arrived at this conclusion through several years of exceptional results. Even though we conduct contrast training on Tuesdays and Thursdays, we also mandate a full day's rest from lifting on those days, which is adequate.

The time for lifting on Mondays, Wednesdays and Fridays is limited to eighty minutes, which gives us forty minutes for movement training. Having a sixty-yard, five-lane track and a 40 X 50 foot agility turf area in the weight room at ECU has enabled us to utilize every available minute. The forty minutes of movement includes twenty minutes of efficient speed "drilling" and functional strengthening. Speed drilling encompasses several sub-categories, including postural drills with overhead resistance, stride separation drills, acceleration pattern drills and motor learning sequences. The turf segment is twenty minutes long and includes change of direction, hip mobility, foot quickness and reactives. We flip at twenty minutes.

We also include lower leg strengthening and reflex response on Monday and vertical multi-jumps on Friday—either included in a superset or as part of the forty-minute segment. From 2008 to 2010, with this program as our foundation at UNC, we were able to achieve three eight-win seasons, three bowl appearances and a bowl victory over Tennessee. The 2010 season was particularly notable because so many of our starters were ruled ineligible due to an NCAA investigation. Our system of training produced an explosive football team that racked up eight victories despite the absence of multiple starters. Nine seniors from that team would be drafted. Today our ECU players continue to put up very respectable numbers using the same program we fine-tuned at UNC. We need to constantly evaluate what we do with athletes and continue to seek more favorable training results, and those results must be transferred to the field. The main thing is the main thing.

Weekly Breakdown
Monday

Strength and power development:

- Max effort power clean
- Barbell step up
- Push press
- Posterior chain (KB)
- Shoulder prehab sequence
- Turkish get ups
- Neck isos

Speed Development:

- Speed drilling
- Lower leg sequences
- Horizontal multi-jumps
- Functional strength work
- Turf segment

Tuesday

- Contrast sled training
- High tempo position specifics

Wednesday

Strength and power development:
- Hang snatch
- Max effort bench press
- Box squat (Tendo unit and band tension) plus jumps
- DB incline
- RDL
- Pulling circuit
- Glute ham raise
- Get up –sit up

Speed Development:
- Speed drilling
- Acceleration pattern work
- multi starts
- Turf segment

Thursday
- Contrast sled training
- High tempo position specifics

Friday

Strength and Power Development:
- Max effort back squat
- Block clean (Tendo unit) / Power clean (cluster singles)
- Dynamic bench press and swing
- Push jerk and posterior shoulder
- Pulling circuit
- Med ball core
- Neck Isos

Speed Development:
- Speed drilling
- Vertical multi-jumps
- Functional strengthening
- Turf segment

Most strength and conditioning coaches who work with football can expect to put in at least a 12-hour day. I generally go to work at about 5 a.m. and come home at about 7 p.m. At least thirty weekends a year are tied up with recruiting presentations, games, clinics or other commitments. That grueling schedule leaves very little time to think about anything else. When I left UNC, I received a sizable check for the vacations I never took. At least that was some restitution I could offer my wife, who raised our children with minimal support. Dollars only go so far.

In this profession, you barely have time to grab a bite to eat as you move from one training group to the next. My assistants and I used to joke that since we only had time to eat seeds and nuts in the summer, we were starting to resemble some kind of bird species. In this environment of organized chaos within the confines of the weight room, it is dumbfounding when someone approaches you and informs you that the NCAA is going to interrogate you and you have the right to an attorney. What could you possibly offer up as information beyond the nature of training program that you are incarcerated with for sixty to eighty hours a week?

When the investigation of the UNC football program started in 2010, I had spent close to ten years grinding in an effort to bring a steady stream of pride to the UNC football faithful. My staff and I had poured our guts into the place, and I felt stupid and naïve, not to mention angry at the whole situation. I was angry toward the whole building for somehow being subjected to whatever was going on. I'm still angry because of the incredible number of hours spent in an attempt to maximize the potential of the players who ended up suspended.

Our mission as coaches was to vindicate the struggle that had marked our early years in Chapel Hill. We were extremely determined to succeed, and it seemed like things were headed in a very favorable direction. Unfortunately, a handful of athletes got wrapped up in a selfish mentality that only they could really explain, and sadly they took others down with them. Moving toward the 2010 season, we had an incredible amount of talent across the board. Coach Davis had gone the extra mile with these young men in every aspect of their daily athletic experience; the player's lounge looked like something that would be featured on NFL Cribs, and it was near a well-stocked cafeteria. An elaborate brunch was provided, along with a dinner featuring several professional chefs who conducted regular written surveys to make sure everyone was happy.

One of the first things Butch had done when he arrived was to make sure everyone had enough gear. I was very much in favor of that because it meant the players would have two changes of clothes for training. As coaches, we became well stocked with gear as well. When I left UNC, I had an abundance of complimentary clothing, most of which I never unfolded. The clothing package from the Music City Bowl was a wardrobe in itself and it even included several pair of tailored dress slacks. Little things like that do matter—they make you want to come back and work even harder.

Butch also peppered the building with Tar Heels who were also current or former NFL players. Any recruit who stepped foot in that building got the feeling that he could make it into the league if he just put on that Carolina blue jersey. Those three stooges who followed Butch around with their tablets got it right. It was impressive how effectively he could spend money in a way that he would get a return. The football boosters recognized that he knew something about presentation, and they were willing to step up the funding for whatever Butch wanted to do next.

Coach Davis was a master in just about every aspect of the business—fundraising, P.R., marketing, recruiting and retaining staff, and of course, the game itself. He knew all three sides of the ball expertly, and he was always a head coach who liked to be involved in every aspect of practice. I was impressed with the way the man worked, both on and off the field. He wanted things done and they got done. He might have left under a cloud, but UNC football is still reaping the benefits from Butch's vision and influence.

The rising senior class in 2010 included boatloads of talent and many future NFL players, featuring Marvin Austin, Greg Little, Da'Norris Searcy, Johnny White, Kendrick Burney, Robert Quinn, T.J. Yates, Ryan Taylor, Zach Pianalto, Bruce Carter, Quan Sturdivant and Shaun Draughn. Quite a group. Bunting actually signed Searcy, White, Burney, Carter, Draughn, Sturdivant, Taylor and Yates, so let's give credit where credit is due. Underclassmen from that squad who would one day play in the NFL included Zach Brown, Gio Bernard, Jon Cooper, Travis Bond, Brennan Williams, Eric Highsmith and Quinton Coples.

Obviously, many of those seniors could have declared for the draft in the spring of 2010…but not so fast.

Butch Davis scheduled a meeting with these players, and we all knew the power of his influence. What would the deal require if he convinced them all to stick around? Would the "entitlement" factor increase? Would we all be forced to express our indebtedness to them? Surely they wouldn't continue to put their plates under the couches in the players' lounge after they took their food in there to eat. Would they be willing to attend study hall? I know they wouldn't dare disrespect the study hall monitors. Would they show up for treatment and doctors appointments? Where would they park?

Things have become really complicated since I was a student athlete at Salem. We didn't have any kind of infraction list. I knew people who chose not to do the right things at times, but certainly not to the extent where they faced a weekly tally of expected poor behavior. I worry about the future sometimes. The list of player infractions went well into double figures. I dream sometimes that I'll go to work and see collegiate football players who are 100 percent accountable and understand the value and power of principle-centered living. Recent history, unfortunately, would classify that dream as utopian.

As a strength coach, I'm not sure where the lesson is in this situation. When people perceive themselves as being collectively unleashed, an avalanche of hedonistic thinking is loosed, and it snowballs with zero regard for consequences. I suppose when a young man is twenty years old and he perceives himself to be a millionaire in less than a year, he loses his regard for a degree. His social status is enhanced, study hall attendance is one of the last things on his mind and he seeks to avoid all types of physical discomfort. These effects are multiplied if he spends most of his time with eight or ten other athletes with the same mindset, and if an agent gets in his ear he might be inclined to believe any idea he floats his way.

I knew our program was taking a turn in the wrong direction the day I was asked to take it easy on the seniors during the winter program. You combine that lax attitude with the mandate from the compliance office that punitive action for training infractions could only occur during regular workout sessions, and suddenly you're in the middle of a nut house. When twenty-five players show up to train and seven have to be punished for missing study hall or class, and you multiply that by seven weeks, you have a team morale issue because the other players know that the wheels are falling off. Anger can't even describe the way this decline made me feel; it was more like rage.

The moral of this story for the strength coach is related to the theme of this book. If you haven't figured it out yet, it's discipline. In a situation like that one, when we were clearly in the path of the storm, there were only two basic choices in order to keep receiving a paycheck—to compromise, or to start sending out resumes. There was another sub-choice, too—to isolate and minimize the problem by pouring yourself into the good men of the program (while sending out resumes). That was the route I took, and it ended up being the right one.

Despite the turbulence, there were plenty of young guys in that program who were still working very hard toward a great season. We had a chance to beat LSU in the first game with close to a dozen starters missing—we were knocking on their door at the 3-yard line on the final drive. We managed to win eight games that season, including a Music City Bowl victory over Tennessee. A lot of unsuspecting players stepped up when the need was the greatest, and it was encouraging to see that our in-season training program helped keep us competitive. We saw great effort in the weight room the entire season. You have to keep looking for rainbows.

When I felt the ground shifting beneath me that season, I started to talk to a company that bid on the strength coaching positions proposed for the United States Marine Corp Special Operations, or MARSOC. By the time the 2010 season ended, I was already deep into the placement process. Shortly after the bowl game, I was offered a position as lead strength and conditioning coach at Camp LeJeune, and I accepted it. Soon after that, I informed Coach Davis that I was leaving. That was a tough day for me, because I was truly in line with about ninety-five percent of what he stood for. He was a great coach to work for, and my staff and I had been motivated to achieve his vision. Later that night, I got a call to meet with UNC athletic director Dick Baddour, and he offered me a new contract. I accepted, and I decided to turn down the job with the Marines.

A few weeks later, I got an unexpected opportunity to return home to ECU. I had thought about going back to Greenville often, and the timing was impeccable, since Coach Davis and Mr. Baddour had just gone the extra mile for me. What a perfect scenario for a multiple bridge inferno—just my luck.

Greenville is a very unique football town. Like anywhere else, you have to win to be respected, but despite that you get the feeling that people genuinely care about you and want to see you succeed. In Pirate Country, I always felt that I was more than just a guy who prescribed the right combination of sets and reps. I had to emotionally endure five games against the Pirates as a Tar Heel, and I coached even harder those weeks because I didn't want to hear the talk. That one game every year typically gave me a three-week headache. I couldn't deny the deep emotional ties we still felt with Greenville. My kids spent their whole childhood there. My wife had heart surgery there. Dad and I landscaped my yard together. It ran deep.

The UNC experience forced me to work harder than I had ever worked in my life. I needed to vindicate the struggle that had led to Coach Bunting's departure, and I felt a strong need to go out of there a winner. As it turned out, we couldn't have written a sweeter ending. I had always wanted to beat Tennessee, and we did that in a bowl game. On top of that, on Christmas Day my family and I ended up honky tonking in downtown Nashville with Kellie Pickler, who got up and sang "Stand By Your Man" and "You Ain't Woman Enough to Take My Man." My wife loves those songs.

It was a great ending.

Foundational Perspectives

1. As a coach you need to clearly define your goals. As it stands, your destiny as a strength and conditioning coach is connected to winning. That's it. Remember that.

2. Try to continually find areas where your program is improving. If the team is not winning, you still need to find ways of winning in the weight room.

3. Coach movement. I think that this is a weakness in our profession. The transfer of training to the field is crucial to success. Master the individual drills that are used in your football program.

4. Acceleration improves with increased force application. Speed bounding over hurdles and acceleration pattern drills provide visual cues for projecting the hips. It works.

5. Self-image is the key to human behavior. Expand the self-image and we expand the possible. Thank you, Zig Ziglar.

6. Players will get weary of hearing the same things from the same people. They enjoy hearing the successful experiences of other individuals outside the program.

7. As a strength coach, you will need a very intelligent plan and an ingenious approach to maximize results and minimize the distraction of the undisciplined.

8. Research all the little things about the profession. Learn the NCAA manual inside and out. Be aware of issues and precedents. Remember though, you must find a way to develop a winning football team. Losing equals joblessness.

9. A three-day program can produce exceptional results if you can set it up to facilitate the correct balance of training. Know where to put your money.

10. Learn to golf. Very few strength coaches can hit a golf ball. You can learn to hit it well enough to spend quality time with a lot of people surrounding the program. That's good.

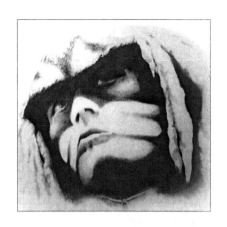

CHAPTER FIVE
SPIRIT LEADER

Let's revisit the dog soldier. The dog soldiers of the Cheyenne Indians were the final hope of survival through the magnitude of frequent battles. Some returned from battle and others were lost. If they returned, they were inducted into the highly revered "society of the bear." The phrase, "you can stake your life on it," was born of their commitment. The strength of spirit that connects with a commitment to a purpose is one of many astonishing characteristics of human behavior. Coaching enables you to observe the incredible power of the human spirit. Not only are you able to witness it, you can be part of the process. People usually don't achieve anything extraordinary unless they are strongly compelled. That type of motivation can come from within, but most of the time it is the result of some extrinsic force. That force can take the shape of deliberate coaching, a situation of duress, an unrelenting faith in God or combination of the above.

This chapter is devoted to the recognition of exceptional courage and overachievement. Even the people in this chapter who had exceptional talent had to overcome significant adversity to achieve what they did. There are also examples of incredible accomplishment of a few businessmen and other leaders within the "Pirate Nation." It takes a village to build a program. Collegiate athletics couldn't exist without the generosity of the ultra-achievers in the community. Every one of these individuals would agree that they only arrived at their destination through faith. Success, courage, perseverance—all who exhibit these qualities should be honored as part of their own special "society of the bear." They are all unique examples of overachievement.

RUFFIN MCNEILL

"For I know the plans I have for you," declares the Lord, "plans to prosper you and not to harm you, plans to give you hope and a future."

JEREMIAH 29:11

Ruffin McNeill just keeps making history—on the football field and otherwise. But even as he helps take down barriers and set new standards for excellence, he has been guided by timeless principles like perseverance, respect and integrity.

"My mom taught me to be sure you carry yourself in a proper way, to respect everyone, and if you respect everyone you should have respect back from that individual," he said. That lesson is all the more inspiring when you consider that Ruffin's parents were two of the first teachers in Lumberton, North Carolina to teach in integrated schools and faced plenty of opposition along the way.

Among the milestones McNeill has been part of:

* He was the first African-American from his high school to earn a college scholarship when he committed to ECU in 1976.
* He was the first African-American head coach at his high school and at East Carolina.
* At Texas Tech in 2007, he was the first African-American to be named a coordinator.

"Being the first minority coach, a lot of responsibility comes with it," he said. "I think the life training that I had was by God's plan, because it taught me how to be the first. I've tried to carry myself in a manner my mom and dad would be very proud of. I know I have to make sure I do things at a high level. I know that I can possibly set the trail for another young coach to have a chance if I do a great job."

Through an extraordinary career as a player and a coach, McNeill faced several turning points that set his course back to ECU. The first was as a multisport high school athlete who hoped to earn a football scholarship but pursued college basketball because he didn't think he was receiving any interest from college coaches.

Until McNeill's high school hired a new head coach, and he called Ruff in one day and showed him a drawer full of college letters addressed to him—inquiries the previous coach had never told him about. That epiphany put him back into the recruiting pool, and in one game he chased down Mitchell Strickland, one of the state's top running backs—and came away with a big tackle in a game where several college coaches were in attendance—to watch the running back.

ECU head coach Pat Dye was in the stands that night, and while everyone around him was discussing the yardage Strickland had gained Dye had a different question: "Who was the guy who just ran him down?" Soon, McNeill was a Pirate.

During his first year at Texas Tech, his new team played his alma mater in the Galleryfurniture.com Bowl in Houston. The Pirates defeated the Red Raiders 40-27, which was a rough loss for McNeill but also revolutionized the way he prepared for bowl games, a shift in philosophy that would pay off down the road.

The Texas Tech football program had a turbulent season in 2009 when head coach Mike Leach was under fire, and five days before his team's Alamo Bowl matchup with Michigan State McNeill learned that Leach had been suspended and he would be the acting head coach for the bowl game. Texas Tech pulled out a win, and McNeill gained national attention for his grace under fire. Seventeen days later he was introduced as the new head coach at East Carolina.

Coming off of his best record at ECU in 2012, McNeill earned a three-year contract extension and an opportunity to lead the Pirates to new heights. He is hoping to be at the center of a few more historic milestones in the Pirate Nation.

JEFF KERR

"Blessed is the man who perseveres under trial."

JAMES 1:12

Jeff was injured in high school. He had an ACL tear, which he obviously spent a great deal of time rehabilitating. Any time a player has that type of injury coming out of high school, he is viewed as a risk. Pirates take risks, so we took Jeff. He came strolling in at about 198 pounds, looking like Ichabod Crane. When I saw his frame I was a little concerned, because I knew it would be difficult for him to gain weight. It didn't take long to recognize the reason we signed him. He would try to hit you so hard that he would often hurt himself in the process. Soon he earned the nickname "Wood."

Unfortunately, Jeff's injury in high school was just the beginning of the adversity ahead of him. He had a tough time staying healthy. His injury history is in itself worthy of the record books. This is how it looked from his collegiate senior year working back to high school:

11-20-99	Dislocated left pinkie
9-25-99	Left shoulder, mild separation
9-21-99	Grade 1 concussion

9-4-99	Right elbow sprain
4-20-99	Nose laceration (three stitches)
11-5-98	Right talus fracture, surgery 2-18-99
10-13-98	Grade 1 concussion
6-3-98	Mononucleosis
11-22-97	Skin laceration (six stitches)
11-1-97	Grade 2 concussion
9-18-97	Right elbow fracture
8-27-97	Right hand, third metacarpal fx, surgery
9-7-96	Left ACL tear, surgery 9/30/96
8-22-96	Left knee, grade 2 MCL sprain
10-18-95	Left wrist fracture, casted
8-19-95	Left ring finger flexor tendon treat, surgery 8/23/95

Don't forget the ACL tear in fall 1993 during high school. Let's review. That's five surgeries, including both knees, three concussions, four fractures, two lacerations, a dislocation, a separation and a case of mono. Any mother who considered allowing her son to go out for Pop Warner should not read this report.

Jeff was never frustrated to the point of rethinking football. Even with all he had to go through, he was consistently in attack mode. It was his nature. He had a ferocious work ethic in the weight room and he was never satisfied just to make a time while conditioning. He had to win. He expected everyone around him to give the same type of effort, and with that expectation he was laying the groundwork for being one of the most effective leaders in the history of the program.

When Jeff approached his senior year, we were keeping our fingers crossed that he would stay healthy. He had trained particularly hard during the offseason. Jeff had played the previous two seasons at 215-225 pounds, but something finally began to work for him, between cutting down on running and taking in more calories. He got up to 235 pounds.

Jeff was one of a special group of seniors—vocal leaders who wanted badly to win. They had an exceptional final season. He ended up fourth on the all-time list for tackles with 371. This was a great accomplishment, especially when you consider what he endured with injuries. He later became my assistant at UNC.

DUANE LEDFORD

"Do you see a man skilled in his work? He will serve before kings."
PROVERBS 22:29

Duane came in as a freshman as somewhat of a "tweener". We couldn't figure out exactly where he would fit in as he advanced in the program. He could possibly be a linebacker or a defensive end. He was athletic, but maybe not enough to run sideline to sideline. He wasn't big enough for us to visualize him as a lineman who could put his hand on the ground. Over a period of time, he started to gain weight and strength. I think the staff looked at him as a young man with very solid character and a strong work ethic—someone who could finish a game for you someday.

As time progressed, Duane started to embody two words I love to live by—relentless and fanatical. He trained that way in the weight room, and he was also working very hard to gain weight. Duane had a good physique, but I started to notice that he was getting fat around the mid-section. I told him that we needed to take a look at his diet. We sat down and looked at all of the foods and how much he was eating. I couldn't find a problem. Just when I was about to advise some additional cardio, I thought to ask him about his consumption of beverages. So I said to Duane, "Tell me what you drink." His response was, "Sweet tea." So I said, "How much do you drink in one day?" He said, "Oh, probably about two gallons." Well, there it was!

Duane continued to progress and gain weight, and he was starting to put up some incredible numbers. He was benching well over 400 and squatting well over 600. He hang cleaned 420 his junior year. The problem was that he still wasn't really settling into a solid role on defense. At some point, someone recognized that he was up to 290 pounds and could probably be a great offensive lineman. As he approached his senior year, Duane was excited to fulfill his new role, and he was working overtime to get it done. It had been a long road to get there, but finally he found the goal he had been working toward all along. With his strength, athleticism and foot quickness, he became very productive that year as an offensive lineman. He would later sign with the San Francisco 49ers. Duane would make several NFL rosters, and he spent two years with the 49ers. He also worked as a graduate assistant for me in strength and conditioning at UNC between teams. Duane is one of the finest young men I have had the privilege to coach, and he is currently the offensive line coach for Appalachian State.

The scripture reads "Do you see a man skilled in his work?" The skill that Duane developed was the result of years of sacrifice and commitment. He maintained a great attitude and had faith and confidence in his abilities. He was coachable and hung his hat on every word of advice. Steve Shankweiler converted him into an offensive lineman with great mastery in a very short time. It's not an easy task to be considered a professional at anything after only one year of apprenticeship. That is exactly what Duane was able to accomplish.

DAVID THORNTON

"Whatever you put your hand to, do it with your might."

ECCLESIASTES 9:10

One of the things that I relish about my time at UNC is the opportunity to coach David Thornton. In our first meeting moving into the offseason program, I put a quote on the board that emphasized the fact that if a man truly aspires to call himself a Christian, there is only one way to conduct his preparation. David responded to this, because he was already a living example of this command. He had joined the program as a walk on weighing 185 pounds, and he had been so hard pressed financially at times that he lived in his car.

It would be difficult to match the enthusiasm and energy of this young man. I don't think I've ever been around a player anywhere who had such a contagious spirit on a daily basis. He was a vocal leader from the front. He was always looking to lift someone up. His commitment in the weight room paid dividends, as he was able to build himself up to 230 pounds. Jon Tenuta was highly impressed with David and had previously coached a long list of great defensive players. DT had the right coaches, and his coachability would no doubt help him to optimize his leadership skills.

David was voted team MVP, and he was selected to second team All-ACC. He was viewed as an NFL draft prospect, but no one realized how his character would elevate his value. When you go from a walk-on status to fourth round draft choice, you have defeated the odds and accomplished something extraordinary. He did it with his spirit. Anyone who met him for ten minutes would recognize it. In 2003 he led the Colts in tackles with 145. He joined the Tennessee Titans in 2006 and retired from the NFL in 2011. He is currently employed with the Colts. David had a very special commitment to living a Christian life, and he was always determined to infect those around him with his joy and enthusiasm. That quality influenced the Colts to bring him back as the player engagement consultant.

DAVID AND DAREN HART

"Stand firm then, with the belt of truth buckled around your waist, and the breastplate of righteousness in place."

EPHESIANS 6:14

The Hart twins came to East Carolina as defensive backs. When they reported as freshmen, they were each 175-180 pounds in a 5'9" frame. They weren't exceptionally strong or fast, and they didn't jump very high. For athletes to excel at the Division I level, they have to possess a tremendous football instinct to overcome these types of physical deficiencies. They must be relentless in their commitment to improve their physical attributes. They will also need to be students of the game. In other words, they will need to model themselves after the Hart twins.

Anyone who was around these young men quickly realized that they only knew one speed—and winning was an obsession to them. They were like a continuous dynamic one-two punch. They were always together and always energized. If the climate around them was anything less than the Pirate standard they lived by, they weren't afraid to confront the problem. They were always vocal. If you didn't like what one said, you might turn your head away only to get hit with an echo from another direction—the identical sibling. They were highly argumentative toward anything that didn't smell like hard work or a teammate exhibiting less than a one hundred percent commitment.

Early in their careers, they were both either late or absent from some activity. They probably had a legitimate excuse, but I had to keep punitive procedures consistent across the board. The drill was five exercises in consecutive thirty-second bouts with a five round requirement. Usually I had to grind people through the last round because they were fried. The twins were unique. They refused to show any indication of fatigue and actually appeared to get stronger as they progressed. I started to think that I might have to increase the difficulty level of the activity. The truth was, it didn't matter what the activity was, you needed to pack a lunch if you thought you were going to break these guys. They were equal parts tough and stubborn.

I don't think you could ever put a price tag on what these brothers brought to the table through their careers. They were extremely unique. Many times they would beat me to the punch in confronting inappropriate behavior or poor effort. They were even more effective on the field during practice because they knew the defensive scheme and would not tolerate stupidity or those who were unprepared. They were 5-foot-9, but equal to ten feet of competitive spirit. They practiced and played big. They were excellent tacklers and they would hit you. It was always comforting to know that you had an identical pair of pit bulls in your locker room who would not tolerate negative thinking. They made a difference.

RYAN TAYLOR

"And Sampson called unto the Lord, and said, O Lord God, remember me, I pray thee, and strengthen me, I pray thee, only this once, O God, that I may be at once avenged of the Philistines for my two eyes."

JUDGES 16:28

Ryan Taylor came to UNC as a receiver. He didn't look like a tight end and he didn't look like a receiver who was going to blaze by a corner on a go route. He was another classic "tweener"—not great size, not great speed, and easily underestimated. I really identified with Ryan, because I felt like I was looking in a mirror that reflected back to the 1970's when I was his age. I was stubborn, impatient and unconcerned with anything but making sure that I was going to be on the field on game day. I would do whatever it took to get there.

Ryan became a standout on special teams very early, because he would flat out try to knock you in the bleachers on every special teams snap. He was the type of player who wasn't happy just blocking or tackling you. He wanted to let you know who he was. He would try to bury you in the ground or knock you out and then make sure you saw his face. His physical attributes meant that he didn't have a natural place to fit into the scheme, and his frustration at standing on the sideline for many snaps was expressed toward the opponent at every opportunity. They had to wonder at times why he seemed to absolutely despise the fact that they were even on his field.

143

Ryan was a real pain to me on the sideline of every game. He would refuse to get back out of the coach's box, where he continuously paced back and forth like a caged animal. I literally almost had to fight the guy every game. Typically, I would say, "Look idiot, you're not getting in the game until we call up the next special team. Give it up." That would make him even more aggravated, which I actually liked. I liked it because I would watch him go in the game and annihilate the next unsuspecting poor soul. It was great. I really loved to watch the kid because he was the essence of the game. He would hustle and hit. He would have been Wild Billy's favorite.

Ryan experienced a ton of frustration because he went through an extensive period of time as a backup who didn't get a whole lot of playing time. Not only that, but he was eventually moved to defense. Linebacker was just not a natural position for him, and he had been a great lacrosse player, which had somehow impacted his movement. He always looked like he was carrying a lacrosse stick! It was very strange. He took his frustration to the weight room as well. He would come in and complain or look like he just ate a lemon, but he always worked very hard. He got to where he could power clean over 350 lbs and he weighed 245.

Somewhere in the process, Butch Davis entered the picture and moved Ryan back to receiver. He only had one problem, a young receiver named Zack Pianalto. Zack was a great young man, and he played on several NFL teams before landing with the Carolina Panthers in 2013. He was smart, athletic and strong, and he looked the part. Ryan was not as physically imposing as Zack, but he was two steps faster. Anyway, Zack got the nod. Ryan was his backup going into his senior year. Early in the year, Zack was injured. Enter Ryan Taylor. He blocked, ran great routes, caught the ball and usually destroyed people on special teams. Ryan was drafted in the seventh round of the 2011 draft by the Green Bay Packers, and he was still playing there going into his third season. You have to love that story. Like Samson, he just wanted one more shot.

DAVID GARRARD

"And without faith it is impossible to please God, because anyone who comes to him must believe that he exists and that he rewards those who earnestly seek him."

HEBREWS 11:6

I remember Steve Logan watching this young man throw a football at our camp when David was just a sophomore in high school. He would catch your eye in a number of ways; first, because he was huge. He was not a typical-looking high school quarterback. I'm sure many people looked at him and said that he looked very athletic and would make a great tight end. Logan, of course, recognized a great throwing motion when he saw one and had no other plans for David other than throwing the football and running the speed option like a fullback. He assured David of a bright future as a Pirate and a memorable experience wearing the purple and gold. With Logan's reputation for developing quarterbacks, it was a no brainer.

David was the type of athlete that had a presence when he hit the door—a big presence. He weighed in at 268. He had tremendous power in his hips and legs, which was demonstrated many times through his career. He ran over and through people and stood in the pocket and threw the ball with people hanging on him like a clothesline. He really did not appear to be extremely overweight at 268, but that was a little stout for a quarterback.

Somewhere through the middle of his collegiate career, I got that idea that we would start running three miles together. Running that distance was not my favorite activity, but Cliff Yoshida, our defensive line coach, had talked me into it as a noon activity. I'm sure that David had become disciplined in his choice of foods, but over a relatively short period of time, he got down to 235 lbs and he looked great. He really had a unique physical stature for a quarterback. You don't see many players with that type of hip strength. I was recently certified by Titleist Performance Institute for golf fitness. It's interesting to note that the glutes are viewed as the engine for the golf swing. Clearly, the rotary torso action of the quarterback is similar, so it was never a surprise that David threw a rocket.

One thing that always stood out about David Garrard was his level of maturity. He was always very serious about mastering his craft, and he never had an issue with hard work. I once witnessed him running ten 300s in 55 seconds with 30 seconds rest. For a guy of his size, that takes heart and guts. He was also someone who had spiritual conviction. He had a sense of peaceful focus about him that perfectly contributed to his success as a quarterback. He was highly respected by his teammates and was very coachable. Any quarterback, like Jeff Blake, Marcus Crandell and later Matt Ryan, who has been willing to embrace the knowledge of Coach Logan has been highly successful. David's exceptional NFL career goes back to Steve Logan investing himself in the young man all the way back through the recruiting process. David has made his university proud with his level of accomplishment and his character. He has been inducted into the ECU Hall of Fame after an extensive career, highlighted when he started at quarterback for the Jacksonville Jaguars from 2007 to 2010.

EMMANUEL McDANIEL

"Now to him who is able to do immeasurably more than all we ask or imagine, according to his power that is at work within us."

EPHESIANS 3:20

"EMac" is no doubt one of the top overachievers in the history of ECU football. He had a ferocious work ethic and an incredible sense of determination. No one envisioned him to become a starter in Super Bowl XXXV for the New York Giants or to be voted the defensive MVP in an NFC championship.

When he reported back to school after shoulder surgery as a redshirt sophomore, EMac looked like a skeleton off a Jack Sparrow pirate ship. I think he tipped in at about 150 pounds. I antagonized him until he just about slept in the weight room. EMac was always very coachable, with a genuine personality and a strong sense of loyalty. I think those characteristics took him a long way. But of course, you can't play safety in the NFL without talent. Emmanuel had good speed and worked relentlessly on his position-specific skills. He earned first team All-South Independent honors as a senior in 1995. He started in all 11 games and led the team with six interceptions that year. The previous season he had been awarded the most improved defensive player. The rate of his improvement was never a surprise to me. The more success he experienced, the harder he worked. He was hungry and thrived on momentum. At the end of his senior season, he trained as hard as anyone I've ever seen to prepare for a draft with uncertain results. He was selected with the sixteenth pick in the fourth round of the 1996 NFL draft by the Carolina Panthers. His playing career was as follows:

Carolina Panthers 1996, 2002
Indianapolis Colts 1997
Miami Dolphins 1998
New York Giants 1999, 2001

He spent eight years in the NFL as a defensive back and special teams standout. These types of stories should be motivational to any young athlete with a set of wheels and a pulse. This was a guy who not only was able to make a roster, he was able to excel at the highest level. He is currently on my staff.

MARCUS CRANDELL

"You are a lion's cub, Judah; you return from the prey, my son. Like a lion he crouches and lies down, like a lioness—who dares to rouse him?"

GENESIS 49:9

Marcus was a very athletic local Eastern North Carolina recruit who grew up in Robersonville, North Carolina—a very small town that has nonetheless produced some outstanding athletes. I also coached Tremaine Goddard at UNC, who was widely recruited and was also from Robersonville. Both athletes had some similar characteristics. They were extremely humble, always wore a smile and were fierce competitors. "Marc C" could literally light up a room with that huge grin.

Here's another young man who took the coaching from Steve Logan and inevitably blossomed into leader and playmaker at the quarterback position. He was mobile, smart, poised and versatile.

148

Marc was the type of individual who everyone liked. He was extremely personable and never seemed to get bent out of shape no matter how challenging life in football became. Unfortunately, his most formidable challenge came early.

During the second game of the 1993 season against Central Florida, Marcus set up in the pocket and took a devastating hit to his lower leg—so devastating that his foot was turned in another direction. Most people believe that he was taken down by a late hit. This was a season-ending injury, and everyone in the Pirate Nation felt the pain because the young man was so well-liked. It was not pretty. The Pirates would struggle with a very young Perez Mattison at the quarterback position for the remainder of the season. Marcus, of course being Marcus, remained under control and gradually recovered and worked very hard on shaping his body through the rehabilitation process. He was a great example to anyone who needed to learn about overcoming adversity. He would eventually bench press 375 pounds, which is very respectable for a quarterback.

As Marcus developed, he got back to becoming a master of his trade. He would earn a place in the nation's top ten in total offense in 1994 and 1995. He was a 1995 first-team National All-Independent selection. He led ECU to back–to-back bowl appearances in 1994 and 1995. In 1996, he would be named a Unitas Golden Arm candidate and selected to participate in the East-West Shrine game.

Following his collegiate career, Marcus played in the Canadian football league from 1997-1999 and then from 2001-2008. While playing for the Calgary Stampeders, he led them to the 2001 Grey Cup Victory and was the game's MVP. He converted from player to coach, first as an assistant for the Saskatchewan Roughriders and then as the quarterbacks coach for the Edmonton Eskimos.

Marcus came to ECU as local talent who was undersized and developed into a CFL star who passed for over 17,000 yards and 86 touchdowns in his career. That's over nine miles of passing yards. His role has been crucial to the future positive direction of East Carolina Football.

VONTA LEACH

"Whatever you do, work at it with all your heart, as working for the Lord, not for men."

Vonta Leach was highly recruited coming out of high school. When he chose East Carolina there was celebration and excitement in the Pirate Nation. He had a reputation for being tough and physical. The thing that I always liked about Vonta was the fact that he was a nasty guy on the field and had a comical and enjoyable personality off the field. He was the type of kid you just really enjoyed being around. He loved to work and had fun doing it. Guys like that provide the best scenario for a coach, because with them you can maintain a positive environment and keep raising the demand.

I think the attitude that Vonta brought to the table was one of the reasons he has experienced such a high level of success. When you have a player like Vonta—with a strong presence and a demanding personality—it has a tremendous impact on the rest of the team. The reason he is the best blocking fullback in the NFL is because he combines an intimidating, extremely confident attitude with a high level of strength and explosive power. I have never seen him look very worried about any opponent. That quality was in his character. He is just simply at the top of the scale in mental and physical toughness, and that tenacity was recognized very early, in 2000, when he became the first ECU true freshman to be named to the Conference USA All-Freshmen team.

Vonta began his career as an inside linebacker and played behind Pernell Griffin in 2001. He was moved to fullback and helped lead the way for four 100-yard rushing games by ECU running backs. Before the 2003 campaign, the Sporting News rated Vonta as the No. 20 fullback in the nation. Following his senior season, he played in the Blue-Gray Game, where he was named the offensive MVP.

After graduating from ECU in 2004, Vonta signed as an undrafted free agent with the Green Bay Packers. He remained in Green Bay for two years, and then went to New Orleans for a brief stay before finding a home with the Houston Texans. Houston is where he truly made a name for himself as an NFL fullback, remaining there until being picked by Baltimore Ravens in 2011. As a Raven he was a crucial contributor to their Super Bowl XLVII win in 2013. He was named to the NFL Pro Bowl in 2010, 2011 and 2012 and to the AP All-Pro Team in 2010, 2011 and 2012. He is on the NFL top 100 list at No. 45. He has compiled a long list of incredible accomplishments resulting from his strength of character and passion for the game.

DANNY GONZALEZ

"Whosoever works his land will have plenty of bread, but he who follows worthless pursuits lacks sense." PROVERBS 12:11

Danny Gonzalez landed in Greenville from Neptune, New Jersey in 1994. When he joined the Pirates, he had no idea that he would be enduring a long, patient journey as a back-up quarterback. Danny was the type of young man that everyone would like to see marry their daughter. He had an all-American type of appearance and all

of the characteristics to go with it. He was recognized for his academic success, was very well spoken and was a tremendous representative of the athletic program throughout the community. Danny made very few mental mistakes on the field, and he was quick to learn the offense. He was coached by Steve Logan and sometimes appeared to be an expression of Logan as he matured, becoming somewhat like a player-coach. He could have chosen to be frustrated and miserable in his long- term backup role behind Marcus Crandell, but he chose instead to take the high road. Danny was a leader, a friend and means of support when Marcus struggled, and a valued educator of young Pirates hoping to master the offense.

When Danny finally got his opportunity to be the starter, he was very productive, which was no surprise since he was talented and had spent several years in Logan's system. He got an opportunity to play in 1996, and he completed 90 of 172 passes for 1322 yards and a 52.3 completion percentage. In 1997 he went 253 for 431 for 2510 yards and a 58.7 completion percentage. His success was significant enough to land him a contract with the Amsterdam Admirals of the European League in 1999 and the Montreal Alouettes of the Canadian League in 2001. Before playing internationally, he had also signed contracts with the Dallas Cowboys and Miami Dolphins but was released before seeing action.

Some of Danny's other notable accomplishments during his career at ECU included receiving the Jerry T. Brooks award for academic achievement in 1996 and the E.E. Memorial Award for character, scholarship and academic achievement. He was also named Conference USA player-of-the week twice during his senior season.

T.J. YATES

"Consider him who endured such opposition from sinful men, so that you do not grow weary and lose heart."　　　　　HEBREWS 12:3

T.J. Yates was a recruit that John Bunting was very excited about as a future team leader in the UNC program. He was smart, poised and had a good arm. Those were the things I heard about him coming into the program, and after spending some time around him during his first initial workouts, I could see that he was going to be personable and coachable. His lifting experience was somewhat limited, and he had a typical quarterback mentality in the weight room. He probably had one of the steadiest personalities of any athlete I've been around, which is perfect for the position he plays.

T.J. got caught up in the offensive coordinator transition and then the head coach transition, so he definitely went through some things to establish himself. A fresh offensive coordinator named Frank Cignetti enlightened the final season of Coach Bunting's tenure. I don't think that T.J. felt during that brief period that he would have a bright future under Cignetti. Cignetti's opinion of T.J.'s ability wouldn't matter for long, however, since he would be joining the exodus after just one year. What would matter were the opinions of John Shoop and Butch Davis, who would learn that Bunting had recruited a winner and a fierce competitor. What made him a fierce competitor was not his stature or intense appearance. It wasn't his numbers in the weight room. It wasn't his forty time. It was the fact that he was undaunted by the critics and the non-believers. He just calmly pushed through adversity.

T.J. went through a period of time where he was under a barrage of criticism, including remarks from the stands and other unavoidable embarrassments. During a UNC basketball game, a video of T.J. was flashed that had him saying, "I'm T.J. Yates, and I'm a Tar Heel." The response was very predictable and I will always believe that whoever threw that up on the video board knew very well he would be booed. I don't know why that happened, but it should have been avoided.

If it affected T.J., no one ever knew. He proceeded into his senior season and calmly threw for 3,418 yards and 19 touchdowns and led UNC to a Music City Bowl victory. T.J. was selected by the Houston Texans in the fifth round of the 2011 NFL draft and would become the first former UNC quarterback to ever start in an NFL game. This was no doubt a result of his reticent tenacity.

ROBERT JONES

"Consider it pure joy, my brothers and sisters, whenever you face trials of many kinds, because you know that the testing of your faith produces perseverance. Let perseverance finish its work so that you may be mature and complete, not lacking anything." JAMES 1:2-4

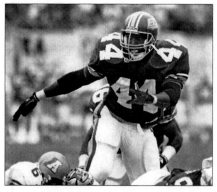

Robert Jones has a very powerful story of overcoming adversity. The hardships that he conquered as a young boy and a young man to eventually be chosen in the first round of the NFL draft are almost unbelievable. The level of emotional pain and loneliness he endured as a child would certainly seem to be insurmountable by any standard, but he found a way to fight through it.

As an infant, while Robert's mother was nursing him in her arms, his father shot and killed her with a shotgun. Robert was unharmed but was found totally covered in his mother's blood. He was the youngest child in a family of eight. After that tragedy, his siblings went multiple directions, and Robert went to live with an uncle. This is the man that Robert began to know as his father. He provided him what he needed to develop a belief in a male figure for a brief period in his childhood. However, when Robert was still a young boy, his uncle made a decision to shoot a gas station attendant as Robert sat in the car, leading to the loss of a second male figure in his life. Robert remembers weeping intensely when the police handcuffed his uncle and led him away.

As time progressed, Robert struggled through adolescence, sometimes staying out until the wee hours of the morning when he was only 13. He was fortunate to involve himself in athletics before life in the streets took him in a direction of no return. He affiliated himself with a player from his high school named Lawrence White, who would play at Virginia Tech. Robert trusted Lawrence and looked up to him, and Lawrence worked to guide and encourage Robert. He would consider him the next significant male figure in his life.

Around this time, Robert also became very close with his high school coach, Billy Boswell. Billy ended up paying Robert's way to Fork Union Military Academy to help him continue his preparation for his collegiate career. After a year at Fork Union, Robert chose East Carolina as the place to advance his football dreams. East Carolina would benefit from that choice, as Robert's career was about to launch at warp speed.

I arrived at ECU before the 1991 season—in time to train the Pirates all summer. Robert was one of the first people I met. He was an impressive sight at 6'3" and 255 pounds. Not only was he formidable physically, he ran a 4.6 forty-yard dash and bench pressed 505 pounds. He would be a major reason that the Pirates would go on to grind out an 11-1 season and bring national attention to the Pirate football program.

Being around Robert and watching the way he interacted with his teammates would never give you any indication of the deep underlying pain that he carried for so many years. He was frequently joking about someone or something that happened around his teammates, and he was talented enough to be entertaining. He seemed to highly enjoy his friends within the team and recently shared with me he thought of them as family. Seldom did any of Robert's family come out to see him play, and he heavily relied on his friends and coaches for support. The tragedies continued within his family. One brother hung himself, one overdosed on cocaine and one committed murder and was sent to prison. Football was truly his saving grace.

Robert would go on to be selected in the first round of the NFL draft, the first Pirate ever to achieve that honor. As a member of the Dallas Cowboys, he was a starter on three Super Bowl teams. Through the transition from collegiate to professional ball, he also lost Billy Boswell and Lawrence White to fatal illnesses. He lost every male figure in his life from shortly after birth to adulthood. Currently he speaks of the great appreciation that he has for all of the coaches like Bill Lewis, Jimmy Johnson, Dave Huxtable, Ron Cooper, Cary Godette and others who demanded nothing less than the very best from him. I was honored to be thrown into the mix. I currently coach Robert's son Isaiah who is a promising wide receiver. Time certainly moves quickly. Robert has been an incredible father for all his children. As you could imagine, the determination level to provide the right influences for them is immense. His son is a model of character. That's not a surprise.

GEORGE KOONCE

"The word of the Lord came to me: 'Son of man, confront Jerusalem with her detestable practices and say, 'This is what the Sovereign Lord says to Jerusalem: Your ancestry and birth were in the land of the Canaanites; your father was an Amorite and your mother a Hittite. On the day you were born your cord was not cut, nor were you washed with water to make you clean, nor were you rubbed with salt or wrapped in cloths. No one looked on you with pity or had compassion enough to do any of these things for you. Rather, you were thrown out into the open field, for on the day you were born you were despised.' Then I passed by and saw you kicking about in your blood, and as you lay there in your blood I said to you, 'Live!'   EZEKIEL 16:1-6

George Koonce graduated from East Carolina shortly before I arrived in 1991. I met him five years later, when he was a starting linebacker for the Green Bay Packers. We became friends in a short period of time, and he asked me if I would be interested in training him in the offseason. I was honored to help George, and we proceeded to put a program together to help his longevity in the league.

George was naturally strong and had good speed for his size. He played at 255 pounds and ran a sub-4.7 forty-yard dash. We trained together and were able to prepare him a total of nine seasons in the NFL; he also added one more in NFL Europe. That's a longer career than the vast majority of players who get the opportunity to play at the next level. I was very proud of George. He reported to training camp in 1999 and bench pressed 315 pounds eighteen times and ran a 4.62 forty. He was subsequently selected to the Muscle and Fitness

All-NFL Strength Team. He had stacked up a long list of accomplishments after signing as a free agent. He was an eight-year starter with the Green Bay Packers and a Super Bowl champ.

Leaving the NFL would be much more traumatic than George ever anticipated. He's quoted as stating, "The tunnel vision and unwavering emotion to living my dream as a professional football player left me completely unprepared for anything else." He felt lost at age 32, and he began to spend time alone contemplating a completely different future than the life he had grown accustomed to. He was having a difficult time with the adjustment, and he started drinking.

During this difficult period, he decided to retreat from reality to his beach house for a few days. After four days of frequent drinking and little sleep, he got in his SUV and began driving. Every thought that entered his mind was self-destructive, and before long he was negotiating a sharp curve in the road at 75 MPH. The vehicle flipped, and George could have easily been fatally injured, but ended up being pried out of the vehicle virtually unharmed. His wife Tunisia stepped in and appealed to George that she was willing to go to any extent to help him redefine his life.

George listened to her and stopped his destructive habits, determined to live differently. As he observed the troublesome aftermath of the experiences of others like himself, he decided to conduct his own study. After an intense study, he wrote his doctoral dissertation on the difficulties that NFL players face when they transition away from the game. The pain wouldn't yet subside for George, as his wife was fighting a lengthy battle with breast cancer. He would lose the one person who convinced him to change his perspective toward the way he viewed his life. Tunisia Koonce lost her battle with breast cancer at age 38, in 2009. George has dedicated his future toward the vision she held for him and the renewed spiritual strength he found from her mere presence.

WALTER WILLIAMS

"From everyone who has been given much, much will be demanded; and from the one who has been entrusted with much, much more will be asked." EZEKIEL 16:1-6

When Walter Williams was growing up on a farm in rural Pitt County, he used to walk the property with his father. But even when Walter was a little guy with short legs, his father walked at his normal brisk pace, so Walter had to run to keep up. When he was working on the farm, he said, he labored so hard he often wondered if his dad was trying to kill him.

But from those early experiences, Williams crafted the life lesson that has dictated every step of his successful career as a businessman. "In life, you can be a floater, you can be a loafer, or you can be aggressive." Williams chose the third option, and through his assertiveness, hard work and attention to detail he built a multimillion-dollar company in Greenville called Trade Oil.

After attending ECU and serving in the U.S. Army for two years, Williams returned to Greenville and took a job teaching the eighth grade, but he and his wife Marie realized that they would need a more substantial income if they wanted to start a family. Soon Taylor Oil hired him to operate some new gas stations in Eastern North Carolina, even though he had never worked in sales before.

Williams hired, trained and supervised employees, first for those first three stores, and for more as the company grew and his leadership yielded dividends. In 1984, after 29 years with Taylor and an increase of the number of stores in his region increased to 28, Williams retired, for less than 24 hours. The next day, he started his own company, starting with two stores.

Over the next two decades, Trade Oil grew to more than 100 stores, and in 2005 the company merged with Williams' brother's family company, Wilco, to create the Trade-Wilco chain of stores. "We just adopted the attitude that if you make enough money to build another location, you should build it," said Williams, who encountered questions from people in his industry who were mystified by Trade Oil's growth through tough economic times. "I outworked 'em. Nobody else was building anything, and I was still building. We're where we are because we had a chip on our shoulder and we didn't know when to quit."

Through it all, Williams has remained steadfastly committed to his alma mater. A member of the Pirate Club since 1966, through Trade Oil he gave the club its first-ever $1 million gift in 1993 during the renovation of Minges Coliseum. In April of 1994 the arena was renamed Williams Arena in honor of his contribution. As first the executive president and later the executive director emeritus of the Pirate Club, he was instrumental in the campaigns to expand Dowdy-Ficklen Stadium and build the Clark-LeClair baseball stadium.

Walter and Marie Williams have also endowed two $150,000 scholarships for basketball and have contributed to both the Spirit of the East Scholarship Endowment and a special leadership scholarship fund for ECU. Williams has also served on the board of trustees for Pitt Community College, and he has given his time to PCC as both an adult education program volunteer and a campaign volunteer for the baseball program's capital campaign.

In all, Williams has donated $1 million each to Williams Arena, the Murphy Center, the basketball practice gym, and Project STEPP, a program designed to provide higher education opportunities to students with learning disabilities. He and Marie also donated $250,000 to help build Clark-LeClair Stadium.

His continued drive to give back, like the work ethic that has brought him to this point, came from his father, who always told him that it was wrong to live in a community unless you were willing to pour back into that community. "He used to say, 'Don't be a parasite. Make things better.'"

PARKER OVERTON

"But one thing I do: Forgetting what is behind and straining toward what is ahead, I press on toward the goal to win the prize for which God has called me heavenward in Christ Jesus." PHILIPPIANS 3:14

When Parker Overton was selling waterskis from behind the meat counter at his father's grocery store, people laughed at his business plan. When he sold his operation to Gander Mountain years later for $67 million, the laughter had subsided.

Overton had started with five skis and a little ad in the newspaper promoting "The Largest Ski Shop on the East Coast." He liked to ski himself, and he knew there was a market for quality watersports equipment in Eastern North Carolina. In 1975, when he started Overton's, his business was worth $400. Over the next 15 years the value of the company had multiplied 900-fold to $367,000, and with its mail-order component it became the largest watersports dealer in the world.

His success story was constructed from unrelenting hard work and a singular dedication to customer service, and Overton also became known for creating opportunities for his employees to advance if they showed the drive and work ethic to succeed. From the time he started working in his father's Greenville grocery store at age 12, separating empty Pepsi bottles from Coke bottles, Overton knew that the secret to making it was working harder than everyone else.

"I didn't get my first Saturday off at the grocery store until I was 21," he said. "I didn't get to compete in a waterski competition until I was 29, because I was working all the time."

When he was growing up, Overton always hoped to do well enough to have a nice car, a boat and possibly an airplane. In fact, he has had five airplanes, which have been earned over a lifetime of paying attention to detail and perpetually believing in the potential of an idea.

But as much as Overton has been able to enjoy his success, he believes strongly that he must give back in equal measure to what he has been given. He has served on a number of boards at ECU and in his community, he was influential in helping secure funding for the new School of Dental Medicine there and he is known for picking up stray dogs who look like they could use a home. He has earned a quiet, tranquil retirement, but he still looks for opportunities to show others what hard work and focus can produce if they press on.

Continued excellence

When you look at individuals who accomplish something extraordinary with perseverance as their primary means of success, you realize that you've witnessed the height of the human experience. Some people make a decision through a life-changing event to become tenacious, some have it ingrained in them by someone in their life and some, I believe, are simply born with it. Whatever ways these individuals acquire it, they all have a common thread in their character. They absolutely and unequivocally refuse to quit.

It would take an entire book to include all of the young athletes I've encountered who demonstrated or acquired these qualities in their characters. As a coach, you want to believe that you've had an impact in this respect probably more than any other. Even if they come in with perseverance, you want to add to what is already there.

It's always interesting to track the success that your athletes experience when football is over. This has become a huge issue with those who complete an NFL career. The statistics indicate that they struggle to adapt to conventional living. Many end up losing their fortune and have little direction.

I coached a defensive back at ECU in the early '90s who was quiet, humble and hardworking. I always used him to demonstrate foot quickness drills, because he had great foot speed. He was very intelligent—he decided to enter the pre-med program and aspired to become a successful physician. He was always personable, coachable and respectful. You would have to believe that he had a great future.

My parents retired to Florida many years ago. During the time I was in Chapel Hill, my dad became very ill with bladder cancer. He was able to defeat it, but shortly afterward he was diagnosed with prostate cancer. He had his prostate removed and developed an almost unbelievable list of complications to the point of barely being able to walk. He bounced from specialist to specialist, and between the new regime at UNC and the twelve-hour distance between us it was very difficult for me to help in any way.

Someone sent him to a facility in Orlando to meet with an orthopedic surgeon who might have an answer. When the surgeon walked in, he noticed my dad was wearing UNC shorts. He said, "Where did you get those shorts?" This sparked a conversation that led to the surgeon informing my dad that he had played at ECU. When my dad told him who he was, the response was, "I'm David Crumbie and Coach Connors was my coach. This is family now. I'm going to make sure you get better." The chances of something like that happening are little to none. It has to be God. I am so thankful for someone like David showing up at such an unbelievable stressful time. He probably saved my dad's life. You just never know how blessings will come your way.

I coached a couple of players who happened to be brothers at ECU. They were special teams players, not your run-of-the-mill kind of guys. Their personalities always jumped off the page. Although their time on the field was somewhat limited, they became as popular and as influential as any four-year starter. I also ran them into the dirt many times, and they were mentally tough. They developed a very strong allegiance to the Pirate program and continued their extreme sense of loyalty through the entire time I've known them.

No matter what these guys were experiencing in their quest to eke out a living, they always seemed happy and upbeat. They were always looking to find a rainbow in the clouds, or turn a bad time into a good time. It was just part of their character. The other thing about them is that they were always dreaming. Sometimes dreamers aren't taken seriously.

One day, I talked to them on the phone and they told me they were having some serious financial challenges and even struggling to pay their rent. They had just borrowed $5000 to buy a painters van. They gutted the van and placed some freezers in it to store seafood. The plan was to go door-to-door selling seafood in hopes of developing a successful sales route in the local community. Of course, they had many other ideas for future growth that some would have found laughable at the time.

Eddie and Nicky Crabtree just kept grinding through the doubters and finding ways to turn a dollar through a relentless approach of getting in front of the right people and emphasizing excellent service. They worked their way into securing military food contracts in the state of North Carolina and from there they skyrocketed into one of the top thirty food suppliers to the military internationally. They have currently involved themselves in an industry of changing food technology, which is considered to be a growing multi-million dollar business. Every time we talk about business, they want to talk about how they made those 300's in preseason camp. Amazing, isn't it?

Rev. Stephen Harrison once gave me a compelling account of a mother giving childbirth. His words painted a powerful picture of the essence of tenacity:

"Every infant ever born drew its first breath because of tenacious teamwork. The face of a woman at the moment she brings her child from deep within the dark warmth of her body into the stark reality of what we call the world, is a portrait of perseverance, the likes of which no man ever approaches.

"For nine long months the child has developed, grown, rested and gained strength, and then at the time of birth it begins to move. It cannot go back, it cannot stop, it must keep going until it emerges exhausted and bloodied, but alive. The first cry of the newborn infant heralds its greatest accomplishment. For nothing else in its life will even come close to approaching the mental, physical and emotional challenges of simply being born. Birth is the mother pushing and the baby stretching. It requires unrelinquishing resolve on the part of the mother and demands that the infant displays that one quality of tenacity that for the rest of its life will mean the difference between life and death; success and failure; victory and defeat."

Foundational Perspectives

1. Tenacity: Diligence, stubbornness
   "But one thing I do: Forgetting what is behind and straining toward what is ahead, I press on toward the goal to win the prize for which God has called me heavenward in Christ Jesus."
   —Philippians 3:14

2. Resolve: Find solutions
   "Set your minds on things above, not on earthly things."
   —Colossians 3:2

3. Heart: Courage and emotion
   "Have I not commanded you? Be strong and courageous. Do not be afraid; do not be discouraged, for the Lord your God will be with you wherever you go."—Joshua 1:9

4. Persistence: Being steadfast
   "Therefore, my dear brothers and sisters, stand firm. Let nothing move you. Always give yourselves fully to the work of the Lord, because you know that your labor in the Lord is not in vain."
   —I Corinthians 15:57-58

5. Relentless: Merciless in competition
   "Do you not know that in a race all the runners run, but only one receives the prize? So run that you may obtain it. Every athlete exercises self-control in all things. They do it to receive a perishable wreath, but we an imperishable. So I do not run aimlessly; I do not box as one beating the air. But I discipline my body and keep it under control, lest after preaching to others I myself should be disqualified."—I Corinthians 9:24-27

6. Fierce: Menacing in the arena
   "I myself will fight against you with an outstretched hand and a mighty arm in furious anger and in great wrath."—Jeremiah 21:5

7. Adamant: Unyielding
   "You will keep in perfect peace those whose minds are steadfast, because they trust in you."—Isaiah 26:3

8. Fanatical: Over-enthusiastic
   "In the same way, faith by itself, if it is not accompanied by action, is dead."—James 2:17

9. Impassioned: Vehement
   "His word was in my heart as a burning fire shut up in my bones."—Jeremiah 20:9

10. Animated: Lively
    "Never be lacking in zeal, but keep your spiritual fervor, serving the Lord."—Romans 12:11

11. Intense: Forceful
    "Therefore we ourselves boast about you in the churches of God for your steadfastness and faith in all your persecutions and in the afflictions that you are enduring."—2 Thessalonians 1:4

12. Grit: Determination
    "For this I toil, struggling with all his energy that he powerfully works within me."—Colossians 1:29

13. Finally, one verse that sums it up is Philippians 2:13: *"For it is God which works in you both to will and to do of his good pleasure."* It is evident that great energy brings pleasure to God.

CHAPTER SIX
NEW DAY

As much as you would like to think that things stay the same, they don't—in strength and conditioning or in any other profession. The world is ever changing, and the modern athlete is drastically different from the ones you played alongside twenty or thirty years ago.

I recently read a presentation that Jimbo Fisher delivered at the American Football Coaches Association convention. It was extremely insightful and on the money (must have been that Salem College education). He talked about the three seasons that we spend coaching each year and referenced the season of development as the one that gets overlooked. He said, "I'm a true believer that your football team is made at this point in the year." He also cited the importance of developing your team's attitude, character and competitiveness. He described today's climate in the following manner:

"Being right and the things you stand for aren't ever going to change over time, but how you do business on a day-to-day basis has to change. To me, that's what tradition is, when your core values don't change, but we have to be able to adapt to the modern player."

You can't just say, "because I said so," to kids anymore; you have to explain why things are done. Our kids today live in an entitlement culture—they believe it's their right to have things. It's this, it's that,

*it's what, it's the me society. It's all about, "What can I do for me?"
How can we, as a coaching staff, take all of these "me" guys and
make them "we"? That's where the offseason comes in."*

Coach Fisher refers to honesty and communication. Those things
have been around for a long time, and I can say with confidence that
I have never compromised them through any offseason. You might
call my words brutally honest at times—you might even call them
antagonistic—but when all is said and done players appreciate the
truth. If you want a team to have a great attitude, then you tolerate
nothing less than complete transparency. Of course, there is also a
clear inverse relationship between team chemistry and team discipline
issues. As issues decrease, chemistry goes up. Fisher also emphasizes
the importance of consistency, especially considering the broken
families that produce so many of our athletes.

"Many of them don't have fathers in their lives," he said. "Eighty-
five percent of your teens in the world are fatherless. They hate
male authority. They resent male authority. They can't deal with it.
Whether you're an administrator, a coach or anybody involved with
an athlete or young man or young lady, we are here for them. They
are not here for us. Not a person in the room would have a job if it
weren't for the kids."

I think these words are righteous and noble, but I also believe that
you can sometimes reach a point of no return. If a player consistently
repeats the same behavior after multiple attempts to educate and
change the behavior, it is probably best for the team to exclude that
player. I've seen athletes respond to reproof and correction with
words like, "hey, I'm a grown man." That response represents an
unwillingness to change, and let's face it, eighteen or nineteen years
of one way of thinking doesn't change overnight. If you tolerate a
disease among your players, no matter how small it might be, you are
jeopardizing your future.

The Florida State coach went on to say, "I remember why I became a coach, and I remember our player development. I remember who they were when they got here and how they evolved into who they became, and I truly believe it's the offseason program and the things you do in player development that are critical."

This is where the strength and conditioning comes in. The guru of charismatic rapport. The magic man who transforms voluntarily into something that appears to be mandatory. The man who is required to smooth talk accountability because reporting poor attendance or using any kind of physical punishment are forbidden. Somewhere in the middle of 'show up and give effort' we must also provide the educational process—providing missing values necessary to winning games and obtaining a degree.

Through all this, we must make sure that the team concept is never compromised. Even the small stuff matters, like making sure that everyone is dressed the same. Should jewelry be permitted? How about different socks? I remember when there was a 'no facial hair' rule for travel at ECU. Would we be going down a crazy and futile road today to attempt to establish such a team concept in the "me" society that Coach Fisher describes? Should we go back and look at that Marine Corps induction speech? Am I just out of touch if I provide an adamant, "hell yes"? I've heard that phrase, 'look good, feel good, play good,' but I kind of like, 'look the same, think the same, play the same and talk the same.' Would most folks respond to that as an outdated mentality? I imagine some would, even if seeing players with different socks still irks my brain.

Jimbo also said: "Most kids in the world, including a lot of the kids we get, come from tough backgrounds. They don't feel like they can control the outcome of their life. They feel that it's already set, that they have to do this or they can only do that. They don't understand that the power of decision making is the greatest power you can have in your life, because it means you control what happens to you. The ability to make decisions is the key thing in life."

I like that statement, and I like the idea that young people can be taught that education at the highest levels provides decision-making power, as do social communication skills. After all, decision-making power is always wielded by other people who grant that power.

At this point, I believe we should refer to a powerful resource in an effort to clarify some of these thoughts and assumptions about young people and maybe even clarify our direction as coaches. That resource is the Bible. 2 Timothy 3:16 is a great place to start: *"All scripture is given by the inspiration of God, and is profitable for doctrine, for reproof, for correction, for instruction in righteousness; that the man of God may be perfect, thoroughly furnished in all good works."*

The reproof from a coach might not be accepted, but if it is in line with the principles outlined in the Bible it should be received with gratitude. I can't think of a better way to impact people than to coach and teach in line with scriptural doctrine. That was the way Steve Logan ran his entire program. It really doesn't matter if that fact was evident to the average observer; Logan's teaching was the proof, because it was truth based in principle. Reproof is only possible when someone becomes convinced that the value they are teaching is true. We can be mindful that today's athlete is not the same as yesterday's. We can also, however, be mindful that scriptural doctrine does not change. We have teaching and reproof if we have proof. This brings forth conviction. We then become corrected and develop discipline, which can be equated with righteousness.

The key here is that the teaching must always line up with Bible. I can be satisfied every day if I am genuinely giving 100 percent to providing righteous teaching, and I will expect that teaching to be accepted. Since God deals with us in grace, we learn that we must provide opportunities for young people to stumble and then to correct their mistakes. The head football coach must make a decision about where the lines get drawn between law and grace.

Because of human nature, the interaction we have with young athletes requires some degree of strategic planning. In my opinion, you will always have individuals who tend to make excuses, attempt to avoid discomfort at all costs, go south if they don't get playing time, skip class, put themselves before the team and consume alcohol—which leads to off-the-field issues. That is just the short list. I remember those same problems cropping up back in the 1960s, but in those years they weren't tolerated for any length of time.

The new training

The most significant challenge that we face as a profession in 2013 is the collective result of the deaths of twenty-one NCAA football players during conditioning workouts since 2000. The most common causes of these incidents were sudden death associated with sickle cell trait, external heat stroke and cardiac conditions. Exertional rhabdomyolysis seems to be on the rise. It is interesting to note that eleven of the 21 deaths occurred during Day 1 or Day 2 of a workout schedule.

The AFCA inter-association task force for preventing sudden death in collegiate conditioning sessions has outlined some very specific recommendations. The first is to acclimatize progressively for utmost safety. We must identify transitional periods, and the task force calls for a written, progressive program of increasing volume, intensity, mode and duration. The work-to-rest ratio should be 1:4 as a good starting place for recovery. Of course, athletes with sickle cell trait or any other condition should always be identified and given a less strenuous regimen.

Any new conditioning activities should be introduced gradually. This applies to any aspect of conditioning, including circuit training. The task force also advises that conditioning or other strenuous activities should not be used as punishment, stating, "physical activity should not be used as retribution, for coercion, or as discipline for unsatisfactory athletic or academic performance or unacceptable behavior."

I don't think that any strength coach I know would be reluctant to comply with any regulation designed to protect athletes from death. To have one of the athletes you see and spend time with every day suddenly die is unimaginable, but many coaches have faced that tragedy. These young men are barely even adults, and no sport on earth is worth the risk of dying. Collegiate athletes are just beginning their lives. If there is any way that we can control the risk, we should move decisively as a profession and get it done. There is one segment in the task force report that is disturbing to those who feel strongly about athletes' welfare. It states, "Unfortunately, the athlete's development, health and safety are sometimes overshadowed by a culture that values making athletes tough, instilling discipline and focusing on success at all costs."

That statement is ridiculous. First, instilling discipline should be the number one goal of every parent, every school, every athletic program, every organization that protects our freedom and every workplace. Why does the report infer that someone who has been trusted with athletes might be comfortable with a method of instilling discipline that would jeopardize safety? I don't know one person who would even give that a thought. Who and where are these people? I have yet to meet these reckless maniacs, and I've been in this profession for three decades.

I have been around some ultra-intense programs, and at no time in my career have I heard that we are going to instill toughness at all costs. Even when our athletes pushed themselves to levels of conditioning that seemed to be extraordinary, it took three months of progressive training to get there. No one ever mentioned "success at all costs." Instead, the discussion was about paying a price for success that was achievable but challenging. If an athlete couldn't reach their goals by the end of the summer, they just didn't get it done. Peer pressure was the toughest thing they had to deal with, not pressure from coaches. The test on reporting date was 16 X 110, which had become the standard across most of the nation.

Are the people who hold the power to hire and fire promoting success at all costs? I would hope not. Are the fans promoting success at all costs? I hope not. Are the large donors promoting success at all costs? Again, I hope not. Most coaches who have any visibility are going to develop a sense of pride relative to whatever success they've had throughout their careers. They will never be comfortable accepting failure. Perhaps the committee should look into the effects of the fear of failure? Fear of failure always seems to roll downhill toward eliminating the lesser folks to avoid the big axe. The head coach might feel pressure to make a change that he is reluctant to make in order to save himself.

OK, time for some sarcastic reality. Here's a scenario: Ruffin McNeill had a 7-1 conference record last year, and some critics responded to that by saying the conference was weak. Let's say, for instance, people considered the Pirates' fourth-quarter performances to be subpar. Would they be comfortable advocating something now considered dangerous like a 1:2 rest relief ratio in conditioning? Surely, they would never say anything like, "Coach Connors, I hope you're running the hell out of those boys, so we can win in the fourth quarter." I suppose people think the Pirate faithful ask questions like, "How is your safety level looking this week?" or "What is your alternative program for asthmatics?" or say things like, "Don't worry about your career or your job or your family, we've got your back if the team looks tired." Unfortunately, we never hear anything like that. Instead we might hear, "Ruff, that strength coach has to go."

Let's look at some scenarios of conditioning prescriptions that would be acceptable within the suggested guidelines. Assume we have a typical summer training scenario.

The first consideration for the strength and conditioning professional will be the starting point of his regimen. This is clearly defined; we can't start until nine weeks back from the reporting date. We also must provide one discretionary week somewhere in the summer, consider the date when summer school ends and also look at where the Fourth of July falls. The Independence Day week is always a distraction and sometimes a momentum killer.

Now, let's back up and look at the fact that we have to provide our athletes with eight discretionary weeks from January 1 until nine weeks out from the reporting date. This means that we're not permitted to run our football team in the month of May. We have to classify that whole month as discretionary time to fulfill the eight-week requirement, which means that our team runs the risk of becoming totally detrained. If an athlete is detrained, and incidentally has sacrificed an entire month of speed training, we find ourselves starting from scratch. This issue takes us back to the task force report and the "transitional period" mandated by the NCAA.

The transitional period is defined as the first seven to ten days of any new conditioning cycle, or at minimum the first four separate days of workouts. These periods are included but not limited to return in January, after Spring Break, return in summer and return after any injury. According to the task force report, "Transition periods should invoke an appropriate work to rest ration for the sport. A 1:4 work to rest ratio (with greater rest permissible) when conducting serial activity of an intense nature, for example, is a good starting place to emphasize recovery."

Now, let's keep in mind that the summer is voluntary, the sports medicine staff has the right to cancel a workout with unchallenged authority and the athlete in many summer programs is not enlisted in any regimented nutrition program. Your program will generally start about June 2 and end around July 25. You want to make the last week of July your discretionary week, because you are a looking at a ghost town on campus after finals anyway. Your running program in 2013 is going to consist of a voluntary seven weeks, and your athletes will most likely be running on fast food fuel. Here's another observation: Is it possible that any of these deaths might have occurred from an athlete's repeated poor decision despite legitimate attempts at education?

Let's just look at a couple of hypothetical situations. You're on the sideline during the first game of the season against a formidable opponent. You observe an empty bottle of "Five Hour Energy" on the ground. After several minutes of investigation, you learn that several athletes had used that product before and during the game. They had definitely been educated, but they chose the stupid road.

One summer, after a stadium workout, a freshman lineman is holding his chest. You immediately approach him and ask what the problem is, and he says he feels like his heart is beating fast. You ask if he has ingested anything, and he replies that his peers gave him some form of pre-workout drink. You send him to the trainer and request re-education for the entire team on the dangers and risks of pre-workout drinks. They definitely had been educated and provided with extensive information concerning poor choices, but all of your guidelines and precautions can be shot down with one poor decision.

As professionals, we must be able to consider task force recommendations and apply them effectively to the existing plan. The following might be a typical summer program specific to our objectives at ECU. It outlines a safe progression for a collegiate athlete:

WEEK 1

Monday

- Dynamic warm up
- Postural drills
- Neural fast leg drills
- Acceleration quotient drill
- Contrast speed bound   2x2/ 2x2
- Contrast sprint   2x2/2x2
- Functional strengthening
- Post flex

-Monday is a day for full speed work. It requires full speed effort and provides time for full recovery. The sprint work is executed at 20 meters or less.

Tuesday (two options)

• Option 1 / 300 yard shuttles in 25 yard increments

Skill	Combo	Line
:63	:67	:72

According to task force guidelines we need four minute rest here before the second shuttle. We then begin position specific drill training.

Option 2/ Power Unit Training

- 300 yards around the field x2

Times:	Skill	Combo	Line
	:55	:60	65

Task force guidelines provide four minutes rest between repetitions.
After the second repetition we would take the 2:30 rest

A. 300 yards around the field x 2	2:30 rest
B. 6 x 40 yard sprint 1:4 RR = 50 seconds	2:30 rest
C. 6 x 20 yard sprint 1:4 RR= 50 seconds	2:30 rest
D. 6 x 20 yard sprint 1:4 RR= 10 seconds	2:30 rest
E. 300 yards around the field x 2 (repeat A)	

Begin position specific skill training

Wednesday (Max Effort Speed Day)

- Dynamic warm up
- Hip drills
- Stride separation drills
- Acceleration quotient drill
- Contrast speed bound (4" mini hurdles)
- Contrast speed
- Functional strengthening
- Post flex

Volume and recovery is the same as Monday

Thursday (2 options)

Option 1

Stadium Progression (2 rounds) 1:4 RR =2:00
- A march
- Lunge
- Sprint
- 3 count pose chop

Option 2
Speed Circuit 1:4 RR= :20- :30 on each rep
(8:00 stations) 2:30 between stations
- Ins and outs
- Sand pit drills
- Prowler push
- Resisted sprint (individual sled)

Friday
110 yard runs-skill
100 yard runs-combo
90 yard runs- line
6 reps- 1:4 RR = :60
Begin position specific skill work

WEEK 2

Monday (Max effort speed training)
same as week 1

Tuesday
Option 1
300 yard shuttle in 25 yard increments x 2
Times remain consistent RI = 1:3 RR
- 3:00 rest between shuttles
- Begin position specific drill training

Option 2 Power Unit Training

A. 300 yard around the field x 2	
Times remain the same	
RI moves to 1:3 RR = 3:00	2:30 rest
B. 6 x 40 yard sprint 1:3 RR :15	2:30 rest
C. 4 x 80 yard sprint 1:3 RR :40	2:30 rest
D. 6 x 20 yard sprint 1:3 RR :8	2:30 rest
E. 300 yards around the field x 2 (repeat A)	

Wednesday (Max Effort Speed Training)
Same as week 1

Thursday
Option 1

Stadium progression (round 2)	(add weighted vest for round 2) 2:00 RI

Option 2

Speed circuit 1:4 RR	
2:00 rest between stations	(8:00 stations)

Friday
110 yard runs – skill
100 yard runs- combo (:15)
90 yard runs – line
8 reps – 1:3 RR :45
Begin position specific skill work

WEEK 3

Monday (Max Effort Speed Day)
Same as week 1
Add one round of contrast speed bound
And contrast sprint   3x2/ 3x2
                                          3x2/ 3x2

Tuesday

Option 1
300 yard shuttles in 25 yd increments x 3
Times remain consistent
RI between reps 1 and 2 1:2 RR 2:00
RI between reps 2 and 3   1:3 RR 3:00
Begin position specific drill training

Option 2 Power Unit Training
A. 300 yards around the field x 2
Times remain the same
RI moves to 1:2 RR 2:00   2:30 rest
B. 6x40 yard sprint 1:3 RR :15   2:30 rest
C. 4x80 yard sprint 1:3 RR :40   2:30 rest
D. 6x20 yard sprint 1:3 RR :8   2:30 rest
E. 300 yards around the field x 2 (repeat A)

Wednesday (Max Effort Speed Training)
Same as week 1
Add one round of contrast speed bound and contrast sprint

Thursday
Option 1
Stadium Progression
2 rounds with weighted vest 2:00 RI

Option 2
Speed circuit 1:4 RR
2:00 rest between stations
(9:00 stations)

Friday
110 yard runs – skill
100 yard runs-combo
90 yard runs- line
10 reps 1:3 RR :45

Begin position specific skill work

WEEK 4

Monday (Max Effort Speed Training)
Same as week 3

Tuesday
Option 1
300 yard shuttles in 25 yard increments x 3
Times remain consistent
(1:30 between shuttles)
Begin position specific drill training

Option 2 Power Unit Training
A. 300 yards around the field x2
Times remain the same
RI moves to 1:1 RR :60   2:00 rest
B. 8x 40 yard sprint 1:3 RR :15   2:00 rest
C. 4x80 yard sprint 1:3 RR :40   2:00 rest
D. 8 x 20 yard sprint 1:3 RR :8   2:00 rest
E. 300 yards around field x 2 (repeat A)

Wednesday (Max Effort Speed Training)
Same as week 3

Thursday
Option 1
Stadium Progression
3 rounds - 2 with weighted vest—last round no vest   2:00 RI

Option 2
Speed circuit 1:3 RR
2:00 rest between stations
10:00 minute stations

Friday
110 yard runs- skill
100 yard runs—combo :15
90 yard run –line
12 reps 1:3 RR   :45
Begin position specific skill work

WEEK 5

Monday (Max Effort Speed Training)
Same as week 4

Tuesday
Option 1
300 shuttles in 25 yd increments x 3
Times remain consistent
:60 rest between shuttle 1 and 2
1:30 rest between shuttle 2 and 3
Begin position specific drill training

Option 2 (Power Unit Training)
Same as week 4

Wednesday (Max Effort Speed Training)
Same as week 4

Thursday
Option 1 Stadium Progression
3 rounds with weighted vest 2:00 RI

Option 2
Same as week 4

Friday
110 yard runs- skill
100 yard runs—combo :15
90 yard run –line
14 reps 1:3 RR :45
Begin position specific skill work

WEEK 6 & 7

Monday (Max Effort Speed Training)
Contrast speed rounds and contrast sprint
moves to
4x2 / 4x2
4x2 / 4x2

Tuesday

Option 1
300 shuttles in 25 yard increments x 4
Rest intervals are 1:30 for all reps
Begin position specific training

Option 2 Power Unit Training
A. 300 yards around the field x 2
Times remain the same

RI :60	2:00 rest
B. 10 x 40 yard sprint 1:3 :15	2:00 rest
C. 4 x 80 yard sprint 1:3 :40	2:00 rest
D. 10 x 20 yard sprint 1:3 :8	2:00 rest

E. 300 yards around the field x 2 (repeat A)

Wednesday (Max Effort Speed Training)
Contrast speed bound and contrast sprint
moves to   4x2 / 4x2
                4x2 / 4x2

Thursday

Option 1 Stadium Progression
3 rounds with weighted vest 2:00 RI

Option 2
Same as week 4

Friday
110 yard runs- skill
100 yard runs—combo :15
90 yard run –line
14 reps 1:3 RR :45

Begin position specific skill work

Seven weeks of a consistent five-day program working anaerobic energy systems is very effective in establishing a significant level of conditioning. The athlete must put forth the effort necessary to favorably adapt to the training. Maximum effort speed days are necessary to maintain a high level of skill and power through acceleration. This training also contributes significantly to speed endurance, as does the power unit concept.

The option days can be alternated from week to week or used as a change up. The standard still progresses with options, whether you choose to use them that week or not. The speed circuit is a very high tempo progression of drills. We have at least a dozen drill options that are interchangeable and effective. Athletes adapt rapidly to consistent forms of progression. A young man who is willing to sell out every day will see incredible results in a short amount of time. I would love to have twelve weeks instead of seven to achieve a higher level of conditioning, but I can't run athletes during the month of May. I can only be in the weight room for safety purposes during that time. Would it be sensible to allow for a longer training period in the summer so that athletes can become better acclimated? I would think so. I think we would better serve the health and safety of the athlete. Just an opinion.

Remember that Coach Fisher said, "because I said so" is no longer a legitimate answer to an athlete's question about what we do? We have to prepare a line of reasoning and provide the "why" behind our methods. The "why" for the summer running program would include the following rationale:

We must continue with absolute speed training. Speed training is very specific, and it is only maintained and improved through consistent full-speed effort.

Four quarters of football requires an athlete to sprint and redirect 200 or more times. We must train speed/endurance.

If you think football is limited to one energy system, you never played defensive back against a high-tempo offense. Train the first two energy systems!

Stadium work develops strength in the muscle groups specific to acceleration.

Metabolic position-specific skill work is the glue connecting conditioning and skill.

The specificity of the conditioning test should be part of the formula. The players will appreciate it on test day.

Since we are looking at changes at today's athletes, it would probably be reasonable to see what some other highly successful coaches have said recently about the characteristics and expectations of today's athlete. Connell Maynor, the head football coach at Winston-Salem State University, said at the AFCA Conference:

"Discipline is the foundation. Your players have to be disciplined. You have to hold them accountable. Treat everybody fairly. Nobody is bigger than the football team. When they see you discipline that "star," that will get them in line. I had a running back last year worth 1,800 yards. He was 6-foot-2, 245 pounds. Everybody said we wouldn't be the same in the running game this year (after he left). I think we rushed for the same number of yards this year; we just did it by committee. Nobody's bigger than the football team. Your star player can be replaced. We still play. We were 13-1 with him and we were 14-1 without him. Nobody is bigger than the football team."

Coach Maynor went on to talk about the fact that so many players are fatherless and so many of them are fathers themselves. Their pursuit of a degree is that much more important, because without education they are likely to repeat that pattern.

ECU coach Ruffin McNeill is the poster coach for the important mission of providing education and guidance to facilitate a successful future for a recruit. He is approachable and always willing to listen. He will give an athlete a fair shake and repeated opportunities to change behavior within reason. He preaches no entitlement and special privilege. His reference to the team as a family and his approach to recruiting are uniquely effective in convincing a single parent to support his or her son in choosing East Carolina University. They trust Ruffin, and that provides piece of mind. Every parent wants to be able to turn his or her son over to a coach who can provide solid direction rooted in personal experience. Coach McNeill was a successful former ECU player, and he has had a long list of experiences that are similar to today's athletes. He has an infectious, energetic, uplifting personality. When he steps into a home, every grandma will fall in love.

If an athlete is walking around campus every day feeling good between his ears, the impact on the team will be significant. Much of what makes him feel good is the ongoing relationship he has with the head coach. That's the guy the players want to hear from. The words of the head coach in meetings, in the media and in one-on-one situations have significant meaning in the life of a collegiate athlete. Most of these young men work extremely hard, and they want to hear their name.

Anytime someone can be recognized for academic achievement, strength and conditioning achievement, study hall attendance and demeanor, athletic achievement, community service or just bring a great person, it is meaningful. If it comes from the man with the plan, it can be equated to a medicinal ray of positive light infused into the part of the brain that decides never to complain or make excuses. We all like to impress the boss. Your boss might not like things about you, but if you receive an occasional compliment along with advice on how to improve, it goes a long way.

Strength and conditioning coaches have a great opportunity to provide players with positive feedback and recognition through developing an award system. The best time for this is at the end of the winter program. If you lift weights like we do, you can award your primary lifts. We recognize the leaders in back squat, push jerk, power clean and bench press. Back squat is a three rep max with knee wraps and a belt. Push jerk is a one rep max. (I have also used maximum wattage.) Power clean is a one rep max.

We do a lot of things with the bench press. Remember, it is the lift that can literally kill you. We had a chart on the wall at UNC that I made out on a dry erase board. I provided slots for names next to the numbers of reps, ranging from 5 to 40, and the names could easily be moved around. This gave us the opportunity to execute the 225 reps test and provide feedback. We tested about once every six weeks. If someone lost strength, we would give him one more phase to get that number restored before we erased it. Everyone who came into the weight room saw that number. We also performed a rep test up to five. After five, the formula to extrapolate a one rep max starts to become inaccurate. If you want an all-time record, it's one rep. (We use three spotters.) You get 1 to 10 points on each test, and the tests are standardized by position groups.

To be able to evaluate the players by using our power quotient, we test the 40-yard dash, vertical jump and broad jump. Those individual tests are also scored from 1 to 10 and standardized by position. The remaining tests would include pro shuttle, three-cone drill, 60-yard shuttle and a number of flexibility screens. They are scored the same way. We also use the Wilkes formula to identify strength levels according to body weight.

The acceleration quotient is the final addition to our system as it stands. If you average six points for all tests, you achieve Iron Pirate. Seven points makes you an Elite Pirate, and eight points earns Super Pirate status. This system facilitates the recognition of many team members and gives you a chance to provide some nice awards that they can keep to remember their careers. Some of these guys I had back in the '90s would do just about anything for a T-shirt. It was the principle of the thing. The total point system for our Pirate Awards includes the following tests and awards:

Point system tests
1. Back squat
2. Push jerk
3. Power clean
4. Bench press
5. Vertical jump
6. Broad jump
7. 40 yard dash
8. 3 cone agility
9. Pro shuttle
10. Long shuttle/linemen—backward overhead shot throw
11. Flexibility screen
12. Power quotient
13. Acceleration quotient

*Top lift by body weight—Trophy
   Back squat
   Power clean
   Push jerk
   Bench press

*Most points scored
*Most improved

We also have testing teams, which can be drafted or assigned. Each individual scores points for the team. We include our injured and surgery players as well, because they can be involved in limited testing. We take the top six team scores for each test, and we award the top four teams overall with trophies.

The purpose of the point system is to provide information to the athlete to help him identify his strengths and weaknesses so that he can know where to invest his future efforts. A football team consists of one hundred and twenty-five players, but since you can only put eleven on the field at one time, many of those individuals will have limited playing time. Off-season programs provide tools to help young men work toward increased playing time and a more significant role in the future.

"New day" coaching strategies suggest that we become tuned in to the background of each athlete and attempt to provide the resources and environment to educate young men beyond football. We've been doing this for years, and we've been aware of these issues for years. The difference at this point, as I understand it, is that the NCAA and the task forces have taken a stand against the more primitive methods. I'm all ears.

Foundational Perspectives

1. There is a consensus out there that young athletes are different than they were in recent history and ever changing.

2. Programs are becoming pro-active in establishing systems of educating the athlete toward better choices through self examination. Some schools are advocating peer oriented programs.

3. We recruit most of our players in the state of North Carolina. Our high school teachers are ranked 46th in the country in compensation. Greenville, North Carolina (our college town) ranks 2nd in the country for unmarried mothers. The challenges might be deeper than we realize.

4. The NCAA has evidently linked deaths in conditioning drills to strength and conditioning programs which seems logical. I would be very interested in a task force report with an intense case by case study. I think this could provide significant further understanding of the issues. There seems to be a long list of variables.

5. Football coaches are still unaware of task force recommendations concerning physical punishment. When are they going to be informed? Strength coaches are directed by the football staff.

6. The summer program is referred to as voluntary but still has an eight hour weekly NCAA limitation on training. Does that make any sense?

7. The strength and conditioning coach is expected to not interact with the head football coach thru the summer months. We can provide no information to the coach about his team for nine weeks. Now let's get this straight. The "modern" athlete who needs fatherly guidance, becomes removed from that figure for nine weeks a year.

8. In my humble opinion, eight discretionary weeks through the winter, followed by a voluntary summer needs to be rethought. Also, if we took a look at what these guys eat in the summer, most of us would wonder how they survive the training. There's no way we are even coming close to providing the best scenario for health and safety. We give them food money, but no education or supervision on how to spend it.

9. The summer conditioning program must be very specific. You have seven weeks to get it done. Your objectives must be very specific.

10. Testing and evaluation and a related point system with awards are necessary to perpetuate a successful program.

11. Don't ever talk to me about toughness and discipline being crucial to success if you want me to believe the task force statement about the overshadowing culture that I should assume I am a member of. Let's not even mention the fourth quarter.

12. The head coach is the man. I want to be an extension of that man. That's who I work for. I need to be able to define the things that he has determined to be a non-negotiable. Once defined, I need the means to never have to compromise those things. I also need to feel encouraged that my personal non-negotiables are inclusive.

CHAPTER SEVEN
WEIGHTS

When I was about twelve years old, I encountered a device called an Exergenie that could be considered my earliest exposure to resistance training. This early innovation was essentially a cylinder with a rope passing through it, and you could adjust the resistance and then work out by pulling the rope through different ranges of movement. A common perception during those days maintained that traditional weight lifting was for freaks and would somehow interfere with an athlete's coordination. Coaches failed to realize that they needed to address a lack of flexibility rather than a lack of coordination.

For an interesting perspective on this history of exercise theory, you can check out a magazine called *Strength and Health* that was actually launched in 1932 and is packed with countless feats of strength, flexibility and athleticism. I have read an issue from 1952, and I was amazed at how much I agreed with the writer, Jule Bacon, as he described the proper way to add strength and bulk. Bacon wrote, "The majority of men wish to gain weight. With approximately half the muscular bulk of the body in the legs and hips, half of your opportunity to gain weight lies in the extremities. If you want strength—and who doesn't?—you can build tremendous power in your legs. He suggests exercise like the deep knee bend (on toes), the squat (flat-footed), leg press and leg curl, all of which bear some similarities to movements still employed today. Another exercise mentioned in the magazine was a movement that track and field guru Boo Schexnayder today calls yielding squat jumps. One of the magazine's contributors, John Grimek, reportedly used 200 pounds for that exercise—comparable to many of today's top athletes.

Of course, not every recommendation in *Strength and Health* has stood the test of time. Consider the "York health shoe," also known as the "iron boot." The magazine gives ten basic exercises using this device, and the public was so convinced of the shoes' effectiveness that 200,000 pair were sold between 1937 and 1952.

Another expert from that era, Bob Hoffman, advertised twenty-four instructional courses in the magazine. Readers who purchased his comprehensive package would receive programs like "The Power Course," "The Swing Bell System," "A Super Abdominal Course," "The Neck Developing Course" and even one called "An Unusual Course." Hoffman also offered the York Set system of weight training, including instruction in the Compound System, the Double Progressive System and others. His complete package cost $5—a steal for such a wealth of training options.

It's fascinating to me, especially because these ideas went out of vogue in the decades to follow, that Hoffman's programs feature a variety of Olympic lifting concepts, powerlifting-type exercises and a significant amount of bodybuilding. It's just the type of program I prefer today, in 2013. In other news, Hoffman also offered a publication entitled, "Successful Happy Marriage," with the headline, "When it comes to sex, are you groping in the dark?" When he wasn't selling comprehensive workout programs or marketing products like plastic suits for muscle definition and half leopard-half latex bikini briefs for men, Hoffman could also fix what was ailing any marriage.

One unique and unsettling feature of those early magazines was their tendency to depict experts scantily clad and in unorthodox body positions. So even if those gurus were certainly on to something, the presentation set the correlation between weight training and athletic performance back years, or even decades. But if you can get past those pictures, you can find examples of stability, flexibility, balance and athleticism that would even stand out in today's fitness-crazed culture. It seems that "strongmen" were also acrobats during that era. Even with those glimmers of truth, however, the connection between strength training and performance wasn't fully understood until the 1980s. To counter solid teaching like Hoffman's, people were having discussions back then about topics like avoiding training before activity, limiting in-season training and the possibility that a basketball jump shot could be distorted by too much bench press.

The emergence of the Arthur Jones Nautilus Training Equipment and Concepts Revolution, better known as Nautilus, in the early 1970s ignited the trend of exercise machines. The Nautilus people crafted a tremendous marketing campaign touting the almost-magical value of the system's uniquely shaped cam, which was supposed to match the strength curve specific to human capacity. A companion to this concept was a training theory known as "one set to failure," in which an athlete could fry his whole body in thirty to forty minutes. The trainer would assist his subject in brutal attacks on each muscle group using a four second count on the eccentric movement, forced reps, negative-only reps, negative accentuated reps or super sets—all Nautilus concepts that pushed people past their limits at different levels. Garbage cans were advisable during this program.

Since the nature of football coaches is to shun rest and maintain a high-grinding tempo to increase toughness, they loved this philosophy. Dan Riley, who became the Penn State strength and conditioning coach in 1977 and later spent 27 years coaching in the NFL, burst onto the scene in State College determined to prove that "one set to failure" in a variety of rotations could revolutionize the toughness and hypertrophy levels of his players. Thus the controversy of machines versus free weights was born. Another school that went the machine route was the University of Michigan, and once an athletic program shelled out multiple thousands of dollars on a machine that could only train one athlete at a time they were determined to justify the method and verify the result. What was the result? Hypertrophy, conditioning and toughness were the expectation, and in my opinion those goals were accomplished.

In 1992, I traveled to Penn State to interview for the Director of Strength and Conditioning position. We had just completed an 11-1 season at ECU and had ended the season ranked ninth in the nation and a National Coach of the Year award for Bill Lewis. I showed up in Joe Paterno's office with a video of the program I had used to great success with the Pirates—squats, snatches, power cleans and other exercises that were the complete antithesis of the high-intensity, "one set to failure" approach.

Of course, I grew up in Pennsylvania, and my Dad coached at the Penn State football camp every summer. It was a huge honor just to be interviewed. Still, I had to stay true to my own beliefs, and it quickly became evident that Penn State and I were not a good fit. I took a tour of their weight room, and it looked like a machine graveyard—every imaginable type of machine, no free weights to be found. When Paterno asked me what I thought after the tour, I went for honesty. I told him that I would need to clean house on the facility and start over if I took the job. The PSU sports medicine guy was the only other person in the room, and when I said that he looked at me like I had stolen his lunch. I knew I was dead. Later, after it was clear to me that I was staying at ECU, Joe Pa sent me a nice note that I appreciated but forced me to seriously question his knowledge of training principles. He also thanked me for giving him an education in powerlifting, even though I never mentioned that subject during the interview.

I chose not to tell Paterno that I had managed a Nautilus fitness center for three years in the '80s, when I was working as the linebacker coach at Tennessee Military Institute. Our Nautilus circuit at that fitness center was typical for the Nautilus gyms of that day—we started clients at the multi-hip machine, worked through the largest muscle groups and finished with bicep and tricep isolation. I used Nautilus as a supplement to powerlifting training in those days, because I have always been intrigued with the idea of pushing the limits of the body's pain tolerance.

I had a friend there who liked to dream up the hardest workout possible, using supersets to failure. It was brutal. Saturday was deadlift day, so we were already smoked as we exited the free weight room and entered the Nautilus facility. I considered it excellent assistance work, and it kept me in shape, but I never found a sequence that came close to the ruthless circuit during my college years, which included power cleans, deadlifts, the dreaded squat machine and, of course, Billy Cannons. Crossfit might look intense on ESPN, but it would have been a nice change-up day for us at Salem. My collegiate experience, however, is exactly why I think Crossfit is questionable for any of my objectives. My back has never been the same after being forced to do power cleans in the middle of a circuit.

Get under some weight—it's required

We did have some free weights at TMI Academy, and it was during those years that I began a career in powerlifting. I got into powerlifting because I missed football and I wanted to compete, and East Tennessee was a hotbed for the sport. One powerlifting team, based in Chattanooga, featured some national contenders, and Doc

Kreis and his band of brothers were making a national impression in Nashville. In Knoxville Jody and Joe Cummins and Doug Furness were big names on the powerlifting circuit. I entered three or four meets a year for a few years, and I had some success at the 181-pound weight class.

The powerlifting mentality is one all its own. I've seen some good athletes succeed at competitions, and I've also seen lifters succeed even though they were pretty mediocre athletes. I never got into much discussion with people in that community about steroids, but at that time I would guess that most of the competitors were enhanced in some way. Even if they were taking something, my goal was always the same—to place in the top three in my weight class. The decisions they made that gave them an unfair edge would affect only them, not me, because there was no reason to take that kind of a risk just to win a larger trophy. My ego was in check as a powerlifter, because I was self-actualized through college football.

Today I view golf in much the same way I viewed powerlifting back in the '80s. I enjoyed it when I had time for it, but above all I needed to feed my family. I am proud of some of my accomplishments from that hobby, though. My best lifts in the 181-pound class were a 385-pound bench press, 630-pound squat and 640-pound dead lift, which put me right in what they referred to as "elite." That was my goal—to reach elite without any enhancement, and I was able to get there.

No powerlifting competition was as memorable for me as the one I entered in a federal prison. I was coaching at Bucknell, and I got the crazy idea to compete in a meet at the Pittsburgh Federal Penitentiary. Federal Pen was competing against Greensburgh Prison, and I was there as an independent. Most of my opponents that day were in for murder. I was positioned smack in the middle of the yard with them. I saw one guy smoking a cigarette, getting mentally prepared for his attempt, and I noticed some striking scars in his side—in the shape of bullet holes. Another dude's nickname was "Swampman." Swampman was in the pen for multiple murders in Pennsylvania, and he was also charged in Mississippi. He could also deadlift more than 800 pounds. His last attempt was somewhere around 850, and after he pulled it, he screamed, "Nobody f***s with Swampman! Nobody!" My last deadlift attempt earned me second place in the 198-pound class, but after pulling the lift I didn't hang around for accolades because I was taking points away from one of the teams. I got out of there ASAP, declining the offer to stay and shower.

Right before I went to attempt my last lift, one of the teams started screaming at me that I shouldn't pull the lift, because if I did I would take points away from them. They were trying to intimidate me, but I pulled the lift anyway, and impulsively screamed back at them. But I quickly realized where I was and cut that behavior short.

My experience in powerlifting was invaluable to me as a strength coach. I think it's very difficult to teach athletes techniques for gaining strength unless you've been under some weight yourself. But I also believe that if your experience as a strength coach is limited to powerlifting, you need to work overtime in other areas to optimize and balance your coaching approach.

Meat and potatoes

There are several key methods of strength training that can enhance athletic performance, and a good strength coach should be well-versed in all of them. To develop foundational strength, you need a routine of multi-joint, freeform exercises like the back squat, front squat, barbell step-up, push press, power clean, block clean, push jerk, bench press, incline press and dumbbell variation presses. The primary barbell pressing movements are traditionally those that can be plugged into various models. Those traditional models, applied over the years, have been referred to as periodization.

Current models for college coaches have moved away from this concept, because the training phases specifically applied to collegiate schedules are reduced. Our current methods involve six to eight week cycles using three week mini-cycles, or max effort training. Max effort training is directed toward straining through heavy weight. It's a simple rationale—we are working to get strong and target fast twitch muscle fiber. We must be technically sound and familiar with the weight on the bar.

We want to have a good feel for the resistance level that we are hoping to achieve during a particular training session. This ultimate goal should already be evident during warm-up sets, so that through the entire workout we are training with the correct weight and with the objective of successfully completing every set. The goals we set seem very simple, but they are more difficult to achieve than one might assume. Each athlete must be closely supervised, and the sets must be timed with the end result in mind—the specific objective for that day.

Percentage value training is never an exact science, but it is as close to perfect as we're likely to get in this profession. Because every aspect of this training is measured, a deliberate coach is a necessity. The coach must closely calculate and micromanage progressive strength gains to prevent injury and optimize results. Any implementation of the Olympic lifts requires a high level of coaching. In our program, we have evolved to the implementation of the block clean, power clean and hang snatch. The block clean resistance level is usually dictated by the speed of the bar measured by a Fitrodyne or "Tendo Unit." This device is attached to the bar and can be adjusted to measure speed or wattage.

We dictate resistance with speed. For example, 1.2 meters per second of resistance is relatively 79 to 82 percent of the one-repetition maximum.

Some people have advocated for bar speed with lighter resistance, as opposed to grinding through heavy weight every time you show up. The expert opinions that I value most in this profession advocate a balance of the two methods to best maximize power. This blend has worked very well for me in producing favorable numbers with our four primary exercises.

I place a high value on testing those four—back squat, push jerk, power clean and bench press. The progressive resistance models that I favor have been successfully applied to those four exercises through the years I have been designing my program. I have also separated these models into categories of progressions. I believe that the vast majority of college athletes are drastically undertrained, especially if they participated in three different sports in high school. These athletes have simply not put in the time in the weight room to significantly advance, with the possible exception of the bench press. Coaches must be aware that there is a tremendous amount of room for development in these young athletes.

One of my favorite sayings is, "I believe what I see." Strength training results are not within the spiritual realm. Faith doesn't rack a power clean. Confidence might help, but pure training is what gets you there. There are no shortcuts; you have to put in the work. I am not from the school of thought that sees a smooth set of ten leg presses as the answer. I can't subscribe to that philosophy, because I've seen too many athletes over the years reap significant benefits from something different.

I have found the recipes mentioned in this chapter to be very beneficial in producing record-breaking test results for each lift. In our offseason, these progressions have generally produced between

35 and 40 players who can squat over 500 pounds and between 10 and 15 who can squat over 600 pounds. The testing is a three-repetition maximum with knee wraps. Jason Brown tripled 700 pounds for me at UNC, and that's about as high as we needed to go. A recent graduate hit 700 for a single in 2012 at ECU without wraps. Both of them are still alive and well.

We use a one-repetition maximum for power clean. During the last testing phase at ECU, we produced 41 players at 300-plus and seven at 350-plus. During my tenure at UNC Jason Brown hit 419, Robert Quinn and Bruce Carter 405, Madison Hedgecock 385 and Johnny White 374—all current or former NFL players. I would re-emphasize that this is a power clean, not a hang clean.

Bench press is necessary, but it is still one of my least favorite lifts, because if you get stupid it can be extremely dangerous. Half of the civilized world lifts too heavy, and most people have no clue about the mechanics of lifting properly. Using our system, I've had as many as twenty-four players lift over 400 pounds off a three-repetition maximum. Big deal.

I love the push jerk because it's a total body experience. I've tested a one-repetition maximum and also wattage using the Tendo unit, and the highest wattage occurs at about 76 to 79 percent of a one RM. I was impressed when an athlete jerked 405, and he is also alive and well.

I would also point out that you would see zero "deloading" weeks in these progressions. The NCAA gives me two 6-8 week offseason training periods each year, with only one being mandatory. Because the NCAA provides an inordinate amount of discretionary time, each year amounts to an excessive "deload." I'll emphasize again that I have seen a large number of athletes become exceptionally strong using these progressions:

Recipes
Methods of Strength and Power Development as Applied to the Primary Lifts (1-2 Days Per Week)

LEVEL 1

A. Three-Week Mini-Cycle (9 week program)

Week 1	Week 2	Week 3
5 x 55%	4 x 55%	4 x 55%
5 x 64%	3 x 67%	3 x 67%
5 x 76%	3 x 79%	3 x 79%
4 x 79%	3 x 85%	3 x 85%
3 x 82%	3 x 85%	2 x 88%
3 x 85%	2 x 88%	1 x 91%
8 x 64%	1 x 91%	1 x 94%
8 x 64%	6 x 70%	4 x 76%
	6 x 70%	4 x 76%
	6 x 70%	4 x 76%

B. Calculated Performance Method 3

Warm-up sets are calculated off a three-rep max, and emphasis is placed on completion of repetitions without assistance.

5 x 61%
3 x 70%
2 x 82%
1 x 91%
3 Rep Max
2 x 3 (3 RM weight -10 lbs)
2 x 3 (3 RM weight -20 lbs)

C. Calculated Performance Method 6

5 x 61%
3 x 70%
2 x 82%
1 x 91%

6 Rep Max

2 x 6 (6 RM weight -10 lbs)

2 x 6 (6 RM weight -20 lbs)

D. Level 5's Concept (Level Work Sets)

All sets are five reps, and the total tonnage is calculated from a total of four work sets. The objective is to achieve as much total tonnage as possible with four work sets. The challenge is to achieve all reps successfully. Achievement levels are standardized by position.

8 x 55%

5 x 61%

3 x 67%

2 x 73%

4 x 5 at standardized level weight

LEVEL 2

A. Three-Phase Wave-Volume

Phase 1	Phase 2	Phase 3
5 x 55%	4 x 61%	3 x 67%
5 x 61%	4 x 67%	3 x 73%
5 x 67%	4 x 73%	3 x 79%
5 x 76%	4 x 82%	3 x 88%
5 x 70%	4 x 76%	3 x 82%
5 x 85%	4 x 88%	3 x 94%

Each phase is a 3-week adaptation

B. Eighty Percent Build Up

Phase 1	Phase 2	Phase 3	Phase 4
3:00 rest for work sets	3:30 rest for work sets	4:00 rest for work sets	5:00 rest for work sets
5 x 61%	5 x 61%	5 x 61%	5 x 61%
3 x 67%	3 x 67%	3 x 67%	3 x 67%

2 x 76%	2 x 76%	2 x 76%	2 x 76%
12 x 3 @80%	8 x 4 @80%	6 x 5 @80%	4 x 6 @80%

Each phase is a 2-week adaptation

LEVEL 3

A. Max Effort Meso-Cycle

Phase 1	Phase 2	Phase 3
5 x 58%	4 x 61%	3 x 64%
4 x 64%	3 x 70%	3 x 73%
3 x 73%	2 x 76%	2 x 79%
1 x 79%	1 x 82%	1 x 85%
5 x (82-85%)	4 x (85-88%)	3 x (88-91%)
3 x 5 @76%	3 x 4 @79%	3 x 3 @82%

Each phase is a 2-week adaptation

B. Integrated System

Max effort training with component and variation movements related to foundational strength.

C. Special Category

1. Rep Goal Progression

   Phase 1—55 reps at 73% of 1 RM

   Phase 2—45 reps at 76% of 1 RM

   Phase 3—36 reps at 79% of 1 RM

   Phase 4—28 reps at 82% of 1 RM

   Phase 5—21 reps at 85% of 1 RM

   Phase 6—15 reps at 88% of 1 RM

   Execute designated number or reps in less than 15 minutes

2. Cluster Single Method

Each rotation is one repetition with approximately 30 seconds rest at the designated percentage of 1 RM.

3 Singles at Progressive Percentages

61% 1+1+1
67% 1+1+1
73% 1+1+1
79% 1+1+1
85% 1+1+1
91% 1+1+1

3. Twenties Concept

Twenty is the goal for total reps, first set is done to failure then immediately drop 5% and continue to do the maximum number of reps. Repeat until a goal of 20 reps is met. If 19 reps are achieved, perform a minimum of two reps in the final set.

Strength development phases are used within a four-day split push-pull, four-day split upper/lower schedule, or a three-day total body program.

Three-week mini-cycles have been a great tool for us in developing strength with the redshirt athletes within a fifteen-week cycle. We have also used three rounds of three weeks using some discretionary time, with the assumption that the work would get done.

I have also used the "heavy set first" concept successfully for a number of years. It's a philosophy that requires a progression of warm-up sets followed by a maximum set and several knock down sets. With this progression, we use a relatively new concept known as APRE, in which sets are calculated off of the weight used for the heavy set. We calculate off of the one-repetition maximum and look for 76 percent for a top set of six or 88 percent for a top set of three. I like those progressions for in-season training.

The Level 5's Concept has worked very well for us in incremental strength gains, particularly with bench press. It is a warm-up sequence followed by four level sets of five repetitions, and it calculates total tonnage lifted for the four work sets. Any rep not achieved is deducted from the total, a rule that gives the athlete motivation to achieve his reps. Since the whole world tries to bench press too heavy, this program has some appeal. It includes position group standard for tonnage achievement, which provides a goal and a reason not to miss a rep.

The Wave Concept is simply progressive sets with a knockdown set and a meaningful rest before attempting the heavy set. It features maximum effort with the volume and higher intensity in the warm-up as opposed to a knockdown set following the max effort attempt.

Eighty Percent Build-up is a revised version of the old Bulgarian progression. We have seen a tremendous level of success with this progression over extended training periods using three-week phases. We have also used the first four training phases as a foundation and added two phases of traditional work with low reps.

Maximum Effort Cycle training can be implemented in triples or by using the mesocycle method, moving from five to three reps on the max effort set and knockdowns. Our typical three-day program includes a max effort power clean on Monday, bench press on Wednesday and back squat on Friday. With power clean, we use a ten-second minimum between reps; if you can't execute the rep, the set doesn't count. This is a very effective program if you want to make significant gains in a short time period.

The Integrated System of training is similar to the Westside-Barbell Conjugate Method in that we use variation and component exercises. I still believe that most collegiate athletes are not much above the novice category when it comes to development. They need more volume and time to adapt to each exercise. For example, we see gains using the double chain on bench press, as an alternative, but we feel that we still need four to six weeks to adapt.

The Twenties Concept in the special category is Jon Kolb's old knockdown burn-out death sequence. The idea is to totally fatigue the muscle groups targeted for that session. If it is executed properly, you can get crushed in a short period of time. There is a flavor of the old Steeler bench routine in this sequence.

I could include ten more pages of experimental progressions that I have either personally experienced or coached someone through. These include countless examples of periodization, rotational periodization, max-effort options, mini-cycles, muscular endurance and hypertrophy schemes, to name a few. The bottom line? You have to adapt to the weight and move forward incrementally with some sense of realism as you continue to strain through new levels of resistance. It takes time, effort, consistency and coaching to develop exceptional strength relative to an athlete's true potential.

Side dish supreme

One of the more recent trends that has gained relevance in strength training is the use of kettlebells. My exposure and education to this fantastic tool came via Steve Watterson and Anthony DiLuglio from the Art of Strength in Providence, R.I. When I visited, Steve had been using the system successfully with the Tennessee Titans. I've known him for a long time, and I regard him as one of the best in the business. He is the only strength coach I know with an assistant head coach title, and he certainly deserves it.

After visiting Steve and learning the nuts and bolts of kettlebells, including a hands-on session with him and his wife in his garage, I was sold. As I understand it, this training method originated with the Soviet military, and most people in this business are familiar with kettlebell pioneer Pavel Tsatsouline and the rigorous certification system he offers. I survived Wild Billy, five years of college football and the police academy, so I don't need somebody to get in my face to teach me a kettlebell snatch. I get it.

When I was coaching at UNC, I brought DiLuglio in twice to

teach my staff kettlebell concepts, and he did an incredible job. We incorporated his corrective strategy assessment and also adopted the creative concept of fifty minute high-tempo total body training. We were so sold on the concept of kettlebells that we developed a training program divided into three categories—basic programs, anaerobic emphasis and maximum strength. These workouts have been a significant addition to our total program and a much more productive option for special conditioning projects. Not only that, they are much more exciting than a treadmill.

Another key function of kettlebells is for training injured athletes. We can perform isolateral total body work as well as explosive isolateral work, and the portable aspect of the kettlebells makes them optimal for training during practice. Kettlebells and our sand pit have proved to be a productive combination to accelerate the rehabilitation process for injured athletes. We also believe that kettlebell work assists in facilitating posterior chain development and shoulder stability.

In most of our training progressions we include kettlebell training to supplement our primary work, and many times we use it in a complex type of application in the form of supersets. We find this to be an excellent method of increasing work capacity. One warning—technique is extremely important in learning kettlebell movements. We want them to always be driven from the hips. Performing these exercises improperly can result in low back pain and injury, so it is strongly advisable for every coach to be trained by kettlebell experts.

Now we need to ask ourselves a crucial question in regard to developing high levels of strength and power via straining through heavy weight: When is enough weight enough? For example, if a program is able to recruit freakish fast-twitch quality athletes with exceptional game skills, should there be any red flags in the developmental process? I think that's a great question.

Let's go back and re-emphasize the fact that elite high school athletes are usually significantly undertrained due to three-sport participation and self-perceived status. Many of them are weak from the sternum down, and that fact alone should justify six-and-a-half good training phases (the basic number available to the collegiate football player).

Safety is of paramount importance in a strength training program, and a safe training environment comes from the properly supervised progression of resistance and teaching. Athletes need to be coached every day and advised in detail about the proper resistance levels for each set. An athlete who is technically sound and progressively trained by an educated coach should not experience any type of injury in the process of getting stronger. Coaches should take all physical weaknesses and strengths into consideration when setting the developmental goals for an athletes.

One vital consideration is the joint areas, which should be approached in a balanced manner. The current buzz is all about posterior chain and firing of the glutes. It seems that you can appear more knowledgeable in 2013 if you include a barrage of glute-firing jargon in your repertoire, but the trendy language keeps changing. Ten years ago it was all about engaging the core, and twenty years ago I listened to a talk on super slow motion training. What's next? I'm all ears.

Deliberate Practice—The Real Deal

If we want to put limits on strength development against a sliding scale of talent levels, we run the risk of treading the waters of underdevelopment. Recent research has illustrated that genetic factors are no longer as compelling as was once believed, and those findings have birthed the concept of deliberate practice. The name associated with this research is Anders Ericsson, a professor at Florida State. His findings, which state that genetics have been overestimated and the influence of hard training overestimated, should be a breath of fresh air to strength coaches everywhere. This new information gives a resurgence to the power of overachievement, and it should convince aspiring young athletes that even far-reaching goals are achievable with great coaching and hard work. The research indicates that we have not even come close to understanding our "actualized potential" in strength development. David Schenk gives encouragement to coaches hoping to push their athletes to excellence in his book *The Genius in All of Us:*

Our abilities are not set in genetic stone. They are soft and sculptable, far into adulthood. With humility, with hope, and with extraordinary determination, greatness is something to which any kid—of any age—can aspire.

It is practice that doesn't take no for an answer; practice that perseveres; the type of practice where the individual keeps raising the bar of what he or she considers success."

For deliberate practice to work, the demands have to be serious and sustained. Simply playing lots of chess or soccer or golf isn't enough. Simply taking lessons from a wonderful teacher is not enough. Deliberate practice requires a mindset of never, ever being satisfied with your current ability. It requires a constant self-critique, a pathological relentlessness, a passion to aim consistently just beyond one's capability so that daily disappointment and failure is actually desired, and a never ending resolve to dust oneself off and try again and again and again.

It requires enormous, life altering amounts of time—a daily grinding commitment to becoming better. In the long term, the results can be highly satisfying. But in the short term, from day to day and month to month, there's nothing particularly fun about the process or the substantial sacrifices involved.

In studies, Ericsson found a clear distinction between leisure players who tend to enjoy themselves casually much of the time, and dedicated achievers, who become glued to the gritty process of getting better.

Anyone who aspires to be an effective strength coach should be revitalized by these findings. The belief in an athlete's boundless potential increases the value and meaning of the knowledge and expertise that a good coach brings to the table each day. We already know that it takes years and possibly even decades to optimize strength; the strongest people in the world are well beyond college age. For at least twenty years I had the goal of a 400-pound bench press. When did I finally accomplish it? At age forty-one. That goal was realized after about 2,500 upper body training sessions—a dizzying number of sets and reps over two decades.

My point here is that we need to have the knowledge to treat strength training as a specific art form—a vehicle for an athlete to optimize performance. If we decide that an athlete doesn't need to bench press more than 400 pounds to become the best he can be at his particular athletic pursuit, then we don't need to push him to lift more. We might decide that we can affect speed through fifteen years of strengthening the muscle groups that propel the body forward. We might take an athlete who needs to gain 60 pounds to make it in the NFL and craft a five-year plan of strength and hypertrophy that gets him there. We can take an eighth grader and construct a road map of development that will lead him to a scholarship he would not have received otherwise. We can rehabilitate injuries that might have rendered an athlete dysfunctional without strength training. Knowledge of deliberate practice findings can demonstrate the redeeming value of long, hard commitment, and the promise of these results can be a catalyst for the young athlete.

For me, it was about my ninth grade year when I recognized that some type of weightlifting and conditioning program would make me better prepared as an athlete. I believed that I could become a collegiate football player, but I needed a plan. Of course, the sophistication of training has come light years since then.

The statement that Shenk makes concerning the process is powerful. He maintains that non-achievers seem to be missing one or more of the following aspects—style, intensity of practice, technique, mindset or response to failure. Physical deficiencies should be identified at a young age so that the process of deliberate training can begin. Ericsson suggests that it takes 10,000 hours and ten years of training to achieve maximum potential. This amount of training requires great coaching, steely commitment and a tremendous level of passion.

The other factor that has a meaningful developmental impact on the athlete is frequent competition. Nietzsche wrote, "Every natural gift must develop itself by contests." Win, lose or draw, with the right kind of coaching and learning experiences we can combine new information with deliberate training on the field or the court. This is the best plan of progressive development.

Weight training is an extensive process that allows even non-athletic types to achieve some impressive feats. Collegiate athletes in my program, particularly football players, have demonstrated consistency by making significant progress in the weight room through their career. It's refreshing to note that they undergo frequent drug tests, which serve as a strong deterrent to chemical assistance. The key to forward progress in strength training is consistent commitment in a supervised environment.

A few key variables—volume, intensity, frequency and rest—have a significant influence on the objectives and results of a strength training regimen. Whatever type of training program a coach decides to implement will include a combination of those variables. Concepts like maximum strength, maximum power, hypertrophy, muscular endurance and work capacity call for specific combinations of these variables. The training progressions outlined in this chapter are taken from the practical experience of just a few coaches, so countless customized programs could be developed when coaches tweak those important variables.

Generally we say that most programs with the objective of maximum strength and power are working above 80 percent of one RM on primary exercises during most of the time provided by the NCAA. Very seldom would more than five repetitions be prescribed in any given set. Supplementary, auxiliary or assistance work might be directed toward hypertrophy or increased work capacity. These are some of the terms commonly used for the same objective—work that is corollary to primary lifts.

It is vital to provide a multitude of variations to achieve strength training goals because no two athletes respond to training stimuli in exactly the same way. A coach's practical experience can be valuable in understanding general successes within larger groups of athletes, but some athletes in that group might stall using the plan that worked well for their teammates. The best coaches develop programs that provide the highest level of impact for the largest group of athletes; this is particularly important in a sport like football with more than one hundred young men on the roster.

I owned a personal training business for seven years, and when working with individuals or small groups in that setting personalized formulas can be identified and applied at a higher level of success. When we train collegiate athletes, we divide them into pods and assign a coach to each pod. That coach is responsible for tracking each athlete and making sure that the sets and repetitions are executed with optimal production. Deliberate coaching leads to fruitful training.

The very best weight training programs are led by coaches who micromanage every technical and tactical aspect along the way.

Shenk provides some striking examples of exceptional achievement over time with repetition of training in realms beyond athletics. Mozart's first seven piano concertos, written from ages eleven to sixteen, contained almost nothing original. According to Shenk, "Symphony No. 29, written ten years after his first symphony, was his first of real stature." The first Mozart piano concerto that was considered truly great was his 271st completed composition.

Now, Wolfgang Amadeus doesn't look like he ever touched a weight, but if he did he probably would have made remarkable progress. It's about the "want to," which is something that man clearly possessed at an early age. Other great examples of perseverance throughout history abound—in a variety of disciplines and all over the world. Any time you want to discuss maximum strength gains you are talking about defying some common assumptions about genetics. It's about the "want to."

An athlete with the right coach can target the muscle groups specific to speed, gain thirty pounds of lean mass, improve hip rotary power, increase work capacity and become incredibly injury-resistant. If you approach it properly, strength training is an endless vista of untapped development. A well-crafted program can develop the muscle groups that enhance posture and can facilitate leg drive. Both of those factors will improve speed for the athlete. We can discover systems of training that simultaneously develop strength and speed.

After twenty-five years of this pursuit, I can eyeball an athlete and visualize the result four years down the road. I can watch someone run and diagnose a weakness. I can also observe summer football camp and accurately advise a coach on who would be deserving of a scholarship. It's an art, no doubt, but it has been fine-tuned through years in the trenches. It's also a skill that is typically underappreciated, misrepresented and seldom understood. You can find five people on every street corner in America who think they are an expert in strength and conditioning, but in fact the mysteries of human athletic performance are difficult to unlock. Free weights are associated with negative and mysterious conceptions propagated by strange and mysterious people. I keep a bunch in my garage (weights, not mysterious people), and I see a new canvas and watercolors every time I step into that environment..

Foundational Perspectives

1. A strength training program should begin with foundational lifts that involve large muscle groups. These are referred to as free form, multi-joint, closed-chain movement.

2. The back squat has no equal.

3. The low bar back squat is superior to the high bar back squat.

4. The power clean is a lift that must be coached every day, every set, every repetition. An improper rack position is enemy #1 and very common with football players. If it isn't fixed, you have a problem and possibly a future injury.

5. Use weight that you can handle when you bench. No one will listen, but let's say it anyway.

6. Train for muscular balance in all the major joint areas.

7. Fire the glutes. (I am required to include this statement, but it is, in fact, very important.)

8. Strain through heavy weight for each major muscle group once a week. You are only as strong as the weight you can lift today.

9. Foundational progressive strength development is necessary to optimize maximum power.

10. The jerk is a great exercise. Don't allow overhead protesters to ruin your day.

11. Kettlebells are a tremendous tool. Just so you know.

12. Deliberate practice is a concept that should revitalize the energy level of coaches nationwide. The athlete continues to make progress for ten years or 10,000 hours with great coaching. The coach is key.

13. "Ultra achievers are irrepressible and resilient. You have to want it, want it so bad you will never give up, so bad that you are ready to sacrifice time, money, sleep, friendships, even your reputation. ("People may—and many will—think of you as odd.")" (Excerpt from David Schenk's *The Genius in All of Us*)

14. "Uncommon achievement requires an uncommon level of personal motivation and a massive amount of faith."—*The Genius in All of Us*

15. Strength training is a long, hard, grinding process. As you make progress, you must become consumed with reaching new levels of achievement (thousands of reps over a decade, with no more than 72 hours off). It's a lifestyle. We knew this about strength training for quite some time before the research establishing deliberate practice.

16. Strength coaches are overzealous individuals. They are cordial to each other at clinics and conferences, but have no problem taking someone's job when football coaches get hired and fired. Bob Hoffman didn't seem to care much for Joe Weider. They both probably thought they knew just a little more than each other and didn't like compromising their guru status to any other perceived guru. Sounds familiar.

CHAPTER EIGHT
FAST AND FURIOUS

Let's review the finer details of the total speed program. We've talked a lot in previous chapters about acceleration mechanics and the fact that we have customized our program to target posterior chain development. The rationale is that we wanted to optimize strength in the muscle groups that concentrically contract to overcome inertia. All said and done, we know that the primary engine is comprised of the quadriceps femoris, the glutes and the hamstrings. The hamstrings also optimally function in a reactive manner "at speed". We also know that there has been recent information focusing on the importance of the adductors because of recent EMG studies. Another important point of awareness for those of us who work with football is the number of athletes with "knotted up" hip flexors, which impact glute activation and prevent the hips from opening up to optimize force production. You will notice that speed concepts are re-emphasized throughout this book. That is a purposeful attempt to convince the reader that speed training is king.

When we put young athletes on a line and ask them to run, most take too many steps to cover ground. They have very poor arm stroke and stride separation. They bend at the waist and suffer from swing leg block, and most have also neglected the key principle of working to enhance flexibility equal to enhancing strength. The individuals who ran track through high school are more advanced with posture and arm stroke but unfortunately are cyclical kind of creatures of habit. They typically cycle the heel through acceleration, which means that they don't get their feet back to the ground. Again, we have to understand that to get back to the ground we have to keep the feet close to the ground.

Another concept that can be very beneficial in our training is referred to as "coupling." This indicates that hip flexion and extension are linked together, which lends credibility to drills that require a scissors action. We perform stationary scissors drills on flat ground and boxes. We also execute moving scissors drills with an overhead object, which progress from a dowel to a heavy medicine ball.

We have a series of drills and postural cues that are executed in a "tall hips" position whereby we work to eliminate anterior pelvic tilt and stay tall on the stance leg. Some coaches cue athletes to take slack out of the muscle. This is an interesting concept that assists in stiffening tendons and ligaments, therefore building a tighter elastic suspension. Remember that 52 percent of energy return comes from the lower leg. This would suggest that we incorporate a significant level of lower leg stiffening techniques such as single leg hops and bounds into the total program.

Motor learning skills apply to the process of working toward perfection in the technical aspects of sprinting. The set of drills referred to as "fast leg" would be included in this category. These type of drills are excellent for neural activation at maximum speed movement without the burden of stress placed upon the hamstrings in a full speed sprint. The difference in application for football would be a piston-like fast leg movement as opposed to cyclical action.

Most strength and conditioning coaches have been studying maximum velocity track concepts because they have been attending clinics and consultations from track people. I think track people do an excellent job conveying maximum velocity mechanics, but they do very little with refining a detailed method of teaching acceleration concepts. That's why I decided to take it upon myself to develop my own system with that goal in mind. Football is a game of acceleration and deceleration, and it also requires the athlete to come to balance and restart. Power angles must be set and reset. There will be instances when the athlete will have to open up and run, and those instances are directly related to the position group. For example, I played defensive back. What I learned long ago is that if I'm running with a takeoff route and the receiver has me by three yards, I have to open my hips and initiate violent arm strokes to gain ground. When he looks back for the ball and starts to shut down his arm stroke, I can gain ground immediately. Obviously, as a defensive back, the athlete would need to understand the application of tall, open running.

Now remember the need to open up and run doesn't mean you confuse training cues. Acceleration cues do not jive with maximum velocity cues. Just coach "tall and open." If you incorporate a drill such as a partner tempo run, your athletes will learn how to open up. Don't coach anything cyclical. I counted thirty-two players on our current team that run a sub 4.6 forty indoors under exactly the same conditions every time we test. That's great team speed. It's fact, not fiction. Remember to believe what you see. If you like what you see you are probably doing something right.

The following information is general in nature and has served our program very well over the years. It includes a more in-depth explanation of Kevin McNair's speed terminology, and many of these concepts are taken specifically from Loren Seagrave. The list of speed drills and bounding is specific to our program. The five-day breakdown is more suited for the winter program. It is another option that could be applicable to a four-day split strength training program with a heavy platform day placed on Monday and the running following the lift on that day.

Speed Training Guidelines

When we train for pure speed, we use important guidelines to optimize the training adaptation. It is extremely necessary to direct close attention to specific objectives and prescribe accordingly.

1. To develop speed, we must be in an optimal state of excitability of the central nervous system and not in a state of fatigue.
2. Speed exercises should be performed when athletes are fully recovered.
3. Duration of rest is dictated by two factors:
   a. Changes in excitability of the central nervous system
   b. Elimination of oxygen debt
4. Excitability of the CNS must be maintained; however, breathing should be normal for the repetition.
5. It is important to understand that after several repetitions, fatigue has a cumulative impact and speed drops considerably.
6. Exceptional levels of coordination permit optimal relaxation of muscles. Muscle tension slows movements.
7. Speed is taught from simple to more complex movements.
8. Drills to emphasize body position are done slow, then fast. Much of the drill package is performed at less than maximal speed to enable the athlete to warm up.
9. Every repetition in an "absolute" speed workout should be performed at maximum speed.
10. We prefer contrast training methods for a single workout following dynamic movements, neural drills, and power work.

11. Contrast training includes moderate resistance modalities that do not compromise maximum speed more than 10-15 percent for speed bounding and sprinting. Resistance modalities for acceleration strength work can be progressed.

12. When properly administered, it is possible to perform speed training daily.

    a. Muscle stores of creatine-phosphate are not exceeded.

    b. Recovery time is adequate.

    c. Anaerobic threshold is not exceeded.

13. When athletes are less than fully recovered, it is more advisable to perform speed-endurance or sport-specific endurance work.

14. Training toward absolute speed objectives should continue for six to eight weeks.

15. Teaching begins with proper alignment of body position, because joint angles dictate muscle recruitment.

16. It is important to understand that the ability to accelerate fast and the ability to move at a high velocity are independent from each other.

17. Frequency of movement is related to neural efficiency.

18. Our system includes drills that dictate body position from proper firing sequences and neural drills for improving coordination.

19. Acceleration training is 90 percent of our linear speed package.

20. Top end training is useful to skill players and can also serve to contribute toward better running technique with all position groups. Keep it simple.

Standard Training Procedures

1. Do not condition on absolute speed days. Thoughtful running should be the objective, to optimize correct motor patterns. Speed/endurance can be incorporated later in a training cycle.

2. Assistance running should be proceeded by an extensive dynamic warm-up and flex. Obviously, this training can be very stressful.

3. An effective option for speed training drills is a training circuit. The stations might include acceleration ladder, sled pull, downhill sprints, and resisted starts. This type of contrast training can be manipulated to develop power or power/endurance.
4. The total volume of a sprint training workout for football should not exceed 600 yards at the highest level. This includes tempo progression and full speed work.
5. Speed/endurance training can be blended into an absolute speed day as athletes become more highly conditioned. For example, the athlete runs eight timed 40's at an average of no more than $^3/_{10}$ above their best 40 time.

Dynamic Warm—Up

Many goals can be accomplished within the warm-up. Not only are we preparing the nervous system to fire, we are practicing proper body position and exactness of movement. It is very important that drills are performed perfectly, so that we can coordinate the system to fire in proper sequence and optimize force application as well as recovery. The warm-up should not be limited to linear movement. It should include movements that prepare all involved muscle groups toward more intense activity.

The following components should be included in the warm-up:
1. Body position and alignment (speed terminology directed toward limiting vertical movement, eliminating rotational movement and maximizing force into the ground.)
2. Leg recovery
3. Preparing for ground striking
4. Force application
5. Arm action
6. Scissors action

On some training days, the coach might have the objective of facilitating recovery. This would be a day that would include up to 80 percent drill work at medium tempo. This can be a very valuable method of maximizing the impact of neural drilling.

The current attitude toward static stretching with regard to the newest research is that it can distort neural activation of the highest expression of power. This indicates that the most optimal time for static stretching is post-workout, but it will be subject to the amount of time available toward the warm-up period. If static stretching is not included in the warm-up, the athlete must be confident that he is ready to run full speed, generally, we feel that this is a twenty-minute process at minimum. Traditional procedures are difficult to break, particularly within coaching circles. We used a modified version of a dynamic warm-up, which included 25 percent static stretching in pre-practice. Football coaches like to see you stretch before practice or a game. It's tradition.

Modified Static/Dynamic Warm -up

Our standard football specific warm-up includes a combination of low intensity jumps, build ups, dynamic mobility movements, active exercises and static stretches. We feel this type of warm-up fires the muscle and prepares it specifically for the movement patterns involved in sprinting, agility work, and position specifics.

Connors Lesson Plan For Speed

1. Postural Running: Body position dictates muscle recruitment and muscle recruitment dictates force application. Stride length (the most improvable training factor) is the direct result of force application. This training block will immediately improve your running efficiency.
2. Neural Drills: Sprinting, like any other athletic endeavor, is a motor

learning experience. The proper sequential application of muscle recruitment in conjunction with purposeful force application and recovery of the leg will optimize motor capacity.

3. Acceleration Mechanics: The proper two-point and three-point stance and start will be taught with attention to the overcoming inertia with a violent arm split and pressure on both feet. Athletes will be taught knee punch, leg drive, and how to attack the ground. Emphasis will be placed upon the first twelve yards.

4. Linear Bounding: Athletes will maximize power through exaggerated running. The teaching progression will include ankle, build up, power, fixed leg, single leg, and speed bounding techniques. We will also introduce the mini hurdle and the weighted vest options.

5. Speed Bounding/Blending: Speed bounding is one of the most important components to this system. This is directly related to acceleration and teaches the athlete horizontal direction of the body and maximal stride separation. Blending is an advanced technique designed to combine the development of both stride length and frequency.

6. Tempo Running: This training block is an extension of postural running and is performed with a "tempo partner." This is designed to improve stride frequency, reiterate posture, and competitively pace another athlete with similar level of speed. It can also be performed with resistance modalities.

7. Over-Speed Training: Improving stride frequency is the most challenging aspect of speed training. We will incorporate the proper teaching of safety precautions. The proper warm-up for this drill will be emphasized.

8. Come to Balance/Redirect: The athlete will learn to accelerate, decelerate, and re-accelerate through the application of acceleration mechanics. The game of football consists of repetitive

short bouts of explosive change of direction. We will teach the elimination of false steps, promote excellent posture, and re-emphasize maximal application of force.

9. Resisted Functional Strength Development: We will introduce a number of resisted functional movements designed to primarily strengthen the posterior chain.

10. Resisted Power Development: This training block will include resisted horizontal jumping, speed bounding and other various movements. The athlete will learn to apply force at a higher level in a shorter period of time.

11. Breakaway Drills: These drills are an excellent way to learn to apply acceleration mechanics in a competitive scenario. These are short, explosive drills performed with a partner. They are both programmable and reactive. They can also be linear, lateral, and multi-directional as is the game of football. The drills require a partner and breakaway belts.

12. Hip Flexibility: This station will include a dynamic hurdle series, stationary hurdle series, overhead squats, static flex and hip mobility drills. The ability to bend is crucial to the expression of power and fluidity of movement. This is a very important training component that is undertrained.

13. Competitive Reactives: Athletes will compete and react off each other's movement. They will learn the concept of inside-out pursuit and taking away the cutback. We will teach the concept of maintaining a cushion in an open-field scramble situation. Athletes will tag off on the opponent.

14. Stick Drill: For stride pattern, sticks can be applied to both acceleration and top end speed situations. This concept can assist in reducing the number of steps necessary to running a 40-yard dash. Athletes will learn to project their hips through the air to gain stride length. They will also learn to eliminate casting.

15. Shuttle Training: Learning to run efficient shuttle times is important to individual evaluation at both the high school and collegiate levels. The twenty, sixty and three-cone shuttles will be reviewed in addition to the cone patterns.

Specific Postural Cues

(McNair Speed Vocabulary to Facilitate Body Position)

1. Focus: Keep eyes on the horizontal plane, as if conversing with someone your own height, looking him in the eye. The head is heavy. Where the eyes go, the head goes. Where the head goes, the body goes.

2. Fix : Maintain an arm angle of 90 degrees. When the arm angle opens (straightens out) the arm slows up. When the angle closes the fist points too high to the sky and a vertical component results. We coach a loose 90 degree angle.

3. Rotate: Swing your arm from the shoulder. We don't run elbow to fingertip.

4. Pull: The hard downward and backward action of the arm from the chest height through the pocket below the hip and past the butt is critical to maximizing leg drive. The further the arm is pulled past the butt area behind you, the greater the extension of the leg on the other side. Remember, what you do with the right arm affects the left leg, and what you do with the left arm affects the right leg. You view running as swimming. What you do behind you propels the body forward. The athlete hears the word "pull," and he knows that he is stopping his hand at his hip or butt area, and we want him to clear that area to get as much space as possible between the hand and the butt.

5. Hammer: Imagine your back is to a wall with a nail sticking out of the wall below your waist and you have a hammer in your

hand. You are going to have a downward, backward smash to hammer the nail in with one strong smash. We want a violent rotation through the shoulder, cracking down with the wrist, and hammering the nail back. The word "Hammer" is emphasized in order to put more violence and downward backward force from the shoulder girdle and wrist and arm areas. When the athlete hears the word "Hammer" there is not enough violent force through the shoulder and arm.

6. Arch: There is an upper and lower back arch to maintain erect posture on the run. We want the spine flat and erect in order to have the glutes positioned under the body as the power base of speed to allow extension in the leg. Pinch your shoulder blades back together slightly. Your shoulders should move back slightly in order to have erect posture. The arch flattens the spine and places the glutes in the speed power base position. When an athlete hears the words "upper back arch," he knows the upper torso is hunched over and we want him to take the shoulders back and be erect. When he hears "lower back arch," we want the belt buckle or waistline to go an inch toward the finish line to put the gluteus underneath the body.

7. Snap: Pull your foot back and under the hip in the recovery phase. Any time the foot hits ahead of the hip, you are in a pull rather than a driving position. When the athlete hears the word "snap", his first thought is, to pull the foot back underneath the hip.

8. Punch: Drive your knee out and forward toward the focal point. A forward knee action toward the midline of the body rotates the hips to cover more ground. This slight hip swivel allows you to cover more ground. Knee punch allows hip rotation for greater stride length.

9. Lift: Lift is simply a posterior hip position that is maintained.

The Value of Acceleration Mechanics as Related to Football

- Football is a game of acceleration and re-acceleration with and without resistance.
- Offensive linemen who play on run-oriented teams are constantly in a "drive" mode. Acceleration mechanics relates to body position prior to and during contact.
- Defensive linemen and linebackers are required to accelerate and change direction out of a back pedal in every direction as well as accelerate through a tackle.
- Receivers must accelerate off the line and out of cuts in every direction.
- Running backs must constantly accelerate, decelerate and re-accelerate. They must also have the ability to run away from the opposition.

Acceleration Training

- Pure acceleration mechanics predominate for the first eight to ten strides. Acceleration has been referred to as the positive change in horizontal velocity. It not only can be measured in terms of the initial phase of a sprint, but can also be measured using zones of five or ten meters.
- Stride length increases at a predictable and regular rate during the pure acceleration phase. The increment of increase in stride length is 10-15 percent of the athletes' leg length.
- Proper force application in relationship to the ability to accelerate is vital to projecting upward and forward to optimize effective stride length.
- We want to practice an acceleration pattern that is pre-measured and repetitively performed. We then increase each stride through developing stride separation and more powerful for application.

Resistance Training

Initiating a task that is more difficult than what the athlete can overcome under normal conditions. Training modalities may include:

1. Three percent incline
2. Wooden Sled
3. Individual Sled
   *Acceleration March-Sprint Bound-Low Lunge-Pull Through
4. Prowler
5. Vest
6. Stadium

Pushing the wooden sled and running the stadium have more application toward the natural execution of punch and drive (acceleration) mechanics. Proper alignment from head to contact foot must be maintained.

Weighted sprinting provides an increased stimulus by increasing the momentum that must be overcome in both the vertical and horizontal direction upon landing.

According to Loren Seagrave's *Speed Dynamics,* uphill sprinting forces the foot to strike the ground sooner than it would on flat ground, requiring the force to be exerted over a greater range of motion at the hip joint. This can be a great stimulus to increasing strength and power.

Seagrave also considers sled dragging to be an effective means of training. The angle of resistance line must be considered. If the line is very short, the angle provides a greater resistance to the positive vertical velocities in the drive phase. Shorter cords are more suitable for training acceleration and longer cords are more suitable for training maximum velocity.

Sprinting with a weighted vest increases the training effect in a very specific manner. Loading potential is increased both vertically and horizontally. This increases the spring board mechanism that we are looking for to facilitate the recovery phase and maximize stride length.

Acceleration Cues

Acceleration mechanics are vital to football, according to Seagrave, since football is a game of short bursts against some form of resistance. Drive phase and drive mechanics are emphasized fully during acceleration training. Several coaching cues are applied to this type of emphasis in our training. They originated with McNair's influence.

1. Prolonged foot contact with the ground.
2. Extension of the drive leg to overcome inertia.
3. Feet stay close to the ground.
4. Proper shin angle to facilitate drive.
5. Hips are forward and pelvis is up.
6. Arm drive is violent. Elbows are driven back.
7. Lean does not occur at the waist. Straight line from extended femur to head.
8. Foot position is dorsi-flexed.
9. Big force into the ground.
10. Run tall as you reach the sixth and eighth stride.
11. Hold breath through initial phase.
12. Violent rotation from the shoulder.

Defining Plyometric Training

Plyometric stimulus is realized when the resultant load in one direction, which is greater than must normally be encountered, is abruptly decelerated then re-accelerated in the opposite direction. Plyometric stimulus should evoke a greater force output because of the stretch shortening phenomenon. Upper body exercises, such as reactive medicine ball, are movements that would also be characterized as plyometrics.

Multi Jump Training

Various jumping movements are accompanied by a counter-movement upon initiation, according to *Speed Dynamics,* The counter-movement, along with the loading encountered by each successive jump response, stimulated the receptors inside the muscle to fire because of a rapid stretch of the muscles.

Seagrave also found that force production may be enhanced by utilizing the stored elastic energy produced when a pre-activated muscle is loaded by an external force in conjunction with a major volitional contraction. The weight of the body, the negative vertical velocity and the horizontal velocity experienced at ground contact, which can be expressed as breaking forces, are the various influences on the forces that must be overcome.

Classifications

In-Place Jumps: We use vests and the verti-max unit can be used in performing the majority of the type of activity. With weighted vests, we increase mass while the verti-max increases negative vertical velocity.

Short Response Displacement Jumps
- Standing Long Jump
- Triple Jump
- Continuous Single Leg Hops
- Multiple Hurdle Jumps

Long Response Displacement Jumps
- Straight Leg Bounds
- Speed Bounds
- Power Bounds
- Run-Run Bound
- Single Leg Bound
- Lateral Bound

Alternate Leg Training Favorites: Our multi-jump program involves a limited number of exercises that address both horizontal and lateral movement.

Power Bound: Power bounding is related to the maximum velocity mechanics or a focus on training stride frequency. The athlete attempts to get more vertical space and pause between strides as well as great explosion off the ground. Put big force into the ground and attempt to get off very quickly.

Straight Leg Bound: Knees are slightly bent. Hit the ball of the foot and pull with the top of the hamstring and gluteus. Don't lean back with a "Drum Major" effect. Keep the shoulders one inch ahead of the hips.

Power Skip: Emphasis is placed on driving the leg violently back into the ground and pulling through the hip with the opposite arm. Eye focus and torso position should be the same as it is in regular speed work. Skipping action takes place on every step.

Build-up Bound: Start with ankle flips and gradually widen the stride into full bounding action. Place emphasis on hip flexion and exaggerated shoulder rotation during the full bounding phase.

Fly-In Bound: Run half to three-quarters speed for twenty yards, gradually gaining speed until you reach the chute (two cones). Blast twenty or thirty yards into full speed bound. Gain ground by putting force back into the ground and flexing the hip through an exaggerated range of motion.

Speed Bounding: Speed bounding is related to acceleration training. When we speed bound we keep the feet close to the ground, minimizing vertical projection and maximizing horizontal projection, and prolong the foot contact with the surface to propel us forward.

Maximum Velocity Training

In our program we use this type of training as a starting point in conjunction with speed terminology to set body position. MV drills are conducive to the rapid development of those athletes with no sprint training background. We have one objective in mind—posture.

Ins and Outs

This training is based on the premise that the nervous system cannot integrate high-intensity signals representing maximum output for more than four seconds. Fly in zones are 20 to 30 meters. The athlete accelerates and gradually inhales. When the in-zone marker is reached, the athlete holds his breath and blasts through the zone, getting as many foot contacts as possible in the zone. The "in" zone has been referred to as a peak.

- Initially peaks are 10 meters and "outs" are 20 meters. (2x10 meter peaks/1x20 meter out)
- After four weeks, progress to (3x10 meter peaks/ 2x20 meter outs)
- Increase peaks and decrease outs to 15 meters in the final phase of adaptation. A three peak the limit for the objectives concerning football .
- When the athlete enters the "out" zone, the intensity of recovering the leg is gradually reduced.

Maximum Velocity Cues

This type of training relates to perfect body mechanics at top speed. It has been determined by track experts that sprinters do not achieve top speed or maximum velocity until they reach 30 to 35 meters. Because football is primarily a game of short bursts, maximum velocity training is limited. Again, we use a high level of discretion concerning specific cues.

1. Run tall with pelvis projected forward and up.
2. Punch the knees horizontally, no excessive vertical lift.
3. Rotate from the shoulder, drive the elbows back.
4. Pull low through the pocket.
5. Step over the opposite knee—(heel pops to butt with toe up).
6. Come out of foot plant as quickly as possible. The emphasis is on turnover.

Over-Speed

This type of training is advanced in nature. Athletes with low training experience with regard to speed development can exacerbate existing technical problems, and Seagrave writes that training should not exceed a 10 percent increase in maximum speed. Over-speed methods include a plyometric component horizontally. Increased horizontal momentum has been known to force the system to become more responsive to ground reaction. The body increases the capacity for joint stabilization, particularly at the ankle and knee, through anticipatory firing of antigravity muscles.

In our program we prefer a three percent downhill grade using 30-yard fly-ins. The use of flexi-cord is more difficult to properly administer, particularly with larger groups of athletes. It is important to take precautions against injury with athletes towing other athletes. Also, all brands of flexi-cord may not have the same amount of rubber linear unit measure. Devices like the ultra-speed pacer have non-elastic cord, which allows for safer training. Downhill sprinting has an enhanced plyometric effect because of the vertical distance the center of gravity must fall. Specific coaching points must be emphasized.

1. Towing is extended for 30 meters.
2. The athlete accelerates the thigh and attempts to maximize force production.
3. The athlete, with extreme emphasis on proper technique, attempts to outrun the cable with maximum effort toward stride frequency.
4. As the assistance stimulus is reduced the athlete attempts to maintain the same level of turnover.
5. One of the advantages if this type of training is that the hips are forced into a posterior position, which is optimal for sprinting. Football players can benefit from the postural factor alone, since they commonly have an issue with maintaining a vertical stack position.

6. We are looking for a stiffer suspension off the ground to rapidly recover the leg. The nervous system should adapt to increase horizontal momentum in this manner.

Sled Training

We believe that power walking with an individual sled can be extremely effective in developing functional strength of an athlete. Maintaining posture will dictate the appropriate level of resistance. Maintaining body position is vital to the training effect. We walk anywhere from 25 to 75 yards depending on the specific exercise. The total number of repetitions is between eight and 15.

- Tin Soldier
- Tight Low Pedal
- Wide Pedal
- Lunge Walk
- Dead Man Walking
- Shuffle
- Bear Crawl
- Hip Flexor Walk

Total Consideration for Contrast Training

Contrast training is a five-day breakdown with an emphasis on building acceleration mechanics and work capacity.

Typical Training Day Progression/ Linear Speed

- Warm-Up
- Bounding/ Jumps/ Sand Training
- Neural Drills/ Acceleration Ladder
- Assistance
- Resistance
- Regular

ADR (Acceleration, Deceleration, and Re-Acceleration)

Because the game of football primarily involves multi-directional patterns of deceleration and re-acceleration, we must include this type of training in every session of speed training. We will incorporate this aspect into the "regular" segment of the total training sequence.

Weekly Contrast Training Schedule

Monday
- Dynamic Warm-Up: 10 minutes
- Neural Drills/ Acceleration Ladder: 15 min.
- Sand Bounding/ Jumping: 5 min.
- Sled Walking: 10 min.
- Static Flex: 5 min.

Tuesday
- Dynamic Warm-Up: 10 min.
- Neural Drills: 5 min.
- Bounding/ Multi Jump: 5 min.
- Resisted Speed Bound: 8 min.
- Regular Speed Bound: 8 min.
- Regular Sprints: 8 min.
- Resisted Sprints: 8 min.
- Static Flex: 5 minutes

Wednesday
- Dynamic Warm-Up: 10 min.
- Neural Drills: 20 min.
- Ins and Outs: 10 min.
- Static Flex: 5 min.

Thursday
- Dynamic Warm-Up: 10 min.
- Neural Drills/Acceleration Ladder: 5 min.
- Bounding/ Jumping: 5 min.

- Ultra Speed Pacer: 15 min.
- Uphill Sprints: 5 min.
- ADR: 5 min.
- Static Flex: 5 min.

Friday

- Dynamic Warm-Up: 10 min.
- Neural Drills: 5 min.
- Bounding/ jumping: 5 min.
- Wooden Sled: 10 min.
- Individual Sled Fly-Ins: 10 min.
- ADR: 10 min.
- Static Flex: 5 min.

The Dynamic Warm-Up/ Neural Drill time slot might also be blended for the purpose of efficiency. We attempt to rotate modalities within specific objectives to vary the desired stimulus. The total time allotment set for speed development is approximately 3.7 hours per week during winter training. The objectives during this training phase are directed toward pure speed and power development.

Testing Parameters Relative to Speed

1. Vertical Jump
2. Standing Long Jump
3. Double Leg Jumps (3-5 reps)
4. Hurdle Jumps (5-10 reps)
5. 10 Alt. Leg Bounds from a 5 Step Run
6. 20 Meter Hop (timed/ steps)
7. 30 Meter Fly-In from 20 Meter Run
8. 10-20-40
9. Uphill Distance in 8 seconds
10. Weighted Vest Stadium Sprint

Speed Menu (Options for Lesson Plans)

Extended Dynamic Warm-Up
Neural Drills
- Quick Rhythm
- Three Count Fast Leg Build Up
- Single Leg Fast Leg
- Command Fast Leg

Hip Development
- Mann Run
- Mann Run Resisted
- Pose Chop
    Stationary
    Four Count
    Three Count (MB overload)
    Three Count (Stick + Resistance)
- Scissors march
    Overhead Resisted

Stride Separation
- Stick Drill
- Wall Drill
- Hip Punch- Ankle Resistance
- Suspended Hip Punch
- Target Swing
- Split Lunge (Box-Floor)

Multi Starts
- Supine
- Prone
- One Knee
- Two Knee
- Lateral (Open Step)

- Lateral (Crossover)
- Face away
- Single Knee Lateral (Near Knee)
- Two Point
- Three Point

Acceleration Power

- Contrast Sprint Bound
- Contrast Sprint
- Stadium Bound
- Fly-In Speed Bound
- Fly-In Sprint (Mini Hurdle)

Sprint Bound Index

Plyos

- Vertical Jumps
- Horizontal Jumps
- Single Leg Bounds
- Combo Bounding
- Straight Leg Bound
- Multi Cone Bound

Stationary Drills

- Suspended Run
- Split Lunge + Arm Rotation
- Stationary Chop (Vest)

Functional Strength (Post Workout)

Sled

- Pull Through
- Low Lunge
- March (Counter Balance)
- Bear Crawl

- Tin Soldier
- Lateral Walk
- Deadman Walking
- Low Pedal

Stadium

- March
- Pose Chop
- Lunge
- Bound
- Sprint
- Prowler

Sand Pit

Mann Run	Power Bound	45-degree Wave Drill
3 Step Cut	S. Leg Bound	Kick Slide
Pedal	Combo Bound	Pedal Slide
Weave	3 x BR Jump	
Transitional Survival	Knees to Feet	
Lateral Bound	Pirate Maker	
Speed Bound	Reactive Lateral	

Tempo Options

- Tempo 40
- 100 Meter Walk Backs
- Partner Tempo Run
- 110's
- Man Makers
- Power Unit
- 200-300-400-500-600

Come Forward to Balance

- 45 Open Cross
- Transition
- Lateral Transition
- Reverse 45 Drop

With the right combination of training components that contribute to the improvement of speed, it should become increasingly apparent that your athletes are running stronger and more efficiently. Running "strong" is the term that I like to use to describe the clearly visible improvement that progressively becomes evident with proper training. This can be observed specifically as stronger posture, a solid stance position on each stride, increased power in force application and separation in stride. With football players we can also observe related characteristics of improved hip strength. Offensive linemen can anchor themselves to the ground, defensive linemen noticeably improve hip extension, running backs increase leg drive, etc.

Running strength does not equate with running "stiff" or with poor robotic mechanics. You must be relaxed to be fast and proper mechanics should never be compromised. That's why we include what we refer to as "thoughtful" running into our total program. We want to run relaxed, with great posture and powerful arm stroke.

Developing sprint strength is certainly not limited to the weight room. We include hill running, stadium work, sled work, vest bounding, overhead resisted drilling, run rocket training and any form of a multi-jump as overload training. We want to plan a total program that defines the specificity we need for football speed.

CHAPTER NINE

GET STRONG

Most strength and conditioning coaches use some type of computer program. Veteran strength coaches like myself did not have the good fortune of growing up in this computer era, but others have developed programs that make our lives easier. Rather than sit through computer classes – which I felt would take me off the weight room floor and inevitably force me to sit in a chair – I settled into a program called Power 5.1, and I have used it for a long time. It's great to have everything on paper. Some programs have even evolved to a computer screen on each rack, which illustrates everything we put on paper. It all looks wonderful.

I want to be very clear in stating here that you need a coach at every rack who is focusing on technique, counting every rep and making sure the resistance is correct for safety and, most importantly, consistent progress. Technology is no substitute for excellent coaching. Don't ever assume that an athlete knows anything. You must coach every rep. As your coachable athletes cooperate and develop, you will probably be able to back off slightly, but you will always have those who are much less coachable and who look for ways to make things easier. Those individuals must be treated like technical fifth graders until they demonstrate mature behavior. The coaching never ends.

This chapter primarily includes the training progressions we use to maximize and maintain strength through the training year. We use a combination of barbell, dumbbell and kettlebell exercises, with limited use of what you might refer to as machines. We also train the neck with a combination of techniques that are not included on this list. Core strengthening is very frequent, as in most programs, and we still regard many of our multijoint movements as exercises that force the athlete to engage the core.

These training programs will include some exercises and concepts that need some clarification. For example, we do box squats off a box using band tension and a tendo unit to measure bar speed in meters per second. We also use a plus sign to indicate coupling of exercises, which can be referred to as supersets or complex training. Obviously, the final chapters of this book are program-oriented. The reader will need a basic understanding of strength and conditioning concepts. The primary exercises will reflect progressive changes in volume and intensity so that there is a gradual adaptation to each phase. The concepts discussed in chapter seven will be found in some form within each training phase. For example, max effort training will be featured in the winter program as applied to power clean, bench press and back squat.

The in-season phase is divided into two groups – travel and non-travel. Many members of the non-travel squad are redshirt freshmen who need a year of development. They lift six days a week, and the travel squad lifts four days a week. The travel squad athletes do heavy lower body work every Monday, heavy upper body work every Wednesday and pulling and core with group stretching and foam rolling on Thursday. Sunday is a day for light running to promote recovery and rack lockouts, which are less stressful to the shoulders because of the limited range of movement. They also do light to medium high box step ups on Sunday to loosen up the hips.

The offseason phase, which begins in January, is the three-day program that we discussed in chapter four. If we look at the daily breakdown, we can see that there is a linear segment and an agility and change of direction segment. The two-hour block is divided into 80 minutes of strength training and two twenty-minute blocks of movement training. Tuesday and Thursday are dedicated to speed training and position specifics.

The kettlebell programs can be used as a supplementary method of developing anaerobic conditioning, in addition to total body strength and work capacity. Each program is named so that it can be identified to elicit a specific training effect.

Let's also note here that we use a contingency approach. The four-day split program for the summer provides for exclusive upper body days, because this particular team needs upper body strength. We might provide a different type of split, based on team needs, if our objectives change. If I had a strong, slow team like I had at Bucknell many years ago, the summer program would be three days of lifting and five days of speed training. If I thought the offensive linemen on a football team were obese and poorly conditioned, I would have them perform kettlebell workouts as a form of supplementary training using a high tempo approach.

One of the trends in training today is the popularity of "strongman" lifts and competitive scenarios. I think competitive scenarios are great if properly planned and conducted. During the 1990s at ECU, we had a competitive day as a finale to our winter program. It was referred to as "War Day." Every competitive scenario was scored, and much of it was combative. The offense was competing with the defense, and the loser had to perform 100 up-downs. The winner got a cheap T-shirt. The competitive level was off the chart. It was a very effective tool for our program. I would not, however, use such events as farmer's walk, tire flip, keg toss or heavy stone lift as staples of my program.

The NCAA provides very limited time for me to train our team. I feel that every minute must be planned to specifically train the attributes that win football games. I fail to see how I might consistently execute strongman events with 100 athletes whereby I could assess their progress in acquiring foundational strength. I also refuse to compromise any time allocated to improving linear speed, foot quickness, reactive ability or position-specific drilling. Again, I think it could be a good changeup and might be suitable for competitive options, but I see a limited value given our time limitations. I have included an outline of "War Day" at the end of this chapter, as well as another competitive option we have named the Gridiron Grind.

Any double or triple number indicates multiple sets

SUMMER PROGRAM: Week 1

1 rep max/exercise	Set 1 RP x WT	Set 2 RP x WT	Set 3 RP x WT	Set 4 RP x WT	Set 5 RP x WT	Set 6 RP x WT
MONDAY						
Bench Press	5 x 205	5 x 225	5 x 245	55 x 270	5 x 280	
DB Incline + Pull-up	8 x 100	8 x 100	8 x 100	8 x 100		
Push Jerk + W	5 x 170	4 x 185	3 x 220	3 x 230	3 x 230	3 x 230
Skull Crusher + DB Ext	10 x 150	10 x 150	10 x 150	10 x 150		
BB Curl	10 x 115	10 x 115	10 x 115	10 x 115		
Iso Push-up Sequence	4 sets x 10 reps					
Pull Circuit	4 sets x 10 reps					
Floor Core	200 reps					
TUESDAY						
Power Clean	5 x 165	5 x 185	55 x 205	55 x 220	5 x 230	
Box SQ-Bands + TU + HJ	2 x 215	2 x 235	22 x 245	22 x 255	2 x 270	2 x 280
Step up + KB swing	5 x 160	5 x 160	5 x 160	5 x 160		
Double KB Sumo	4 sets x 10 reps					
Glute Ham + Hip Bridge	4 sets x 10 reps					
BB Single Leg RDL	10 x 100	10 x 105	10 x 110	10 x 115		
MB 1	4 sets x 20 reps					
Renegade Row	4 sets x 20 reps					
THURSDAY						
Dbl Chain B PR + P Up	3 x 160	3 x 180	3 x 195	33 x 205	3 x 210	3 x 220
BB Incline + DKB Row	10 x 170	10 x 175	10 x 185	10 x 190		
Push Press + Ext Rot	3 x 140	3 x 155	2 x 170	2 x 180	22 x 195	2 x 200
Shld Pre-Hab Circuit	4 sets x 20 reps					
Bamboo PR + PL Raise	4 sets x 10 reps					
Strip Curl	4 sets x 10 reps					
Get Up Sit Up	4 sets x 10 reps					
Turkish Get Up	4 sets x 5 reps					
FRIDAY						
Cluster Single P CL	111 x 185	111 x 205	111 x 220	111 x 240	111 x 260	111 x 275
Parallel Squat		5 x 295	4 x 355	3 x 380	33 x 395	3 x 410
Pistol Squat + Box Jump	4 sets x 5 reps					
Runner	2 sets x 40 reps, 2 sets x 30 reps					
Bear Jumps	4 sets x 10 reps					
KB Swings + KBSL Dead	4 sets x 8 reps					
Hip Thrust	4 sets x 8 reps					
Floor Core	200 reps					

SUMMER PROGRAM: Week 2

1 rep max/exercise	Set 1 RP x WT	Set 2 RP x WT	Set 3 RP x WT	Set 4 RP x WT	Set 5 RP x WT	Set 6 RP x WT
MONDAY						
Bench Press	5 x 205	5x 225	5x245	55 x270	5x 280	
DB Incline + Pull-up	8 x 100	8 x 100	8 x 100	8 x 100		
Push Jerk + W	5 x 170	4 x 185	3 x 225	3 x 230	3 x 230	3 x 230
Skull Crusher + DB Ext	10 x 150	10 x 150	10 x 150	10 x 150		
BB Curl	10 x 115	10 x 115	10 x 115	10 x 115		
Iso Push-up Sequence	4 sets x 10 reps					
Pull Circuit	4 sets x 10 reps					
Floor Core	200 reps					
TUESDAY						
Power Clean	5 x 170	5 x 185	55 x 205	55 x 225	5 x 230	
Box SQ-Bands + TU + HJ	2 x 215	2 x 240	22 x 250	22 x 260	2 x 270	2 x 280
Step up + KB swing	5 x 160	5 x 160	5 x 160	5 x 160		
Double KB Sumo	4 sets x 10 reps					
Glute Ham + Hip Bridge	4 sets x 10 reps					
BB Single Leg RDL	10 x 100	10 x 105	10 x 110	10 x 115		
MB 1	4 sets x 20 reps					
Renegade Row	4 sets x 20 reps					
THURSDAY						
Dbl Chain B PR + P Up	3 x 160	3 x 180	3 x 195	33 x 205	3 x 215	3 x 220
BB Incline + DKB Row	10 x 170	10 x 180	10 x 185	10 x 195		
Push Press + Ext Rot	3 x 145	3 x 155	2 x 170	2 x 185	22 x 195	2 x 205
Shld Pre-Hab Circuit	4 sets x 20 reps					
Bamboo PR + PL Raise	4 sets x 10 reps					
Strip Curl	4 sets x 10 reps					
Get Up Sit Up	4 sets x 10 reps					
Turkish Get Up	4 sets x 5 reps					
FRIDAY						
Cluster Single P CL	111 x 185	111 x 205	111 x 225	111 x 240	111 x 260	111 x 280
Parallel Squat		5 x 295	4 x 355	3 x 385	33 x 400	3 x 415
Pistol Squat +Box Jump	4 sets x 5 reps					
Runner	2 sets x 40 reps, 2 sets x 30 reps					
Bear Jumps	4 sets x 10 reps					
KB Swings + KBSL Dead	4 sets x 8 reps					
Hip Thrust	4 sets x 8 reps					
Floor Core	200 reps					

SUMMER PROGRAM: Week 3

1 rep max/exercise	Set 1 RP x WT	Set 2 RP x WT	Set 3 RP x WT	Set 4 RP x WT	Set 5 RP x WT	Set 6 RP x WT
MONDAY						
Bench Press	5 X 205	5 X 230	4 X 260	444 X 280	4 X 295	
DB Incline + Pull-up	8 X 100	8 X 100	8 X 100	8 X 100		
Push Jerk + W	5 X 170	4 X 190	3 X 225	3 X 235	3 X 235	3 X 235
Skull Crusher + DB Ext	10 X 150	10 X 150	10 X 150	10 X 150		
BB Curl	10 X 115	10 X 115	10 X 115	10 X 115		
Iso Push-up Sequence	4 sets X 10 reps					
Pull Circuit	4 sets X 10 reps					
Floor Core	200 reps					
TUESDAY						
Power Clean	5 X 180	5 X 190	55 X 205	55 X 235	5 X 245	
Box SQ-Bands + TU + HJ	2 X 220	2 X 240	22 X 250	22 X 260	2 X 270	2 X 280
Step up + KB swing	5 X 160	5 X 160	5 X 160	5 X 160		
Double KB Sumo	4 sets X 10 reps					
Glute Ham + Hip Bridge	4 sets X 10 reps					
BB Single Leg RDL	10 X 100	10 X 105	10 X 110	10 X 115		
MB 1	4 sets X 20 reps					
Renegade Row	4 sets X 20 reps					
THURSDAY						
Dbl Chain B PR + P Up	3 X 165	3 X 180	3 X 200	33 X 205	3 X 215	3 X 225
BB Incline + DKB Row	10 X 170	10 X 180	10 X 185	10 X 195		
Push Press + Ext Rot	3 X 145	3 X 160	2 X 170	2 X 185	22 X 200	2 X 205
Shld Pre-Hab Circuit	4 sets X 20 reps					
Bamboo PR + PL Raise	4 sets X 10 reps					
Strip Curl	4 sets X 10 reps					
Get Up Sit Up	4 sets X 10 reps					
Turkish Get Up	4 sets X 5 reps					
FRIDAY						
Cluster Single P CL	111 X 190	111 X 210	111 X 225	111 X 245	111 X 265	111 X 280
Parallel Squat		5 X 300	4 X 355	3 X 385	33 X 400	3 X 415
Pistol Squat + Box Jump	4 sets X 5 reps					
Runner	2 sets X 40 reps, 2 sets X 30 reps					
Bear Jumps	4 sets X 10 reps					
KB Swings + KBSL Dead	4 sets X 8 reps					
Hip Thrust	4 sets X 8 reps					
Floor Core	200 reps					

SUMMER PROGRAM: Week 4

1 rep max/exercise	Set 1 RP x WT	Set 2 RP x WT	Set 3 RP x WT	Set 4 RP x WT	Set 5 RP x WT	Set 6 RP x WT
MONDAY						
Bench Press	5 X 210	5 X 230	4 X 265	444 X 285	4 X 295	
DB Incline + Pull-up	8 X 100	8 X 100	8 X 100	8 X 100		
Push Jerk + W	5 X 180	4 X 200	3 X 235	3 X 245	3 X 245	3 X 245
Skull Crusher + DB Ext	10 X 150	10 X 150	10 X 150	10 X 150		
BB Curl	10 X 115	10 X 115	10 X 115	10 X 115		
Iso Push-up Sequence	4 sets X 10 reps					
Pull Circuit	4 sets X 10 reps					
Floor Core	2 sets X 40 reps, 2 sets X 30 reps					
TUESDAY						
Power Clean	5 X 180	5 X 190	55 X 210	55 X 235	5 X 245	
Box SQ-Bands + TU + HJ	2 X 220	2 X 240	22 X 250	22 X 265	2 X 275	2 X 285
Step up + KB swing	5 X 160	5 X 160	5 X 160	5 X 160		
Double KB Sumo	4 sets X 10 reps					
Glute Ham + Hip Bridge	4 sets X 10 reps					
BB Single Leg RDL	10 X 100	10 X 105	10 X 110	10 X 115		
MB 1	4 sets X 20 reps					
Renegade Row	4 sets X 20 reps					
THURSDAY						
Dbl Chain B PR + P Up	3 X 165	3 X 180	3 X 200	33 X 210	3 X 215	3 X 225
BB Incline + DKB Row	10 X 175	10 X 180	10 X 190	10 X 195		
Push Press + Ext Rot	3 X 145	3 X 160	2 X 170	2 X 185	22 X 200	2 X 205
Shld Pre-Hab Circuit	4 sets X 20 reps					
Bamboo PR + PL Raise	4 sets X 10 reps					
Strip Curl	4 sets X 10 reps					
Get Up Sit Up	4 sets X 10 reps					
Turkish Get Up	4 sets X 5 reps					
FRIDAY						
Cluster Single P CL	111 X 190	111 X 210	111 X 230	111 X 250	111 X 265	111 X 285
Parallel Squat		5 X 300	4 X 360	3 X 390	33 X 405	3 X 420
Pistol Squat + Box Jump	4 sets X 5 reps					
Runner	2 sets X 40 reps, 2 sets X 30 reps					
Bear Jumps	4 sets X 10 reps					
KB Swings + KBSL Dead	4 sets X 8 reps					
Hip Thrust	4 sets X 8 reps					
Floor Core	200 reps					

SUMMER PROGRAM: Week 5

1 rep max/exercise	Set 1 RP x WT	Set 2 RP x WT	Set 3 RP x WT	Set 4 RP x WT	Set 5 RP x WT	Set 6 RP x WT
MONDAY						
Bench Press	5 X 210	5 X 230	4 X 265	44 X 285	444 X 310	
DB Incline + Pull-up	8 X 100	8 X 100	8 X 100	8 X 100		
Push Jerk + W	5 X 180	4 X 200	3 X 240	3 X 245	3 X 245	3 X 245
Skull Crusher + DB Ext	10 X 150	10 X 150	10 X 150	10 X 150		
BB Curl	10 X 115	10 X 115	10 X 115	10 X 115		
Iso Push-up Sequence	4 sets X 10 reps					
Pull Circuit	4 sets X 10 reps					
Floor Core	2 sets X 40 reps, 2 sets X 30 reps					
TUESDAY						
Power Clean	5 X 190	4 X 230	3 X 245	33 X 255	3 X 265	
Box SQ-Bands + TU + HJ	2 X 220	2 X 245	22 X 255	22 X 265	2 X 275	2 X 285
Step up + KB swing	5 X 160	5 X 160	5 X 160	5 X 160		
Double KB Sumo	4 sets X 10 reps					
Glute Ham + Hip Bridge	4 sets X 10 reps					
BB Single Leg RDL	10 X 100	10 X 105	10 X 110	10 X 115		
MB 1	4 sets X 20 reps					
Renegade Row	4 sets X 20 reps					
THURSDAY						
Dbl Chain B PR + P Up	3 X 165	3 X 185	3 X 200	33 X 210	3 X 220	3 X 225
BB Incline + DKB Row	10 X 175	10 X 185	10 X 190	10 X 200		
Push Press + Ext Rot	3 X 145	3 X 160	2 X 175	2 X 185	22 X 200	2 X 210
Shld Pre-Hab Circuit	4 sets X 20 reps					
Bamboo PR + PL Raise	4 sets X 10 reps					
Strip Curl	4 sets X 10 reps					
Get Up Sit Up	4 sets X 10 reps					
Turkish Get Up	4 sets X 5 reps					
FRIDAY						
Cluster Single P CL	111 X 195	111 X 210	111 X 230	111 X 250	111 X 270	111 X 290
Parallel Squat		5 X 300	4 X 360	3 X 390	33 X 405	3 X 420
Pistol Squat + Box Jump	4 sets X 5 reps					
Runner	2 sets X 40 reps, 2 sets X 30 reps					
Bear Jumps	4 sets X 10 reps					
KB Swings + KBSL Dead	4 sets X 8 reps					
Hip Thrust	4 sets X 8 reps					
Floor Core	200 reps					

SUMMER PROGRAM: Week 6

1 rep max/exercise	Set 1 RP x WT	Set 2 RP x WT	Set 3 RP x WT	Set 4 RP x WT	Set 5 RP x WT	Set 6 RP x WT
MONDAY						
Bench Press	5 X 210	5 X 235	4 X 265	44 X 290	444 X 310	
DB Incline + Pull-up	8 X 100	8 X 100	8 X 100	8 X 100		
Push Jerk + W	5 X 190	4 X 210	2 X 250	2 X 270	2 X 270	2 X 270
Skull Crusher + DB Ext	10 X 150	10 X 150	10 X 150	10 X 150		
BB Curl	10 X 115	10 X 115	10 X 115	10 X 115		
Iso Push-up Sequence	4 sets X 10 reps					
Pull Circuit	4 sets X 10 reps					
Floor Core	200 reps					
TUESDAY						
Power Clean	5 X 190	4 X 230	3 X 250	33 X 260	3 X 270	
Box SQ-Bands + TU + HJ	2 X 225	2 X 245	22 X 255	22 X 265	2 X 275	2 X 290
Step up + KB swing	5 X 160	5 X 160	5 X 160	5 X 160		
Double KB Sumo	4 sets X 10 reps					
Glute Ham + Hip Bridge	4 sets X 10 reps					
BB Single Leg RDL	10 X 100	10 X 105	10 X 110	10 X 115		
MB 1	4 sets X 20 reps					
Renegade Row	4 sets X 20 reps					
THURSDAY						
Dbl Chain B PR + P Up	3 X 170	3 X 185	3 X 205	33 X 210	3 X 220	3 X 230
BB Incline + DKB Row	10 X 175	10 X 185	10 X 190	10 X 200		
Push Press + Ext Rot	3 X 145	3 X 160	2 X 175	2 X 190	22 X 200	2 X 210
Shld Pre-Hab Circuit	4 sets X 20 reps					
Bamboo PR + PL Raise	4 sets X 10 reps					
Strip Curl	4 sets X 10 reps					
Get Up Sit Up	4 sets X 10 reps					
Turkish Get Up	4 sets X 5 reps					
FRIDAY						
Cluster Single P CL	111 X 195	111 X 215	111 X 235	111 X 255	111 X 270	111 X 290
Parallel Squat		5 X 305	4 X 365	3 X 390	33 X 410	3 X 425
Pistol Squat + Box Jump	4 sets X 5 reps					
Runner	2 sets X 40 reps, 2 sets X 30 reps					
Bear Jumps	4 sets X 10 reps					
KB Swings + KBSL Dead	4 sets X 8 reps					
Hip Thrust	4 sets X 8 reps					
Floor Core	200 reps					

SUMMER PROGRAM: Week 7

1 rep max/exercise	Set 1 RP x WT	Set 2 RP x WT	Set 3 RP x WT	Set 4 RP x WT	Set 5 RP x WT	Set 6 RP x WT
MONDAY						
Bench Press	4 X 235	4 X 255	3 X 280	3 X 300	33 X 310	33 X 325
DB Incline + Pull-up	8 X 100	8 X 100	8 X 100	8 X 100		
Push Jerk + W	5 X 195	4 X 215	2 X 250	2 X 270	2 X 270	2 X 270
Skull Crusher + DB Ext	10 X 150	10 X 150	10 X 150	10 X 150		
BB Curl	10 X 115	10 X 115	10 X 115	10 X 115		
Iso Push-up Sequence	4 sets X 10 reps					
Pull Circuit	4 sets X 10 reps					
Floor Core	200 reps					
TUESDAY						
Power Clean	5 X 195	4 X 230	3 X 250	22 X 270	22 X 280	2 X 290
Box SQ-Bands + TU + HJ	2 X 225	2 X 245	22 X 255	22 X 270	2 X 280	2 X 290
Step up + KB swing	5 X 160	5 X 160	5 X 160	5 X 160		
Double KB Sumo	4 sets X 10 reps					
Glute Ham + Hip Bridge	4 sets X 10 reps					
BB Single Leg RDL	10 X 100	10 X 105	10 X 110	10 X 115		
MB 1	4 sets X 20 reps					
Renegade Row	4 sets X 20 reps					
THURSDAY						
Dbl Chain B PR + P Up	3 X 170	3 X 185	3 X 205	33 X 215	3 X 220	3 X 230
BB Incline + DKB Row	10 X 180	10 X 185	10 X 195	10 X 205		
Push Press + Ext Rot	3 X 150	3 X 160	2 X 175	2 X 190	22 X 205	2 X 210
Shld Pre-Hab Circuit	4 sets X 20 reps					
Bamboo PR + PL Raise	4 sets X 10 reps					
Strip Curl	4 sets X 10 reps					
Get Up Sit Up	4 sets X 10 reps					
Turkish Get Up	4 sets X 5 reps					
FRIDAY						
Cluster Single P CL	111 X 195	111 X 215	111 X 235	111 X 255	111 X 275	111 X 295
Parallel Squat		5 X 305	4 X 365	3 X 390	33 X 410	3 X 425
Pistol Squat + Box Jump	4 sets X 5 reps					
Runner	2 sets X 40 reps, 2 sets X 30 reps					
Bear Jumps	4 sets X 10 reps					
KB Swings + KBSL Dead	4 sets X 8 reps					
Hip Thrust	4 sets X 8 reps					
Floor Core	200 reps					

SUMMER PROGRAM: Week 8

1 rep max/exercise	Set 1 RP x WT	Set 2 RP x WT	Set 3 RP x WT	Set 4 RP x WT	Set 5 RP x WT	Set 6 RP x WT
MONDAY						
Bench Press	4 X 235	4 X 260	3 X 280	3 X 305	33 X 315	33 X 325
DB Incline + Pull-up	8 X 100	8 X 100	8 X 100	8 X 100		
Push Jerk + W	5 X 195	4 X 215	2 X 255	2 X 270	2 X 270	2 X 270
Skull Crusher + DB Ext	10 X 150	10 X 150	10 X 150	10 X 150		
BB Curl	10 X 115	10 X 115	10 X 115	10 X 115		
Iso Push-up Sequence	4 sets X 10 reps					
Pull Circuit	4 sets X 10 reps					
Floor Core	200 reps					
TUESDAY						
Power Clean	5 X 195	4 X 235	3 X 255	22 X 270	22 X 280	2 X 290
Box SQ-Bands + TU + HJ	2 X 225	2 X 250	22 X 260	22 X 270	2 X 280	2 X 290
Step up + KB swing	5 X 160	5 X 160	5 X 160	5 X 160		
Double KB Sumo	4 sets X 10 reps					
Glute Ham + Hip Bridge	4 sets X 10 reps					
BB Single Leg RDL	10 X 100	10 X 105	10 X 110	10 X 115		
MB 1	4 sets X 20 reps					
Renegade Row	4 sets X 20 reps					
THURSDAY						
Dbl Chain B PR + P Up	3 X 170	3 X 190	3 X 205	33 X 215	3 X 225	3 X 235
BB Incline + DKB Row	10 X 180	10 X 190	10 X 195	10 X 205		
Push Press + Ext Rot	3 X 150	3 X 165	2 X 175	2 X 190	22 X 205	2 X 210
Shld Pre-Hab Circuit	4 sets X 20 reps					
Bamboo PR + PL Raise	4 sets X 10 reps					
Strip Curl	4 sets X 10 reps					
Get Up Sit Up	4 sets X 10 reps					
Turkish Get Up	4 sets X 5 reps					
FRIDAY						
Cluster Single P CL	111 X 200	111 X 220	111 X 240	111 X 260	111 X 280	111 X 295
Parallel Squat		5 X 305	4 X 365	3 X 400	33 X 415	3 X 430
Pistol Squat + Box Jump	4 sets X 5 reps					
Runner	2 sets X 40 reps, 2 sets X 30 reps					
Bear Jumps	4 sets X 10 reps					
KB Swings + KBSL Dead	4 sets X 8 reps					
Hip Thrust	4 sets X 8 reps					
Floor Core	200 reps					

SUMMER PROGRAM: Week 9

1 rep max/exercise	Set 1 RP x WT	Set 2 RP x WT	Set 3 RP x WT	Set 4 RP x WT	Set 5 RP x WT	Set 6 RP x WT
MONDAY						
Bench Press	4 X 240	4 X 260	3 X 285	3 X 305	33 X 315	33 X 330
DB Incline + Pull-up	8 X 100	8 X 100	8 X 100	8 X 100		
Push Jerk + W	3 X 205	3 X 225	2 X 245	2 X 265	22 X 285	2 X 295
Skull Crusher + DB Ext	10 X 150	10 X 150	10 X 150	10 X 150		
BB Curl	10 X 115	10 X 115	10 X 115	10 X 115		
Iso Push-up Sequence	4 sets X 10 reps					
Pull Circuit	4 sets X 10 reps					
Floor Core	200 reps					
TUESDAY						
Power Clean	5 X 195	4 X 235	3 X 255	22 X 275	22 X 285	2 X 295
Box SQ-Bands + TU + HJ	2 X 225	2 X 250	22 X 260	22 X 270	2 X 285	2 X 290
Step up + KB swing	5 X 160	5 X 160	5 X 160	5 X 160		
Double KB Sumo	4 sets X 10 reps					
Glute Ham + Hip Bridge	4 sets X 10 reps					
BB Single Leg RDL	10 X 100	10 X 105	10 X 110	10 X 115		
MB 1	4 sets X 20 reps					
Renegade Row	4 sets X 20 reps					
THURSDAY						
Dbl Chain B PR + P Up	3 X 175	3 X 190	3 X 210	33 X 215	3 X 225	3 X 235
BB Incline + DKB Row	10 X 180	10 X 190	10 X 200	10 X 205		
Push Press + Ext Rot	3 X 150	3 X 165	2 X 180	2 X 195	22 X 205	2 X 215
Shld Pre-Hab Circuit	4 sets X 20 reps					
Bamboo PR + PL Raise	4 sets X 10 reps					
Strip Curl	4 sets X 10 reps					
Get Up Sit Up	4 sets X 10 reps					
Turkish Get Up	4 sets X 5 reps					
FRIDAY						
Cluster Single P CL	111 X 200	111 X 220	111 X 240	111 X 260	111 X 280	111 X 300
Parallel Squat		5 X 310	4 X 370	3 X 400	33 X 415	3 X 430
Pistol Squat + Box Jump	4 sets X 5 reps					
Runner	2 sets X 40 reps, 2 sets X 30 reps					
Bear Jumps	4 sets X 10 reps					
KB Swings + KBSL Dead	4 sets X 8 reps					
Hip Thrust	4 sets X 8 reps					
Floor Core	200 reps					

SUMMER PROGRAM: Week 10

1 rep max/exercise	Set 1 RP x WT	Set 2 RP x WT	Set 3 RP x WT	Set 4 RP x WT	Set 5 RP x WT	Set 6 RP x WT
MONDAY						
Bench Press	4 X 240	4 X 260	2 X 285	2 X 310	2 X 330	22 X 350
DB Incline + Pull-up	8 X 100	8 X 100	8 X 100	8 X 100		
Push Jerk + W	3 X 210	3 X 230	2 X 245	2 X 265	22 X 285	2 X 295
Skull Crusher + DB Ext	10 X 150	10 X 150	10 X 150	10 X 150		
BB Curl	10 X 115	10 X 115	10 X 115	10 X 115		
Iso Push-up Sequence	4 sets X 10 reps					
Pull Circuit	4 sets X 10 reps					
Floor Core	200 reps					
TUESDAY						
Power Clean	4 X 210	3 X 245	22 X 265	2 X 285	11 X 295	1 X 305
Box SQ-Bands + TU + HJ	2 X 230	2 X 250	22 X 260	22 X 275	2 X 285	2 X 295
Step up + KB swing	5 X 160	5 X 160	5 X 160	5 X 160		
Double KB Sumo	4 sets X 10 reps					
Glute Ham + Hip Bridge	4 sets X 10 reps					
BB Single Leg RDL	10 X 100	10 X 105	10 X 110	10 X 115		
MB 1	4 sets X 20 reps					
Renegade Row	4 sets X 20 reps					
THURSDAY						
Dbl Chain B PR + P Up	3 X 175	3 X 190	3 X 210	33 X 220	3 X 230	3 X 235
BB Incline + DKB Row	10 X 180	10 X 190	10 X 200	10 X 210		
Push Press + Ext Rot	3 X 150	3 X 165	2 X 180	2 X 195	22 X 210	2 X 215
Shld Pre-Hab Circuit	4 sets X 20 reps					
Bamboo PR + PL Raise	4 sets X 10 reps					
Strip Curl	4 sets X 10 reps					
Get Up Sit Up	4 sets X 10 reps					
Turkish Get Up	4 sets X 5 reps					
FRIDAY						
Cluster Single P CL	111 X 205	111 X 225	111 X 245	111 X 265	111 X 285	111 X 305
Parallel Squat		5 X 310	4 X 370	3 X 400	33 X 420	3 X 435
Pistol Squat + Box Jump	4 sets X 5 reps					
Runner	2 sets X 40 reps, 2 sets X 30 reps					
Bear Jumps	4 sets X 10 reps					
KB Swings + KBSL Dead	4 sets X 8 reps					
Hip Thrust	4 sets X 8 reps					
Floor Core	200 reps					

SUMMER PROGRAM: Week 11

1 rep max/exercise	Set 1 RP x WT	Set 2 RP x WT	Set 3 RP x WT	Set 4 RP x WT	Set 5 RP x WT	Set 6 RP x WT
MONDAY						
Bench Press	4 X 240	3 X 265	2 X 285	2 X 310	2 X 330	22 X 355
DB Incline + Pull-up	8 X 100	8 X 100	8 X 100	8 X 100		
Push Jerk + W	3 X 210	3 X 230	2 X 250	2 X 270	22 X 290	2 X 300
Skull Crusher + DB Ext	10 X 150	10 X 150	10 X 150	10 X 150		
BB Curl	10 X 115	10 X 115	10 X 115	10 X 115		
Iso Push-up Sequence	4 sets X 10 reps					
Pull Circuit	4 sets X 10 reps					
Floor Core	200 reps					
TUESDAY						
Power Clean	4 X 210	3 X 250	22 X 270	2 X 290	11 X 300	1 X 310
Box SQ-Bands + TU + HJ	2 X 230	2 X 255	22 X 265	22 X 275	2 X 285	2 X 300
Step up + KB swing	5 X 160	5 X 160	5 X 160	5 X 160		
Double KB Sumo	4 sets X 10 reps					
Glute Ham + Hip Bridge	4 sets X 10 reps					
BB Single Leg RDL	10 X 100	10 X 105	10 X 110	10 X 115		
MB 1	4 sets X 20 reps					
Renegade Row	4 sets X 20 reps					
THURSDAY						
Dbl Chain B PR + P Up	3 X 175	3 X 195	3 X 210	33 X 220	3 X 230	3 X 240
BB Incline + DKB Row	10 X 185	10 X 195	10 X 200	10 X 210		
Push Press + Ext Rot	3 X 155	3 X 165	2 X 180	2 X 195	22 X 210	2 X 215
Shld Pre-Hab Circuit	4 sets X 20 reps					
Bamboo PR + PL Raise	4 sets X 10 reps					
Strip Curl	4 sets X 10 reps					
Get Up Sit Up	4 sets X 10 reps					
Turkish Get Up	4 sets X 5 reps					
FRIDAY						
Cluster Single P CL	111 X 205	111 X 225	111 X 245	111 X 265	111 X 285	111 X 305
Parallel Squat		5 X 310	4 X 375	3 X 405	33 X 420	3 X 435
Pistol Squat + Box Jump	4 sets X 5 reps					
Runner	2 sets X 40 reps, 2 sets X 30 reps					
Bear Jumps	4 sets X 10 reps					
KB Swings + KBSL Dead	4 sets X 8 reps					
Hip Thrust	4 sets X 8 reps					
Floor Core	200 reps					

SUMMER PROGRAM: Week 12

1 rep max/exercise	Set 1 RP x WT	Set 2 RP x WT	Set 3 RP x WT	Set 4 RP x WT	Set 5 RP x WT	Set 6 RP x WT
MONDAY						
Bench Press	4 X 245	3 X 265	2 X 290	2 X 310	2 X 335	22 X 355
DB Incline + Pull-up	8 X 100	8 X 100	8 X 100	8 X 100		
Push Jerk + W	3 X 210	3 X 230	2 X 250	2 X 270	22 X 290	2 X 300
Skull Crusher + DB Ext	10 X 150	10 X 150	10 X 150	10 X 150		
BB Curl	10 X 115	10 X 115	10 X 115	10 X 115		
Iso Push-up Sequence	4 sets X 10 reps					
Pull Circuit	4 sets X 10 reps					
Floor Core	200 reps					
TUESDAY						
Power Clean	4 X 210	3 X 250	22 X 270	2 X 290	11 X 300	1 X 310
Box SQ-Bands + TU + HJ	2 X 230	2 X 255	22 X 265	22 X 275	2 X 290	2 X 300
Step up + KB swing	5 X 160	5 X 160	5 X 160	5 X 160		
Double KB Sumo	4 sets X 10 reps					
Glute Ham + Hip Bridge	4 sets X 10 reps					
BB Single Leg RDL	10 X 100	10 X 105	10 X 110	10 X 115		
MB 1	4 sets X 20 reps					
Renegade Row	4 sets X 20 reps					
THURSDAY						
Dbl Chain B PR + P Up	3 X 175	3 X 195	3 X 215	33 X 225	3 X 230	3 X 240
BB Incline + DKB Row	10 X 185	10 X 195	10 X 205	10 X 210		
Push Press + Ext Rot	3 X 155	3 X 170	2 X 180	2 X 195	22 X 210	2 X 220
Shld Pre-Hab Circuit	4 sets X 20 reps					
Bamboo PR + PL Raise	4 sets X 10 reps					
Strip Curl	4 sets X 10 reps					
Get Up Sit Up	4 sets X 10 reps					
Turkish Get Up	4 sets X 5 reps					
FRIDAY						
Cluster Single P CL	111 X 205	111 X 230	111 X 250	111 X 270	111 X 290	111 X 310
Parallel Squat		5 X 310	4 X 375	3 X 405	33 X 420	3 X 440
Pistol Squat + Box Jump	4 sets X 5 reps					
Runner	2 sets X 40 reps, 2 sets X 30 reps					
Bear Jumps	4 sets X 10 reps					
KB Swings + KBSL Dead	4 sets X 8 reps					
Hip Thrust	4 sets X 8 reps					
Floor Core	200 reps					

IN SEASON DEVELOPMENTAL SQUAD: Week 1

1 rep max/exercise	Set 1 RP x WT	Set 2 RP x WT	Set 3 RP x WT	Set 4 RP x WT	Set 5 RP x WT	Set 6 RP x WT
SUNDAY						
Push Jerk	55 x 145	55 x 155	5 x 160			
Front Squat	5 x 200	5 x 210	555 x 240	5 x 250		
Bench Press	5 x 180	5 x 200	5 x 220	55 x 240	55 x 250	
Basic Pirate	5 sets x 5 reps					
MONDAY						
Power Clean	5 x 145	5 x 165	55 x 180	55 x 195	5 x 205	
BB Snatch	3 x 150	3 x 150	3 x 155	3 x 155	3 x 165	3 x 165
Horizontal Jumps	5 sets x 5 reps					
SKB SLDL	4 sets x 10 reps					
SKB LCY Swing	4 sets x 10 reps					
BB RDL	10 x 195	10 x 195	10 x 195	10 x 195		
BB Shrug	4 sets x 20 reps					
BB Curl	4 sets x 10 reps					
Wrist Curls	4 sets x 20 reps					
Abdominals	200 reps					
TUESDAY						
Bench Press	5 x 180	5 x 200	5 x 220	55 x 240	55 x 250	
DB Incline	5 x 105	5 x 105	5 x 110	5 x 110	5 x 115	
BB Step-up	5 x 170	5 x 170	5 x 180	5 x 180	5 x 185	
Runner	2 sets x 40 reps, 2 sets x 30 reps					
Close Grip Bench	10 x 150	10 x 150	10 x 150	10 x 150		
Band Pre Hab	4 sets x 20 reps					
Get Up Sit Up	4 sets x 10 reps					
WEDNESDAY						
Block Clean	3 x 200	3 x 200	3 x 205	3 x 205	3 x 215	3 x 215
Box Jump	5 sets x 5 reps					
SKB Dead Clean	5 sets x 5 reps					
DBL KB Row	4 sets x 10 reps					
BB Shrug	4 sets x 10 reps					
Strip Curl	4 sets x 10 reps					
Plank Sequence	4 sets x 10 reps					
Top Down Get Down	5 sets x 5 reps					
THURSDAY						
Push Jerk	55 x 145	55 x 155	5 x 160			
Board Press	5 x 220	5 x 240	5 x 265	55 x 285	5 x 300	
Parallel Squat	5 x 260	5 x 290	5 x 320	55 x 350	55 x 365	
Incline Fly Press	4 sets x 10 reps					
KB Seesaw Press	4 sets x 10 reps					
Pistol Squat	4 sets x 10 reps					
MB 1	3 sets x 30 reps					
FRIDAY						
Hang Snatch	3 x 170	3 x 170	3 x 175	3 x 175	3 x 185	3 x 185
Squat Clean	3 x 185	3 x 185	3 x 190	3 x 190	3 x 195	3 x 195
Bear Jumps	4 sets x 10 reps					
BB RDL	10 x 195	10 x 195	10 x 195	10 x 195		
Glute Ham Raise	4 sets x 10 reps					
BB Row	4 sets x 10 reps					
Rev Lat Pull	4 sets x 10 reps					
BB Curl	4 sets x 10 reps					
Grip Sequence	3 sets x 30 reps					

IN SEASON DEVELOPMENTAL SQUAD: Week 2

1 rep max/exercise	Set 1 RP x WT	Set 2 RP x WT	Set 3 RP x WT	Set 4 RP x WT	Set 5 RP x WT	Set 6 RP x WT
SUNDAY						
Push Jerk	55 x 150	55 x 155	5 x 165			
Front Squat	5 x 200	5 x 210	555 x 240	5 x 250		
Bench Press	5 x 180	5 x 200	5 x 220	55 x 240	55 x 250	
Basic Pirate	5 sets x 5 reps					
MONDAY						
Power Clean	5 x 150	5 x 165	55 x 180	55 x 195	5 x 205	
BB Snatch	3 x 150	3 x 150	3 x 160	3 x 160	3 x 165	3 x 165
Horizontal Jumps	5 sets x 5 reps					
SKB SLDL	4 sets x 10 reps					
SKB LCY Swing	4 sets x 10 reps					
BB RDL	10 x 195	10 x 195	10 x 195	10 x 195		
BB Shrug	4 sets x 20 reps					
BB Curl	4 sets x 10 reps					
Wrist Curls	4 sets x 20 reps					
Abdominals	200 reps					
TUESDAY						
Bench Press	5 x 180	5 x 200	5 x 220	55 x 240	55 x 250	
DB Incline	5 x 105	5 x 105	5 x 110	5 x 110	5 x 115	
BB Step-up	5 x 170	5 x 170	5 x 180	5 x 180	5 x 185	
Runner	2 sets x 40 reps, 2 sets x 30 reps					
Close Grip Bench	10 x 150	10 x 150	10 x 150	10 x 150		
Band Pre Hab	4 sets x 20 reps					
Get Up Sit Up	4 sets x 10 reps					
WEDNESDAY						
Block Clean	3 x 200	3 x 200	3 x 205	3 x 205	3 x 215	3 x 215
Box Jump	5 sets x 5 reps					
SKB Dead Clean	5 sets x 5 reps					
DBL KB Row	4 sets x 10 reps					
BB Shrug	4 sets x 10 reps					
Strip Curl	4 sets x 10 reps					
Plank Sequence	4 sets x 10 reps					
Top Down Get Down	5 sets x 5 reps					
THURSDAY						
Push Jerk	55 x 150	55 x 155	5 x 165			
Board Press	5 x 220	5 x 245	5 x 265	55 x 290	5 x 300	
Parallel Squat	5 x 265	5 x 290	5 x 320	55 x 350	55 x 365	
Incline Fly Press	4 sets x 10 reps					
KB Seesaw Press	4 sets x 10 reps					
Pistol Squat	4 sets x 10 reps					
MB 1	3 sets x 30 reps					
FRIDAY						
Hang Snatch	3 x 170	3 x 170	3 x 180	3 x 180	3 x 185	3 x 185
Squat Clean	3 x 185	3 x 185	3 x 190	3 x 190	3 x 200	3 x 200
Bear Jumps	4 sets x 10 reps					
BB RDL	10 x 195	10 x 195	10 x 195	10 x 195		
Glute Ham Raise	4 sets x 10 reps					
BB Row	4 sets x 10 reps					
Rev Lat Pull	4 sets x 10 reps					
BB Curl	4 sets x 10 reps					
Grip Sequence	3 sets x 30 reps					

IN SEASON DEVELOPMENTAL SQUAD: Week 3

1 rep max/exercise	Set 1 RP x WT	Set 2 RP x WT	Set 3 RP x WT	Set 4 RP x WT	Set 5 RP x WT	Set 6 RP x WT
SUNDAY						
Push Jerk	55 X 150	55 X 155	5 X 165			
Front Squat	5 X 200	5 X 210	555 X 240	5 X 255		
Bench Press	5 X 180	5 X 200	5 X 220	55 X 240	55 X 250	
Basic Pirate	5 sets X 5 reps					
MONDAY						
Power Clean	5 X 150	5 X 165	55 X 180	55 X 200	5 X 205	
BB Snatch	3 X 155	3 X 155	3 X 160	3 X 160	3 X 165	3 X 165
Horizontal Jumps	5 sets X 5 reps					
SKB SLDL	4 sets X 10 reps					
SKB LCY Swing	4 sets X 10 reps					
BB RDL	10 X 195	10 X 195	10 X 195	10 X 195		
BB Shrug	4 sets X 20 reps					
BB Curl	4 sets X 10 reps					
Wrist Curls	4 sets X 20 reps					
Abdominals	200 reps					
TUESDAY						
Bench Press	5 X 180	5 X 200	5 X 220	55 X 240	55 X 250	
DB Incline	5 X 105	5 X 105	5 X 110	5 X 110	5 X 115	
BB Step-up	5 X 170	5 X 170	5 X 180	5 X 180	5 X 185	
Runner	2 sets X 40 reps, 2 sets X 30 reps					
Close Grip Bench	10 X 150	10 X 150	10 X 150	10 X 150		
Band Pre Hab	4 sets X 20 reps					
Get Up Sit Up	4 sets X 10 reps					
WEDNESDAY						
Block Clean	3 X 200	3 X 200	3 X 210	3 X 210	3 X 215	3 X 215
Box Jump	5 sets X 5 reps					
SKB Dead Clean	5 sets X 5 reps					
DBL KB Row	4 sets X 10 reps					
BB Shrug	4 sets X 10 reps					
Strip Curl	4 sets X 10 reps					
Plank Sequence	4 sets X 10 reps					
Top Down Get Down	5 sets X 5 reps					
THURSDAY						
Push Jerk	55 X 150	55 X 155	5 X 165			
Board Press	5 X 220	5 X 245	5 X 265	55 X 290	5 X 300	
Parallel Squat	5 X 265	5 X 295	5 X 320	55 X 350	55 X 365	
Incline Fly Press	4 sets X 10 reps					
KB Seesaw Press	4 sets X 10 reps					
Pistol Squat	4 sets X 10 reps					
MB 1	3 sets X 30 reps					
FRIDAY						
Hang Snatch	3 X 175	3 X 175	3 X 180	3 X 180	3 X 185	3 X 185
Squat Clean	3 X 185	3 X 185	3 X 195	3 X 195	3 X 200	3 X 200
Bear Jumps	4 sets X 10 reps					
BB RDL	10 X 195	10 X 195	10 X 195	10 X 195		
Glute Ham Raise	4 sets X 10 reps					
BB Row	4 sets X 10 reps					
Rev Lat Pull	4 sets X 10 reps					
BB Curl	4 sets X 10 reps					
Grip Sequence	3 sets X 30 reps					

IN SEASON DEVELOPMENTAL SQUAD: Week 4

1 rep max/exercise	Set 1 RP x WT	Set 2 RP x WT	Set 3 RP x WT	Set 4 RP x WT	Set 5 RP x WT	Set 6 RP x WT
SUNDAY						
Push Jerk	55 X 160	55 X 165	5 X 175			
Front Squat	5 X 200	5 X 225	555 X 255	5 X 265		
Bench Press	5 X 180	5 X 200	5 X 220	555 X 250	5 X 260	
Basic Pirate	5 sets X 5 reps					
MONDAY						
Power Clean	5 X 150	5 X 165	4 X 185	33 X 200	33 X 215	
BB Snatch	3 X 155	3 X 155	3 X 160	3 X 160	3 X 170	3 X 170
Horizontal Jumps	5 sets X 5 reps					
SKB SLDL	4 sets X 10 reps					
SKB LCY Swing	4 sets X 10 reps					
BB RDL	10 X 195	10 X 195	10 X 195	10 X 195		
BB Shrug	4 sets X 20 reps					
BB Curl	4 sets X 10 reps					
Wrist Curls	4 sets X 20 reps					
Abdominals	200 reps					
TUESDAY						
Bench Press	5 X 180	5 X 200	5 X 220	55 X 250	55 X 260	
DB Incline	5 X 105	5 X 105	5 X 110	5 X 110	5 X 115	
BB Step-up	5 X 170	5 X 170	5 X 180	5 X 180	5 X 185	
Runner	2 sets X 40 reps, 2 sets X 30 reps					
Close Grip Bench	10 X 150	10 X 150	10 X 150	10 X 150		
Band Pre Hab	4 sets X 20 reps					
Get Up Sit Up	4 sets X 10 reps					
WEDNESDAY						
Block Clean	3 X 200	3 X 200	3 X 210	3 X 210	3 X 215	3 X 215
Box Jump	5 sets X 5 reps					
SKB Dead Clean	5 sets X 5 reps					
DBL KB Row	4 sets X 10 reps					
BB Shrug	4 sets X 10 reps					
Strip Curl	4 sets X 10 reps					
Plank Sequence	4 sets X 10 reps					
Top Down Get Down	5 sets X 5 reps					
THURSDAY						
Push Jerk	44 X 160	44 X 165	33 X 175			
Board Press	5 X 220	5 X 245	4 X 280	444 X 305	4 X 315	
Parallel Squat	5 X 265	5 X 295	4 X 325	33 X 355	33 X 380	
Incline Fly Press	4 sets X 10 reps					
KB Seesaw Press	4 sets X 10 reps					
Pistol Squat	4 sets X 10 reps					
MB 1	3 sets X 30 reps					
FRIDAY						
Hang Snatch	3 X 175	3 X 175	3 X 180	3 X 180	3 X 185	3 X 185
Squat Clean	3 X 190	3 X 190	3 X 195	3 X 195	3 X 200	3 X 200
Bear Jumps	4 sets X 10 reps					
BB RDL	10 X 195	10 X 195	10 X 195	10 X 195		
Glute Ham Raise	4 sets X 10 reps					
BB Row	4 sets X 10 reps					
Rev Lat Pull	4 sets X 10 reps					
BB Curl	4 sets X 10 reps					
Grip Sequence	3 sets X 30 reps					

IN SEASON DEVELOPMENTAL SQUAD: Week 5

1 rep max/exercise	Set 1 RP x WT	Set 2 RP x WT	Set 3 RP x WT	Set 4 RP x WT	Set 5 RP x WT	Set 6 RP x WT
SUNDAY						
Push Jerk	44 X 160	44 X 170	33 X 175			
Front Squat	5 X 205	5 X 225	555 X 255	5 X 265		
Bench Press	5 X 185	5 X 205	5 X 225	555 X 255	5 X 265	
Basic Pirate	5 sets X 5 reps					
MONDAY						
Power Clean	5 X 150	5 X 170	4 X 185	33 X 200	33 X 220	
BB Snatch	3 X 160	3 X 160	3 X 165	3 X 165	3 X 170	3 X 170
Horizontal Jumps	5 sets X 5 reps					
SKB SLDL	4 sets X 10 reps					
SKB LCY Swing	4 sets X 10 reps					
BB RDL	10 X 195	10 X 195	10 X 195	10 X 195		
BB Shrug	4 sets X 20 reps					
BB Curl	4 sets X 10 reps					
Wrist Curls	4 sets X 20 reps					
Abdominals	200 reps					
TUESDAY						
Bench Press	5 X 185	5 X 205	5 X 225	555 X 255	5 X 265	
DB Incline	5 X 105	5 X 105	5 X 110	5 X 110	5 X 115	
BB Step-up	5 X 170	5 X 170	5 X 180	5 X 180	5 X 185	
Runner	2 sets X 40 reps, 2 sets X 30 reps					
Close Grip Bench	10 X 150	10 X 150	10 X 150	10 X 150		
Band Pre Hab	4 sets X 20 reps					
Get Up Sit Up	4 sets X 10 reps					
WEDNESDAY						
Block Clean	3 X 205	3 X 205	3 X 210	3 X 210	3 X 220	3 X 220
Box Jump	5 sets X 5 reps					
SKB Dead Clean	5 sets X 5 reps					
DBL KB Row	4 sets X 10 reps					
BB Shrug	4 sets X 10 reps					
Strip Curl	4 sets X 10 reps					
Plank Sequence	4 sets X 10 reps					
Top Down Get Down	5 sets X 5 reps					
THURSDAY						
Push Jerk	44 X 160	44 X 170	33 X 175			
Board Press	5 X 225	5 X 245	4 X 280	444 X 305	4 X 315	
Parallel Squat	5 X 265	5 X 295	4 X 325	33 X 355	33 X 385	
Incline Fly Press	4 sets X 10 reps					
KB Seesaw Press	4 sets X 10 reps					
Pistol Squat	4 sets X 10 reps					
MB 1	3 sets X 30 reps					
FRIDAY						
Hang Snatch	3 X 175	3 X 175	3 X 180	3 X 180	3 X 190	3 X 190
Squat Clean	3 X 190	3 X 190	3 X 195	3 X 195	3 X 205	3 X 205
Bear Jumps	4 sets X 10 reps					
BB RDL	10 X 195	10 X 195	10 X 195	10 X 195		
Glute Ham Raise	4 sets X 10 reps					
BB Row	4 sets X 10 reps					
Rev Lat Pull	4 sets X 10 reps					
BB Curl	4 sets X 10 reps					
Grip Sequence	3 sets X 30 reps					

IN SEASON DEVELOPMENTAL SQUAD: Week 6

1 rep max/exercise	Set 1 RP x WT	Set 2 RP x WT	Set 3 RP x WT	Set 4 RP x WT	Set 5 RP x WT	Set 6 RP x WT
SUNDAY						
Push Jerk	44 X 160	44 X 170	33 X 180			
Front Squat	5 X 205	5 X 225	555 X 255	5 X 270		
Bench Press	5 X 185	5 X 205	5 X 225	555 X 255	5 X 265	
Basic Pirate	5 sets X 5 reps					
MONDAY						
Power Clean	5 X 155	5 X 170	4 X 185	33 X 205	33 X 220	
BB Snatch	3 X 160	3 X 160	3 X 165	3 X 165	3 X 170	3 X 170
Horizontal Jumps	5 sets X 5 reps					
SKB SLDL	4 sets X 10 reps					
SKB LCY Swing	4 sets X 10 reps					
BB RDL	10 X 195	10 X 195	10 X 195	10 X 195		
BB Shrug	4 sets X 20 reps					
BB Curl	4 sets X 10 reps					
Wrist Curls	4 sets X 20 reps					
Abdominals	200 reps					
TUESDAY						
Bench Press	5 X 185	5 X 205	5 X 225	555 X 255	5 X 265	
DB Incline	5 X 105	5 X 105	5 X 110	5 X 110	5 X 115	
BB Step-up	5 X 170	5 X 170	5 X 180	5 X 180	5 X 185	
Runner	2 sets X 40 reps, 2 sets X 30 reps					
Close Grip Bench	10 X 150	10 X 150	10 X 150	10 X 150		
Band Pre Hab	4 sets X 20 reps					
Get Up Sit Up	4 sets X 10 reps					
WEDNESDAY						
Block Clean	3 X 205	3 X 205	3 X 210	3 X 210	3 X 220	3 X 220
Box Jump	5 sets X 5 reps					
SKB Dead Clean	5 sets X 5 reps					
DBL KB Row	4 sets X 10 reps					
BB Shrug	4 sets X 10 reps					
Strip Curl	4 sets X 10 reps					
Plank Sequence	4 sets X 10 reps					
Top Down Get Down	5 sets X 5 reps					
THURSDAY						
Push Jerk	44 X 160	44 X 170	33 X 180			
Board Press	5 X 225	5 X 250	4 X 285	444 X 305	4 X 315	
Parallel Squat	5 X 270	5 X 295	4 X 325	33 X 355	33 X 385	
Incline Fly Press	4 sets X 10 reps					
KB Seesaw Press	4 sets X 10 reps					
Pistol Squat	4 sets X 10 reps					
MB 1	3 sets X 30 reps					
FRIDAY						
Hang Snatch	3 X 175	3 X 175	3 X 185	3 X 185	3 X 190	3 X 190
Squat Clean	3 X 190	3 X 190	3 X 200	3 X 200	3 X 205	3 X 205
Bear Jumps	4 sets X 10 reps					
BB RDL	10 X 195	10 X 195	10 X 195	10 X 195		
Glute Ham Raise	4 sets X 10 reps					
BB Row	4 sets X 10 reps					
Rev Lat Pull	4 sets X 10 reps					
BB Curl	4 sets X 10 reps					
Grip Sequence	3 sets X 30 reps					

IN SEASON DEVELOPMENTAL SQUAD: Week 7

1 rep max/exercise	Set 1 RP x WT	Set 2 RP x WT	Set 3 RP x WT	Set 4 RP x WT	Set 5 RP x WT	Set 6 RP x WT
SUNDAY						
Push Jerk	4 x 165	3 x 170	3 x 180	333 x 190		
Front Squat	5 x 215	5 x 235	555 x 270	5 x 280		
Bench Press	5 x 185	5 x 205	4 x 235	44 x 255	444 x 265	
Basic Pirate	5 sets x 5 reps					
MONDAY						
Power Clean	5 x 170	4 x 205	3 x 220	33 x 230	3 x 240	
BB Snatch	3 x 160	3 x 160	3 x 165	3 x 165	3 x 175	3 x 175
Horizontal Jumps	5 sets x 5 reps					
SKB SLDL	4 sets x 10 reps					
SKB LCY Swing	4 sets x 10 reps					
BB RDL	10 x 195	10 x 195	10 x 195	10 x 195		
BB Shrug	4 sets x 20 reps					
BB Curl	4 sets x 10 reps					
Wrist Curls	4 sets x 20 reps					
Abdominals	200 reps					
TUESDAY						
Bench Press	5 x 185	5 x 205	4 x 235	44 x 255	444 x 275	
DB Incline	5 x 105	5 x 105	5 x 110	5 x 110	5 x 115	
BB Step-up	5 x 170	5 x 170	5 x 180	5 x 180	5 x 185	
Runner	2 sets x 40 reps, 2 sets x 30 reps					
Close Grip Bench	10 x 150	10 x 150	10 x 150	10 x 150		
Band Pre Hab	4 sets x 20 reps					
Get Up Sit Up	4 sets x 10 reps					
WEDNESDAY						
Block Clean	3 x 205	3 x 205	3 x 215	3 x 215	3 x 220	3 x 220
Box Jump	5 sets x 5 reps					
SKB Dead Clean	5 sets x 5 reps					
DBL KB Row	4 sets x 10 reps					
BB Shrug	4 sets x 10 reps					
Strip Curl	4 sets x 10 reps					
Plank Sequence	4 sets x 10 reps					
Top Down Get Down	5 sets x 5 reps					
THURSDAY						
Push Jerk	4 x 165	3 x 170	3 x 180	333 x 190		
Board Press	5 x 225	5 x 250	4 x 285	44 x 305	444 x 330	
Parallel Squat	5 x 300	4 x 330	3 x 355	33 x 385	33 x 400	
Incline Fly Press	4 sets x 10 reps					
KB Seesaw Press	4 sets x 10 reps					
Pistol Squat	4 sets x 10 reps					
MB 1	3 sets x 30 reps					
FRIDAY						
Hang Snatch	3 x 175	3 x 175	3 x 185	3 x 185	3 x 190	3 x 190
Squat Clean	3 x 195	3 x 195	3 x 200	3 x 200	3 x 205	3 x 205
Bear Jumps	4 sets x 10 reps					
BB RDL	10 x 195	10 x 195	10 x 195	10 x 195		
Glute Ham Raise	4 sets x 10 reps					
BB Row	4 sets x 10 reps					
Rev Lat Pull	4 sets x 10 reps					
BB Curl	4 sets x 10 reps					
Grip Sequence	3 sets x 30 reps					

IN SEASON DEVELOPMENTAL SQUAD: Week 8

1 rep max/exercise	Set 1 RP x WT	Set 2 RP x WT	Set 3 RP x WT	Set 4 RP x WT	Set 5 RP x WT	Set 6 RP x WT
SUNDAY						
Push Jerk	4 x 165	3 x 175	3 x 180	333 x 190		
Front Squat	5 x 215	5 x 240	555 x 270	5 x 280		
Bench Press	5 x 185	5 x 205	4 x 235	44 x 255	444 x 275	
Basic Pirate	5 sets x 5 reps					
MONDAY						
Power Clean	5 x 170	4 x 205	3 x 220	33 x 230	3 x 240	
BB Snatch	3 x 165	3 x 165	3 x 170	3 x 170	3 x 175	3 x 175
Horizontal Jumps	5 sets x 5 reps					
SKB SLDL	4 sets x 10 reps					
SKB LCY Swing	4 sets x 10 reps					
BB RDL	10 x 195	10 x 195	10 x 195	10 x 195		
BB Shrug	4 sets x 20 reps					
BB Curl	4 sets x 10 reps					
Wrist Curls	4 sets x 20 reps					
Abdominals	200 reps					
TUESDAY						
Bench Press	5 x 185	5 x 205	4 x 235	44 x 255	444 x 275	
DB Incline	5 x 105	5 x 105	5 x 110	5 x 110	5 x 115	
BB Step-up	5 x 170	5 x 170	5 x 180	5 x 180	5 x 185	
Runner	2 sets x 40 reps, 2 sets x 30 reps					
Close Grip Bench	10 x 150	10 x 150	10 x 150	10 x 150		
Band Pre Hab	4 sets x 20 reps					
Get Up Sit Up	4 sets x 10 reps					
WEDNESDAY						
Block Clean	3 x 205	3 x 205	3 x 215	3 x 215	3 x 220	3 x 220
Box Jump	5 sets x 5 reps					
SKB Dead Clean	5 sets x 5 reps					
DBL KB Row	4 sets x 10 reps					
BB Shrug	4 sets x 10 reps					
Strip Curl	4 sets x 10 reps					
Plank Sequence	4 sets x 10 reps					
Top Down Get Down	5 sets x 5 reps					
THURSDAY						
Push Jerk	4 x 165	3 x 175	3 x 180	333 x 190		
Board Press	5 x 225	5 x 250	4 x 285	44 x 310	444 x 330	
Parallel Squat	5 x 300	4 x 330	3 x 360	33 x 390	33 x 405	
Incline Fly Press	4 sets x 10 reps					
KB Seesaw Press	4 sets x 10 reps					
Pistol Squat	4 sets x 10 reps					
MB 1	3 sets x 30 reps					
FRIDAY						
Hang Snatch	3 x 180	3 x 180	3 x 185	3 x 185	3 x 190	3 x 190
Squat Clean	3 x 195	3 x 195	3 x 200	3 x 200	3 x 210	3 x 210
Bear Jumps	4 sets x 10 reps					
BB RDL	10 x 195	10 x 195	10 x 195	10 x 195		
Glute Ham Raise	4 sets x 10 reps					
BB Row	4 sets x 10 reps					
Rev Lat Pull	4 sets x 10 reps					
BB Curl	4 sets x 10 reps					
Grip Sequence	3 sets x 30 reps					

IN SEASON DEVELOPMENTAL SQUAD: Week 9

1 rep max/exercise	Set 1 RP x WT	Set 2 RP x WT	Set 3 RP x WT	Set 4 RP x WT	Set 5 RP x WT	Set 6 RP x WT
SUNDAY						
Push Jerk	4 X 165	3 X 175	2 X 185	22 X 190	222 X 200	
Front Squat	5 X 220	5 X 240	555 X 270	5 X 285		
Bench Press	5 X 185	5 X 205	4 X 240	44 X 260	444 X 280	
Basic Pirate	5 sets X 5 reps					
MONDAY						
Power Clean	5 X 175	4 X 210	3 X 225	33 X 235	3 X 245	
BB Snatch	3 X 165	3 X 165	3 X 170	3 X 170	3 X 175	3 X 175
Horizontal Jumps	5 sets X 5 reps					
SKB SLDL	4 sets X 10 reps					
SKB LCY Swing	4 sets X 10 reps					
BB RDL	10 X 195	10 X 195	10 X 195	10 X 195		
BB Shrug	4 sets X 20 reps					
BB Curl	4 sets X 10 reps					
Wrist Curls	4 sets X 20 reps					
Abdominals	200 reps					
TUESDAY						
Bench Press	5 X 185	5 X 205	4 X 240	44 X 260	444 X 280	
DB Incline	5 X 105	5 X 105	5 X 110	5 X 110	5 X 115	
BB Step-up	5 X 170	5 X 170	5 X 180	5 X 180	5 X 185	
Runner	2 sets X 40 reps, 2 sets X 30 reps					
Close Grip Bench	10 X 150	10 X 150	10 X 150	10 X 150		
Band Pre Hab	4 sets X 20 reps					
Get Up Sit Up	4 sets X 10 reps					
WEDNESDAY						
Block Clean	3 X 205	3 X 205	3 X 215	3 X 215	3 X 225	3 X 225
Box Jump	5 sets X 5 reps					
SKB Dead Clean	5 sets X 5 reps					
DBL KB Row	4 sets X 10 reps					
BB Shrug	4 sets X 10 reps					
Strip Curl	4 sets X 10 reps					
Plank Sequence	4 sets X 10 reps					
Top Down Get Down	5 sets X 5 reps					
THURSDAY						
Push Jerk	4 X 165	3 X 175	2 X 185	22 X 190	222 X 200	
Board Press	5 X 230	5 X 250	4 X 285	44 X 310	444 X 335	
Parallel Squat	5 X 300	4 X 330	3 X 360	33 X 390	33 X 405	
Incline Fly Press	4 sets X 10 reps					
KB Seesaw Press	4 sets X 10 reps					
Pistol Squat	4 sets X 10 reps					
MB 1	3 sets X 30 reps					
FRIDAY						
Hang Snatch	3 X 180	3 X 180	3 X 185	3 X 185	3 X 195	3 X 195
Squat Clean	3 X 195	3 X 195	3 X 205	3 X 205	3 X 210	3 X 210
Bear Jumps	4 sets X 10 reps					
BB RDL	10 X 195	10 X 195	10 X 195	10 X 195		
Glute Ham Raise	4 sets X 10 reps					
BB Row	4 sets X 10 reps					
Rev Lat Pull	4 sets X 10 reps					
BB Curl	4 sets X 10 reps					
Grip Sequence	3 sets X 30 reps					

IN SEASON DEVELOPMENTAL SQUAD: Week 10

1 rep max/exercise	Set 1 RP x WT	Set 2 RP x WT	Set 3 RP x WT	Set 4 RP x WT	Set 5 RP x WT	Set 6 RP x WT
SUNDAY						
Push Jerk	4 x 170	3 x 175	2 x 185	22 x 195	222 x 200	
Front Squat	5 x 230	5 x 250	555 x 285	5 x 295		
Bench Press	4 x 210	4 x 230	3 x 250	3 x 270	33 x 280	33 x 290
Basic Pirate	5 sets x 5 reps					
MONDAY						
Power Clean	5 x 175	4 x 210	3 x 230	22 x 245	22 x 255	2 x 260
BB Snatch	3 x 165	3 x 165	3 x 170	3 x 170	3 x 180	3 x 180
Horizontal Jumps	5 sets x 5 reps					
SKB SLDL	4 sets x 10 reps					
SKB LCY Swing	4 sets x 10 reps					
BB RDL	10 x 195	10 x 195	10 x 195	10 x 195		
BB Shrug	4 sets x 20 reps					
BB Curl	4 sets x 10 reps					
Wrist Curls	4 sets x 20 reps					
Abdominals	200 reps					
TUESDAY						
Bench Press	4 x 210	4 x 230	3 x 250	3 x 270	33 x 280	33 x 290
DB Incline	5 x 105	5 x 105	5 x 110	5 x 110	5 x 115	
BB Step-up	5 x 170	5 x 170	5 x 180	5 x 180	5 x 185	
Runner	2 sets x 40 reps, 2 sets x 30 reps					
Close Grip Bench	10 x 150	10 x 150	10 x 150	10 x 150		
Band Pre Hab	4 sets x 20 reps					
Get Up Sit Up	4 sets x 10 reps					
WEDNESDAY						
Block Clean	3 x 210	3 x 210	3 x 215	3 x 215	3 x 225	3 x 225
Box Jump	5 sets x 5 reps					
SKB Dead Clean	5 sets x 5 reps					
DBL KB Row	4 sets x 10 reps					
BB Shrug	4 sets x 10 reps					
Strip Curl	4 sets x 10 reps					
Plank Sequence	4 sets x 10 reps					
Top Down Get Down	5 sets x 5 reps					
THURSDAY						
Push Jerk	4 x 170	3 x 175	2 x 185	22 x 195	222 x 200	
Board Press	4 x 255	4 x 275	3 x 300	3 x 325	33 x 335	33 x 350
Parallel Squat	5 x 300	4 x 330	3 x 360	2 x 390	22 x 420	22 x 435
Incline Fly Press	4 sets x 10 reps					
KB Seesaw Press	4 sets x 10 reps					
Pistol Squat	4 sets x 10 reps					
MB 1	3 sets x 30 reps					
FRIDAY						
Hang Snatch	3 x 180	3 x 180	3 x 185	3 x 185	3 x 195	3 x 195
Squat Clean	3 x 200	3 x 200	3 x 205	3 x 205	3 x 210	3 x 210
Bear Jumps	4 sets x 10 reps					
BB RDL	10 x 195	10 x 195	10 x 195	10 x 195		
Glute Ham Raise	4 sets x 10 reps					
BB Row	4 sets x 10 reps					
Rev Lat Pull	4 sets x 10 reps					
BB Curl	4 sets x 10 reps					
Grip Sequence	3 sets x 30 reps					

IN SEASON DEVELOPMENTAL SQUAD: Week 11

1 rep max/exercise	Set 1 RP x WT	Set 2 RP x WT	Set 3 RP x WT	Set 4 RP x WT	Set 5 RP x WT	Set 6 RP x WT
SUNDAY						
Push Jerk	4 X 170	3 X 175	2 X 185	22 X 195	222 X 205	
Front Squat	5 X 230	5 X 255	555 X 285	5 X 295		
Bench Press	4 X 210	4 X 230	3 X 250	3 X 270	33 X 280	33 X 290
Basic Pirate	5 sets X 5 reps					
MONDAY						
Power Clean	5 X 175	4 X 210	3 X 230	22 X 245	22 X 255	2 X 265
BB Snatch	3 X 165	3 X 165	3 X 175	3 X 175	3 X 180	3 X 180
Horizontal Jumps	5 sets X 5 reps					
SKB SLDL	4 sets X 10 reps					
SKB LCY Swing	4 sets X 10 reps					
BB RDL	10 X 195	10 X 195	10 X 195	10 X 195		
BB Shrug	4 sets X 20 reps					
BB Curl	4 sets X 10 reps					
Wrist Curls	4 sets X 20 reps					
Abdominals	200 reps					
TUESDAY						
Bench Press	4 X 210	4 X 230	3 X 250	3 X 270	33 X 280	33 X 290
DB Incline	5 X 105	5 X 105	5 X 110	5 X 110	5 X 115	
BB Step-up	5 X 170	5 X 170	5 X 180	5 X 180	5 X 185	
Runner	2 sets X 40 reps, 2 sets X 30 reps					
Close Grip Bench	10 X 150	10 X 150	10 X 150	10 X 150		
Band Pre Hab	4 sets X 20 reps					
Get Up Sit Up	4 sets X 10 reps					
WEDNESDAY						
Block Clean	3 X 210	3 X 210	3 X 215	3 X 215	3 X 225	3 X 225
Box Jump	5 sets X 5 reps					
SKB Dead Clean	5 sets X 5 reps					
DBL KB Row	4 sets X 10 reps					
BB Shrug	4 sets X 10 reps					
Strip Curl	4 sets X 10 reps					
Plank Sequence	4 sets X 10 reps					
Top Down Get Down	5 sets X 5 reps					
THURSDAY						
Push Jerk	4 X 170	3 X 180	2 X 185	22 X 195	222 X 205	
Board Press	4 X 255	4 X 280	3 X 300	3 X 325	33 X 335	33 X 350
Parallel Squat	5 X 305	4 X 335	3 X 365	2 X 395	22 X 420	22 X 435
Incline Fly Press	4 sets X 10 reps					
KB Seesaw Press	4 sets X 10 reps					
Pistol Squat	4 sets X 10 reps					
MB 1	3 sets X 30 reps					
FRIDAY						
Hang Snatch	3 X 180	3 X 180	3 X 190	3 X 190	3 X 195	3 X 195
Squat Clean	3 X 200	3 X 200	3 X 205	3 X 205	3 X 215	3 X 215
Bear Jumps	4 sets X 10 reps					
BB RDL	10 X 195	10 X 195	10 X 195	10 X 195		
Glute Ham Raise	4 sets X 10 reps					
BB Row	4 sets X 10 reps					
Rev Lat Pull	4 sets X 10 reps					
BB Curl	4 sets X 10 reps					
Grip Sequence	3 sets X 30 reps					

IN SEASON DEVELOPMENTAL SQUAD: Week 12

1 rep max/exercise	Set 1 RP x WT	Set 2 RP x WT	Set 3 RP x WT	Set 4 RP x WT	Set 5 RP x WT	Set 6 RP x WT
SUNDAY						
Push Jerk	4 X 170	3 X 180	2 X 190	22 X 195	222 X 205	
Front Squat	5 X 235	5 X 255	555 X 290	5 X 300		
Bench Press	4 X 210	4 X 230	3 X 250	3 X 275	33 X 285	33 X 295
Basic Pirate	5 sets X 5 reps					
MONDAY						
Power Clean	5 X 180	4 X 215	3 X 230	22 X 250	22 X 260	2 X 265
BB Snatch	3 X 170	3 X 170	3 X 175	3 X 175	3 X 180	3 X 180
Horizontal Jumps	5 sets X 5 reps					
SKB SLDL	4 sets X 10 reps					
SKB LCY Swing	4 sets X 10 reps					
BB RDL	10 X 195	10 X 195	10 X 195	10 X 195		
BB Shrug	4 sets X 20 reps					
BB Curl	4 sets X 10 reps					
Wrist Curls	4 sets X 20 reps					
Abdominals	200 reps					
TUESDAY						
Bench Press	4 X 210	4 X 230	3 X 250	3 X 275	33 X 285	33 X 295
DB Incline	5 X 105	5 X 105	5 X 110	5 X 110	5 X 115	
BB Step-up	5 X 170	5 X 170	5 X 180	5 X 180	5 X 185	
Runner	2 sets X 40 reps, 2 sets X 30 reps					
Close Grip Bench	10 X 150	10 X 150	10 X 150	10 X 150		
Band Pre Hab	4 sets X 20 reps					
Get Up Sit Up	4 sets X 10 reps					
WEDNESDAY						
Block Clean	3 X 210	3 X 210	3 X 220	3 X 220	3 X 225	3 X 225
Box Jump	5 sets X 5 reps					
SKB Dead Clean	5 sets X 5 reps					
DBL KB Row	4 sets X 10 reps					
BB Shrug	4 sets X 10 reps					
Strip Curl	4 sets X 10 reps					
Plank Sequence	4 sets X 10 reps					
Top Down Get Down	5 sets X 5 reps					
THURSDAY						
Push Jerk	4 X 170	3 X 180	2 X 190	22 X 195	222 X 205	
Board Press	4 X 255	4 X 280	3 X 305	3 X 325	33 X 340	33 X 350
Parallel Squat	5 X 305	4 X 335	3 X 365	2 X 395	22 X 425	22 X 440
Incline Fly Press	4 sets X 10 reps					
KB Seesaw Press	4 sets X 10 reps					
Pistol Squat	4 sets X 10 reps					
MB 1	3 sets X 30 reps					
FRIDAY						
Hang Snatch	3 X 180	3 X 180	3 X 190	3 X 190	3 X 195	3 X 195
Squat Clean	3 X 200	3 X 200	3 X 210	3 X 210	3 X 215	3 X 215
Bear Jumps	4 sets X 10 reps					
BB RDL	10 X 195	10 X 195	10 X 195	10 X 195		
Glute Ham Raise	4 sets X 10 reps					
BB Row	4 sets X 10 reps					
Rev Lat Pull	4 sets X 10 reps					
BB Curl	4 sets X 10 reps					
Grip Sequence	3 sets X 30 reps					

IN SEASON DEVELOPMENTAL SQUAD: Week 13

1 rep max/exercise	Set 1 RP x WT	Set 2 RP x WT	Set 3 RP x WT	Set 4 RP x WT	Set 5 RP x WT	Set 6 RP x WT
SUNDAY						
Push Jerk	4 X 180	333 X 200	2 X 215	111 X 195	11 X 235	
Front Squat	5 X 245	5 X 265	555 X 300	5 X 310		
Bench Press	4 X 210	3 X 230	2 X 255	2 X 275	2 X 295	2 X 315
Basic Pirate	5 sets X 5 reps					
MONDAY						
Power Clean	4 X 190	3 X 225	22 X 240	2 X 260	11 X 260	1 X 280
BB Snatch	3 X 170	3 X 170	3 X 175	3 X 175	3 X 185	3 X 185
Horizontal Jumps	5 sets X 5 reps					
SKB SLDL	4 sets X 10 reps					
SKB LCY Swing	4 sets X 10 reps					
BB RDL	10 X 195	10 X 195	10 X 195	10 X 195		
BB Shrug	4 sets X 20 reps					
BB Curl	4 sets X 10 reps					
Wrist Curls	4 sets X 20 reps					
Abdominals	200 reps					
TUESDAY						
Bench Press	4 X 210	3 X 230	2 X 255	2 X 275	2 X 295	2 X 315
DB Incline	5 X 105	5 X 105	5 X 110	5 X 110	5 X 115	
BB Step-up	5 X 170	5 X 170	5 X 180	5 X 180	5 X 185	
Runner	2 sets X 40 reps, 2 sets X 30 reps					
Close Grip Bench	10 X 150	10 X 150	10 X 150	10 X 150		
Band Pre Hab	4 sets X 20 reps					
Get Up Sit Up	4 sets X 10 reps					
WEDNESDAY						
Block Clean	3 X 210	3 X 210	3 X 220	3 X 220	3 X 225	3 X 225
Box Jump	5 sets X 5 reps					
SKB Dead Clean	5 sets X 5 reps					
DBL KB Row	4 sets X 10 reps					
BB Shrug	4 sets X 10 reps					
Strip Curl	4 sets X 10 reps					
Plank Sequence	4 sets X 10 reps					
Top Down Get Down	5 sets X 5 reps					
THURSDAY						
Push Jerk	4 X 180	333 X 200	2 X 215	111 X 225	11 X 235	
Board Press	4 X 255	3 X 280	2 X 305	2 X 330	2 X 355	22 X 375
Parallel Squat	5 X 305	2 X 350	2 X 380	1 X 410	11 X 440	11 X 470
Incline Fly Press	4 sets X 10 reps					
KB Seesaw Press	4 sets X 10 reps					
Pistol Squat	4 sets X 10 reps					
MB 1	3 sets X 30 reps					
FRIDAY						
Hang Snatch	3 X 185	3 X 185	3 X 190	3 X 190	3 X 195	3 X 195
Squat Clean	3 X 200	3 X 200	3 X 210	3 X 210	3 X 220	3 X 220
Bear Jumps	4 sets X 10 reps					
BB RDL	10 X 195	10 X 195	10 X 195	10 X 195		
Glute Ham Raise	4 sets X 10 reps					
BB Row	4 sets X 10 reps					
Rev Lat Pull	4 sets X 10 reps					
BB Curl	4 sets X 10 reps					
Grip Sequence	3 sets X 30 reps					

IN SEASON DEVELOPMENTAL SQUAD: Week 14

1 rep max/exercise	Set 1 RP x WT	Set 2 RP x WT	Set 3 RP x WT	Set 4 RP x WT	Set 5 RP x WT	Set 6 RP x WT
SUNDAY						
Push Jerk	4 X 185	333 X 200	2 X 220	111 X 225	11 X 235	
Front Squat	5 X 245	5 X 270	555 X 300	5 X 315		
Bench Press	4 X 210	3 X 235	2 X 255	2 X 275	2 X 295	2 X 315
Basic Pirate	5 sets X 5 reps					
MONDAY						
Power Clean	4 X 190	3 X 225	22 X 245	2 X 260	11 X 270	1 X 280
BB Snatch	3 X 170	3 X 170	3 X 180	3 X 180	3 X 185	3 X 185
Horizontal Jumps	5 sets X 5 reps					
SKB SLDL	4 sets X 10 reps					
SKB LCY Swing	4 sets X 10 reps					
BB RDL	10 X 195	10 X 195	10 X 195	10 X 195		
BB Shrug	4 sets X 20 reps					
BB Curl	4 sets X 10 reps					
Wrist Curls	4 sets X 20 reps					
Abdominals	200 reps					
TUESDAY						
Bench Press	4 X 210	3 X 235	2 X 255	2 X 275	2 X 295	2 X 315
DB Incline	5 X 105	5 X 105	5 X 110	5 X 110	5 X 115	
BB Step-up	5 X 170	5 X 170	5 X 180	5 X 180	5 X 185	
Runner	2 sets X 40 reps, 2 sets X 30 reps					
Close Grip Bench	10 X 150	10 X 150	10 X 150	10 X 150		
Band Pre Hab	4 sets X 20 reps					
Get Up Sit Up	4 sets X 10 reps					
WEDNESDAY						
Block Clean	3 X 210	3 X 210	3 X 220	3 X 220	3 X 230	3 X 230
Box Jump	5 sets X 5 reps					
SKB Dead Clean	5 sets X 5 reps					
DBL KB Row	4 sets X 10 reps					
BB Shrug	4 sets X 10 reps					
Strip Curl	4 sets X 10 reps					
Plank Sequence	4 sets X 10 reps					
Top Down Get Down	5 sets X 5 reps					
THURSDAY						
Push Jerk	4 X 185	333 X 200	2 X 220	111 X 225	11 X 235	
Board Press	4 X 260	3 X 280	2 X 305	2 X 330	2 X 355	22 X 380
Parallel Squat	5 X 305	2 X 350	2 X 380	1 X 410	11 X 445	11 X 475
Incline Fly Press	4 sets X 10 reps					
KB Seesaw Press	4 sets X 10 reps					
Pistol Squat	4 sets X 10 reps					
MB 1	3 sets X 30 reps					
FRIDAY						
Hang Snatch	3 X 185	3 X 185	3 X 190	3 X 190	3 X 200	3 X 200
Squat Clean	3 X 205	3 X 205	3 X 210	3 X 210	3 X 220	3 X 220
Bear Jumps	4 sets X 10 reps					
BB RDL	10 X 195	10 X 195	10 X 195	10 X 195		
Glute Ham Raise	4 sets X 10 reps					
BB Row	4 sets X 10 reps					
Rev Lat Pull	4 sets X 10 reps					
BB Curl	4 sets X 10 reps					
Grip Sequence	3 sets X 30 reps					

IN SEASON DEVELOPMENTAL SQUAD: Week 15

1 rep max/exercise	Set 1 RP x WT	Set 2 RP x WT	Set 3 RP x WT	Set 4 RP x WT	Set 5 RP x WT	Set 6 RP x WT
SUNDAY						
Push Jerk	4 X 185	333 X 205	2 X 220	111 X 230	11 X 240	
Front Squat	5 X 250	5 X 270	555 X 305	5 X 315		
Bench Press	4 X 215	3 X 235	2 X 255	2 X 275	2 X 300	2 X 320
Basic Pirate	5 sets X 5 reps					
MONDAY						
Power Clean	4 X 190	3 X 230	22 X 245	2 X 265	11 X 275	1 X 280
BB Snatch	3 X 175	3 X 175	3 X 180	3 X 180	3 X 185	3 X 185
Horizontal Jumps	5 sets X 5 reps					
SKB SLDL	4 sets X 10 reps					
SKB LCY Swing	4 sets X 10 reps					
BB RDL	10 X 195	10 X 195	10 X 195	10 X 195		
BB Shrug	4 sets X 20 reps					
BB Curl	4 sets X 10 reps					
Wrist Curls	4 sets X 20 reps					
Abdominals	200 reps					
TUESDAY						
Bench Press	4 X 215	3 X 235	2 X 255	2 X 275	2 X 300	2 X 320
DB Incline	5 X 105	5 X 105	5 X 110	5 X 110	5 X 115	
BB Step-up	5 X 170	5 X 170	5 X 180	5 X 180	5 X 185	
Runner	2 sets X 40 reps, 2 sets X 30 reps					
Close Grip Bench	10 X 150	10 X 150	10 X 150	10 X 150		
Band Pre Hab	4 sets X 20 reps					
Get Up Sit Up	4 sets X 10 reps					
WEDNESDAY						
Block Clean	3 X 215	3 X 215	3 X 220	3 X 220	3 X 230	3 X 230
Box Jump	5 sets X 5 reps					
SKB Dead Clean	5 sets X 5 reps					
DBL KB Row	4 sets X 10 reps					
BB Shrug	4 sets X 10 reps					
Strip Curl	4 sets X 10 reps					
Plank Sequence	4 sets X 10 reps					
Top Down Get Down	5 sets X 5 reps					
THURSDAY						
Push Jerk	4 X 185	333 X 205	2 X 220	111 X 230	11 X 240	
Board Press	4 X 260	3 X 285	2 X 310	2 X 330	2 X 355	22 X 380
Parallel Squat	5 X 310	2 X 355	2 X 385	1 X 415	11 X 445	11 X 475
Incline Fly Press	4 sets X 10 reps					
KB Seesaw Press	4 sets X 10 reps					
Pistol Squat	4 sets X 10 reps					
MB 1	3 sets X 30 reps					
FRIDAY						
Hang Snatch	3 X 185	3 X 185	3 X 195	3 X 195	3 X 200	3 X 200
Squat Clean	3 X 205	3 X 205	3 X 215	3 X 215	3 X 220	3 X 220
Bear Jumps	4 sets X 10 reps					
BB RDL	10 X 195	10 X 195	10 X 195	10 X 195		
Glute Ham Raise	4 sets X 10 reps					
BB Row	4 sets X 10 reps					
Rev Lat Pull	4 sets X 10 reps					
BB Curl	4 sets X 10 reps					
Grip Sequence	3 sets X 30 reps					

IN SEASON TRAVEL SQUAD: Week 1

1 rep max/exercise	Set 1 RP x WT	Set 2 RP x WT	Set 3 RP x WT	Set 4 RP x WT	Set 5 RP x WT	Set 6 RP x WT
SUN						
Rack Lockout	3 X 215	3 X 245	3 X 265	3 X 285	3 X 285	3 X 300
DB Incline	4 X 90	333 X 100	2 X 110	111 X 115	11 X 115	
MON						
Power Clean	3 X 185	3 X 210	3 X 230	3 X 230	3 X 245	
Parallel Squat	5 X 275	4 X 305	3 X 365	3 X 380	3 X 380	3 X 380
Runner	2 sets X 40 reps, 2 sets X 30 reps					
BB Step-up	5 X 135	5 X 135	5 X 140	5 X 140	5 X 150	
DBL KB LCY Swing	4 sets X 10 reps					
SKB SLDL	4 sets X 10 reps					
DBL KB Sumo	4 sets X 10 reps					
WED						
Bench Press	3 X 200	3 X 220	3 X 250	3 X 260	3 X 260	3 X 260
Push Press	3 X 140	3 X 155	3 X 175	3 X 185	3 X 185	3 X 185
DB Incline	5 X 110	5 X 110	5 X 110	5 X 110	5 X 115	
THURS						
BB Shrug	4 sets X 20 reps					
DBL KB Row	4 sets X 10 reps					
Band Pre Hab	4 sets X 20 reps					
Upright Row	4 sets X 10 reps					
BB Curl	4 sets X 10 reps					
Grip Sequence	4 sets X 20 reps					
MB2	4 sets X 20 reps					

IN SEASON TRAVEL SQUAD: Week 2

1 rep max/exercise	Set 1 RP x WT	Set 2 RP x WT	Set 3 RP x WT	Set 4 RP x WT	Set 5 RP x WT	Set 6 RP x WT
SUN						
Rack Lockout	3 X 215	3 X 245	3 X 265	3 X 285	3 X 285	3 X 300
MON						
Power Clean	3 X 185	3 X 210	3 X 230	3 X 230	3 X 250	
Parallel Squat	5 X 275	4 X 305	3 X 365	3 X 385	3 X 385	3 X 385
Runner	2 sets X 40 reps, 2 sets X 30 reps					
BB Step-up	5 X 170	5 X 170	5 X 180	5 X 180	5 X 185	
DBL KB LCY Swing	4 sets X 10 reps					
SKB SLDL	4 sets X 10 reps					
DBL KB Sumo	4 sets X 10 reps					
WED						
Bench Press	3 X 200	3 X 220	3 X 250	3 X 260	3 X 260	3 X 260
Push Press	3 X 140	3 X 155	3 X 175	3 X 185	3 X 185	3 X 185
DB Incline	5 X 110	5 X 110	5 X 115	5 X 115	5 X 120	
THURS						
BB Shrug	4 sets X 20 reps					
DBL KB Row	4 sets X 10 reps					
Band Pre Hab	4 sets X 20 reps					
Upright Row	4 sets X 10 reps					
BB Curl	4 sets X 10 reps					
Grip Sequence	4 sets X 20 reps					
MB2	4 sets X 20 reps					

IN SEASON TRAVEL SQUAD: Week 3

1 rep max/exercise		Set 1 RP x WT	Set 2 RP x WT	Set 3 RP x WT	Set 4 RP x WT	Set 5 RP x WT	Set 6 RP x WT
SUN	Rack Lockout	3 X 215	3 X 245	3 X 265	3 X 285	3 X 285	3 X 300
MON	Power Clean	3 X 185	3 X 215	3 X 230	3 X 230	3 X 250	
	Parallel Squat	5 X 280	4 X 310	3 X 370	3 X 385	3 X 385	3 X 385
	Runner	2 sets X 40 reps, 2 sets X 30 reps					
	BB Step-up	5 X 170	5 X 170	5 X 180	5 X 180	5 X 185	
	DBL KB LCY Swing	4 sets X 10 reps					
	SKB SLDL	4 sets X 10 reps					
	DBL KB Sumo	4 sets X 10 reps					
WED	Bench Press	3 X 200	3 X 220	3 X 250	3 X 260	3 X 260	3 X 260
	Push Press	3 X 140	3 X 155	3 X 175	3 X 185	3 X 185	3 X 185
	DB Incline	5 X 110	5 X 110	5 X 115	5 X 115	5 X 120	
THURS	BB Shrug	4 sets X 20 reps					
	DBL KB Row	4 sets X 10 reps					
	Band Pre Hab	4 sets X 20 reps					
	Upright Row	4 sets X 10 reps					
	BB Curl	4 sets X 10 reps					
	Grip Sequence	4 sets X 20 reps					
	MB2	4 sets X 20 reps					

IN SEASON TRAVEL SQUAD: Week 4

1 rep max/exercise		Set 1 RP x WT	Set 2 RP x WT	Set 3 RP x WT	Set 4 RP x WT	Set 5 RP x WT	Set 6 RP x WT
SUN	Rack Lockout	3 X 215	3 X 245	3 X 265	3 X 285	3 X 285	3 X 300
MON	Power Clean	3 X 185	3 X 215	3 X 235	3 X 250	3 X 250	3 X 260
	Parallel Squat	5 X 295	4 X 325	3 X 385	3 X 400	3 X 400	3 X 400
	Runner	2 sets X 40 reps, 2 sets X 30 reps					
	BB Step-up	5 X 170	5 X 170	5 X 180	5 X 180	5 X 185	
	DBL KB LCY Swing	4 sets X 10 reps					
	SKB SLDL	4 sets X 10 reps					
	DBL KB Sumo	4 sets X 10 reps					
WED	Bench Press	3 X 210	3 X 230	3 X 260	333 X 270	2 X 280	
	Push Press	3 X 150	3 X 165	3 X 185	333 X 190	2 X 200	
	DB Incline	5 X 110	5 X 110	5 X 115	5 X 115	5 X 120	
THURS	BB Shrug	4 sets X 20 reps					
	DBL KB Row	4 sets X 10 reps					
	Band Pre Hab	4 sets X 20 reps					
	Upright Row	4 sets X 10 reps					
	BB Curl	4 sets X 10 reps					
	Grip Sequence	4 sets X 20 reps					
	MB2	4 sets X 20 reps					

IN SEASON TRAVEL SQUAD: Week 5

1 rep max/exercise	Set 1 RP x WT	Set 2 RP x WT	Set 3 RP x WT	Set 4 RP x WT	Set 5 RP x WT	Set 6 RP x WT
SUN						
Rack Lockout	3 X 215	3 X 245	3 X 265	3 X 285	3 X 285	3 X 300
MON						
Power Clean	3 X 190	3 X 215	3 X 235	3 X 255	3 X 255	3 X 260
Parallel Squat	5 X 295	4 X 325	3 X 385	3 X 400	3 X 400	3 X 400
Runner	2 sets X 40 reps, 2 sets X 30 reps					
BB Step-up	5 X 170	5 X 170	5 X 180	5 X 180	5 X 185	
DBL KB LCY Swing	4 sets X 10 reps					
SKB SLDL	4 sets X 10 reps					
DBL KB Sumo	4 sets X 10 reps					
WED						
Bench Press	3 X 210	3 X 230	3 X 260	333 X 270	2 X 280	
Push Press	3 X 150	3 X 165	3 X 185	333 X 195	2 X 200	
DB Incline	5 X 115	5 X 115	5 X 115	5 X 115	5 X 120	
THURS						
BB Shrug	4 sets X 20 reps					
DBL KB Row	4 sets X 10 reps					
Band Pre Hab	4 sets X 20 reps					
Upright Row	4 sets X 10 reps					
BB Curl	4 sets X 10 reps					
Grip Sequence	4 sets X 20 reps					
MB2	4 sets X 20 reps					

IN SEASON TRAVEL SQUAD: Week 6

1 rep max/exercise	Set 1 RP x WT	Set 2 RP x WT	Set 3 RP x WT	Set 4 RP x WT	Set 5 RP x WT	Set 6 RP x WT
SUN						
Rack Lockout	3 X 215	3 X 245	3 X 265	3 X 285	3 X 285	3 X 300
MON						
Power Clean	3 X 190	3 X 215	3 X 235	3 X 255	3 X 255	3 X 265
Parallel Squat	5 X 295	4 X 325	3 X 390	3 X 405	3 X 405	3 X 405
Runner	2 sets X 40 reps, 2 sets X 30 reps					
BB Step-up	5 X 170	5 X 170	5 X 180	5 X 180	5 X 185	
DBL KB LCY Swing	4 sets X 10 reps					
SKB SLDL	4 sets X 10 reps					
DBL KB Sumo	4 sets X 10 reps					
WED						
Bench Press	3 X 215	3 X 235	3 X 265	333 X 275	2 X 285	
Push Press	3 X 150	3 X 165	3 X 185	333 X 195	2 X 200	
DB Incline	5 X 115	5 X 115	5 X 120	5 X 120	5 X 125	
THURS						
BB Shrug	4 sets X 20 reps					
DBL KB Row	4 sets X 10 reps					
Band Pre Hab	4 sets X 20 reps					
Upright Row	4 sets X 10 reps					
BB Curl	4 sets X 10 reps					
Grip Sequence	4 sets X 20 reps					
MB2	4 sets X 20 reps					

IN SEASON TRAVEL SQUAD: Week 7

1 rep max/exercise		Set 1 RP x WT	Set 2 RP x WT	Set 3 RP x WT	Set 4 RP x WT	Set 5 RP x WT	Set 6 RP x WT
SUN	Rack Lockout	3 X 215	3 X 245	3 X 265	3 X 285	3 X 285	3 X 300
MON	Power Clean	3 X 200	3 X 230	3 X 250	2 X 265	2 X 265	2 X 275
	Parallel Squat	5 X 315	4 X 345	2 X 405	2 X 435	2 X 435	2 X 435
	Runner	2 sets X 40 reps, 2 sets X 30 reps					
	BB Step-up	5 X 170	5 X 170	5 X 180	5 X 180	5 X 185	
	DBL KB LCY Swing	4 sets X 10 reps					
	SKB SLDL	4 sets X 10 reps					
	DBL KB Sumo	4 sets X 10 reps					
WED	Bench Press	3 X 215	3 X 235	2 X 265	2 X 285	22 X 295	1 X 305
	Push Press	3 X 155	3 X 165	2 X 190	2 X 205	22 X 210	1 X 215
	DB Incline	5 X 115	5 X 115	5 X 120	5 X 120	5 X 125	
THURS	BB Shrug	4 sets X 20 reps					
	DBL KB Row	4 sets X 10 reps					
	Band Pre Hab	4 sets X 20 reps					
	Upright Row	4 sets X 10 reps					
	BB Curl	4 sets X 10 reps					
	Grip Sequence	4 sets X 20 reps					
	MB2	4 sets X 20 reps					

IN SEASON TRAVEL SQUAD: Week 8

1 rep max/exercise		Set 1 RP x WT	Set 2 RP x WT	Set 3 RP x WT	Set 4 RP x WT	Set 5 RP x WT	Set 6 RP x WT
SUN	Rack Lockout	3 X 215	3 X 245	3 X 265	3 X 285	3 X 285	3 X 300
MON	Power Clean	3 X 200	3 X 230	3 X 250	2 X 265	2 X 265	2 X 275
	Parallel Squat	5 X 315	4 X 345	2 X 405	2 X 435	2 X 435	2 X 435
	Runner	2 sets X 40 reps, 2 sets X 30 reps					
	BB Step-up	5 X 170	5 X 170	5 X 180	5 X 180	5 X 185	
	DBL KB LCY Swing	4 sets X 10 reps					
	SKB SLDL	4 sets X 10 reps					
	DBL KB Sumo	4 sets X 10 reps					
WED	Bench Press	3 X 215	3 X 235	2 X 265	2 X 285	22 X 295	1 X 305
	Push Press	3 X 155	3 X 165	2 X 190	2 X 205	22 X 210	1 X 215
	DB Incline	5 X 115	5 X 115	5 X 120	5 X 120	5 X 125	
THURS	BB Shrug	4 sets X 20 reps					
	DBL KB Row	4 sets X 10 reps					
	Band Pre Hab	4 sets X 20 reps					
	Upright Row	4 sets X 10 reps					
	BB Curl	4 sets X 10 reps					
	Grip Sequence	4 sets X 20 reps					
	MB2	4 sets X 20 reps					

IN SEASON TRAVEL SQUAD: Week 9

1 rep max/exercise	Set 1 RP x WT	Set 2 RP x WT	Set 3 RP x WT	Set 4 RP x WT	Set 5 RP x WT	Set 6 RP x WT
SUN						
Rack Lockout	3 X 215	3 X 245	3 X 265	3 X 285	3 X 285	3 X 300
MON						
Power Clean	3 X 200	3 X 230	3 X 250	2 X 270	2 X 270	2 X 275
Parallel Squat	5 X 315	4 X 345	2 X 405	2 X 440	2 X 440	2 X 440
Runner	2 sets X 40 reps, 2 sets X 30 reps					
BB Step-up	5 X 170	5 X 170	5 X 180	5 X 180	5 X 185	
DBL KB LCY Swing	4 sets X 10 reps					
SKB SLDL	4 sets X 10 reps					
DBL KB Sumo	4 sets X 10 reps					
WED						
Bench Press	3 X 215	3 X 235	2 X 265	2 X 285	22 X 295	1 X 305
Push Press	3 X 155	3 X 170	2 X 190	2 X 205	22 X 210	1 X 220
DB Incline	5 X 120	5 X 120	5 X 120	5 X 120	5 X 125	
THURS						
BB Shrug	4 sets X 20 reps					
DBL KB Row	4 sets X 10 reps					
Band Pre Hab	4 sets X 20 reps					
Upright Row	4 sets X 10 reps					
BB Curl	4 sets X 10 reps					
Grip Sequence	4 sets X 20 reps					
MB2	4 sets X 20 reps					

IN SEASON TRAVEL SQUAD: Week 10

1 rep max/exercise	Set 1 RP x WT	Set 2 RP x WT	Set 3 RP x WT	Set 4 RP x WT	Set 5 RP x WT	Set 6 RP x WT
SUN						
Rack Lockout	3 X 215	3 X 245	3 X 265	3 X 285	3 X 285	3 X 300
MON						
Power Clean	3 X 205	3 X 230	2 X 260	2 X 280	2 X 280	2 X 290
Parallel Squat	3 X 330	3 X 360	2 X 395	2 X 425	22 X 455	2 X 470
Runner	2 sets X 40 reps, 2 sets X 30 reps					
BB Step-up	5 X 170	5 X 170	5 X 180	5 X 180	5 X 185	
DBL KB LCY Swing	4 sets X 10 reps					
SKB SLDL	4 sets X 10 reps					
DBL KB Sumo	4 sets X 10 reps					
WED						
Bench Press	3 X 215	3 X 235	2 X 265	2 X 285	22 X 305	1 X 315
Push Press	3 X 155	3 X 170	2 X 190	2 X 205	22 X 220	1 X 225
DB Incline	5 X 120	5 X 120	5 X 125	5 X 125	5 X 130	
THURS						
BB Shrug	4 sets X 20 reps					
DBL KB Row	4 sets X 10 reps					
Band Pre Hab	4 sets X 20 reps					
Upright Row	4 sets X 10 reps					
BB Curl	4 sets X 10 reps					
Grip Sequence	4 sets X 20 reps					
MB2	4 sets X 20 reps					

IN SEASON TRAVEL SQUAD: Week 11

1 rep max/exercise	Set 1 RP x WT	Set 2 RP x WT	Set 3 RP x WT	Set 4 RP x WT	Set 5 RP x WT	Set 6 RP x WT
SUN						
Rack Lockout	3 X 215	3 X 245	3 X 265	3 X 285	3 X 285	3 X 300
MON						
Power Clean	3 X 205	3 X 230	2 X 260	2 X 280	2 X 280	2 X 290
Parallel Squat	3 X 330	3 X 365	2 X 395	2 X 425	22 X 455	2 X 470
Runner	2 sets X 40 reps, 2 sets X 30 reps					
BB Step-up	5 X 170	5 X 170	5 X 180	5 X 180	5 X 185	
DBL KB LCY Swing	4 sets X 10 reps					
SKB SLDL	4 sets X 10 reps					
DBL KB Sumo	4 sets X 10 reps					
WED						
Bench Press	3 X 215	3 X 235	2 X 270	2 X 290	22 X 310	1 X 320
Push Press	3 X 155	3 X 170	2 X 190	2 X 205	22 X 220	1 X 225
DB Incline	5 X 120	5 X 120	5 X 125	5 X 125	5 X 130	
THURS						
BB Shrug	4 sets X 20 reps					
DBL KB Row	4 sets X 10 reps					
Band Pre Hab	4 sets X 20 reps					
Upright Row	4 sets X 10 reps					
BB Curl	4 sets X 10 reps					
Grip Sequence	4 sets X 20 reps					
MB2	4 sets X 20 reps					

IN SEASON TRAVEL SQUAD: Week 12

1 rep max/exercise	Set 1 RP x WT	Set 2 RP x WT	Set 3 RP x WT	Set 4 RP x WT	Set 5 RP x WT	Set 6 RP x WT
SUN						
Rack Lockout	3 X 215	3 X 245	3 X 265	3 X 285	3 X 285	3 X 300
MON						
Power Clean	3 X 205	3 X 235	2 X 260	2 X 280	2 X 280	2 X 290
Parallel Squat	3 X 335	3 X 365	2 X 395	2 X 425	22 X 460	2 X 475
Runner	2 sets X 40 reps, 2 sets X 30 reps					
BB Step-up	5 X 170	5 X 170	5 X 180	5 X 180	5 X 185	
DBL KB LCY Swing	4 sets X 10 reps					
SKB SLDL	4 sets X 10 reps					
DBL KB Sumo	4 sets X 10 reps					
WED						
Bench Press	3 X 220	3 X 240	2 X 270	2 X 290	22 X 310	1 X 320
Push Press	3 X 155	3 X 170	2 X 190	2 X 205	22 X 220	1 X 230
DB Incline	5 X 120	5 X 120	5 X 125	5 X 125	5 X 130	
THURS						
BB Shrug	4 sets X 20 reps					
DBL KB Row	4 sets X 10 reps					
Band Pre Hab	4 sets X 20 reps					
Upright Row	4 sets X 10 reps					
BB Curl	4 sets X 10 reps					
Grip Sequence	4 sets X 20 reps					
MB2	4 sets X 20 reps					

OFF SEASON TRAINING PLANS

MONDAY			
STRENGTH	**TRACK**	**GREEN AREA**	**HARD GAINERS**
M.E. POWER CLEAN	Dynamic W/U	Bag Drills	BLOCK CLEAN
+ Jumps	Stick Drill	Agility Ladder Drills	+ Jumps
DB BENCH PRESS	In's & Out's (*20yds peak zone*)	Tempo Hurdle Drills	BACK SQUAT
+ Band Shuffle	Speed Bound Over Hurdles	Core	STEP-UP
+ Plate Hip Flexor	2 Point Sprints-timed		PISTOL SQUAT
+ Lat Pulldown	4 Count Pose Chop		R.D.L.
FRONT SQUAT	Lunge Jumps		DBL KB SUMO DL
+ Hip Bridge	Lower Leg Drills		DBL KB RACK SQUAT
STEP-UP	Core		GLUTE & HAM
+ Heavy KB Swing			+ KB Swing
PUSH PRESS			PROWLER or SLED
+ BB R.D.L			

TUESDAY	
SPEED	**HARD GAINERS**
DYNAMIC W/U	KB SNATCH
CONTRAST SPRINT BOUNDS WITH SLED	BENCH PRESS
STRAIGHT LEG BOUNDS WITH SLED	INCLINE PRESS
PEDAL WITH SLED	CLOSE GRIP BENCH
LOW LUNGE WITH SLED	PULLING CIRCUIT
POSITION SPECIFIC DRILL WORK	- PULL UP
	- SHRUG
	- BARBELL ROW
	- LOW ROW
	- BARBELL CURL

WEDNESDAY			
STRENGTH	**TRACK**	**GREEN AREA**	**HARD GAINERS**
M.E. BENCH PRESS	Dynamic W/U	Bag Drills	POWER CLEAN
BLOCK CLEAN	Single Leg Fast Leg	Agility Ladder Drills	+ Jumps
+ Jump Sequence	3 Count Fast Leg	Tempo Hurdle Drills	PUSH JERK
RUNNER	Fast Leg Build-Up	Core	SEATED MILITARY PR.
+ DB Incline	3 point Acceleration Bounds		DB REV. PRESS
BARBELL SNATCH	20yds Sprints with Vests		+ Shoulder Series
+ Hip Thrust	Speed Bounds Over Hurdles		PRE-HAB
GLUTE & HAM	Straight Leg Bound (30-40yds)		DOUBLE TROUBLE
+ Sumo KB DL	Scissor March w/ M.B.		or 21 & DONE
S.L. KB DL	Lower Leg Drills		ABSOLUTE SPEED DAY
+ DBL Leg Hip Bridge	Core		

THURSDAY

SPEED	HARD GAINERS
DYNAMIC W/U	DBL DB VINTAGE CLEAN
CONTRAST SPRINT BOUNDS WITH SLED	BOX SQUAT
SAND PIT WORK	FRONT SQUAT
- Contrast Bounds	RUNNER
- Strength Series	BEAR SQUAT
POSITION SPECIFIC DRILL WORK	BANDIT LOOP LUNGE
	KB SWING
	S.L. KB DL

FRIDAY

STRENGTH	TRACK	GREEN AREA	HARD GAINERS
BOARD PRESS W/CHAIN	Wall Series	Bag Drills	BARBELL SNATCH
+ DBL KB ROW	Over & Under MB Hurdle	Agility Ladder Drills	+ Hurdle Jumps
M.E. BACK SQUAT	Stick Drill	Jump Rope Drills	BENCH PRESS
+ Jumps	Speed Bound Over Hurdles	Core	BB INCLINE PRESS
PUSH JERK	Scissor Drills on Boxes		PUSH PRESS
+ BARBELL S.L. DL	Over Speed or Tempo 40yds		SEE SAW PRESS
PISTOL SQUAT	20 in 5 with MB and Bands		SHOULDER SERIES
+ KB DEAD SWING	Lunge Jumps		TRICEPS EXTENSION
	Lower Leg Drills		STADIUM WORK
	Core		

OFF SEASON WINTER: Week 1

1 rep max/exercise	Set 1 RP x WT	Set 2 RP x WT	Set 3 RP x WT	Set 4 RP x WT	Set 5 RP x WT	Set 6 RP x WT
MON						
Power Clean	5 x 190	4 x 210	3 x 250	3 x ME set	333 x 260	
Dynamic Bench Press	2 x 245	2 x 245	2 x 245	2 x 245	222 x 255	
BB Step-up	5 x 210	5 x 210	5 x 220	5 x 220	5 x 230	
Front Squat	3 x 245	3 x 285	3 x 310	3 x 310	3 x 330	
Push Press	55 x 155	55 x 160	5 x 170			
BB RDL	8 x 240	8 x 240	8 x 240	8 x 240		
Abdominals	200 reps					
WED						
Bench Press	3 x 235	3 x 260	2 x 310	1 x 335	3 x ME set	333 x 320
Block Clean	2 x 250	2 x 250	2 x 250	2 x 250	2 x 250	222 x 260
Horizontal Jumps	5 sets x 3 reps					
DBL KB LCY Swing	4 sets x 10 reps					
Runner	1 set x 40 reps, 2 sets x 30 reps, 1 set x 20 reps					
DB Incline	4 sets x 8 reps					
BB Snatch	3 x 140	3 x 160	3 x 175	3 x 190	3 x 190	3 x 195
Box Jump	5 sets x 3 reps					
Get Up Sit Up	4 sets x 20 reps					
FRI						
Parallel Squat	5 x 300	5 x 330	3 x 365	1 x 415	5 x ME set	555 x 430
Board Press	3 x 270	3 x 310	3 x 335	3 x 365	3 x 365	3 x 375
Push Jerk	3 x 185	3 x 210	3 x 230	3 x 245	3 x 245	3 x 255
Pistol Squat	4 sets x 8 reps					
SKB SLDL	4 sets x 8 reps					
BB RDL	8 x 240	8 x 240	8 x 240	8 x 240		
Pull Circuit	4 sets x 10 reps					
Turkish Get Up	4 sets x 5 reps					

STRENGTH COACH

OFF SEASON WINTER: Week 2

1 rep max/exercise	Set 1 RP x WT	Set 2 RP x WT	Set 3 RP x WT	Set 4 RP x WT	Set 5 RP x WT	Set 6 RP x WT
MON						
Power Clean	5 X 190	4 X 210	3 X 255	3 X ME set	333 X 265	
Dynamic Bench Press	2 X 245	2 X 245	2 X 245	2 X 245	222 X 255	
BB Step-up	5 X 215	5 X 215	5 X 225	5 X 225	5 X 230	
Front Squat	3 X 250	3 X 285	3 X 310	3 X 310	3 X 335	
Push Press	55 X 155	55 X 165	5 X 170			
BB RDL	8 X 240	8 X 240	8 X 240	8 X 240		
Abdominals	200 reps					
WED						
Bench Press	3 X 235	3 X 260	2 X 310	1 X 335	3 X ME set	333 X 335
Block Clean	2 X 250	2 X 250	2 X 250	2 X 250	2 X 250	222 X 260
Horizontal Jumps	5 sets X 3 reps					
DBL KB LCY Swing	4 sets X 10 reps					
Runner	1 set X 40 reps, 2 sets X 30 reps, 1 set X 20 reps					
DB Incline	4 sets X 8 reps					
BB Snatch	3 X 140	3 X 160	3 X 175	3 X 190	3 X 190	3 X 195
Box Jump	5 sets X 3 reps					
Get Up Sit Up	4 sets X 20 reps					
FRI						
Parallel Squat	5 X 300	5 X 335	3 X 370	1 X 420	5 X ME set	555 X 435
Board Press	3 X 270	3 X 315	3 X 340	3 X 365	3 X 365	3 X 380
Push Jerk	3 X 185	3 X 210	3 X 230	3 X 245	3 X 245	3 X 255
Pistol Squat	4 sets X 8 reps					
SKB SLDL	4 sets X 8 reps					
BB RDL	8 X 240	8 X 240	8 X 240	8 X 240		
Pull Circuit	4 sets X 10 reps					
Turkish Get Up	4 sets X 5 reps					

OFF SEASON WINTER: Week 3

1 rep max/exercise	Set 1 RP x WT	Set 2 RP x WT	Set 3 RP x WT	Set 4 RP x WT	Set 5 RP x WT	Set 6 RP x WT
MON						
Power Clean	5 X 195	4 X 215	3 X 255	3 X ME set	333 X 280	
Dynamic Bench Press	2 X 245	2 X 245	2 X 245	2 X 245	222 X 255	
BB Step-up	5 X 215	5 X 215	5 X 225	5 X 225	5 X 235	
Front Squat	3 X 255	3 X 290	3 X 315	3 X 315	3 X 340	
Push Press	55 X 155	55 X 165	5 X 175			
BB RDL	8 X 240	8 X 240	8 X 240	8 X 240		
Abdominals	200 reps					
WED						
Bench Press	3 X 235	3 X 260	2 X 315	1 X 340	3 X ME set	333 X 355
Block Clean	2 X 255	2 X 255	2 X 255	2 X 255	2 X 255	222 X 265
Horizontal Jumps	5 sets X 3 reps					
DBL KB LCY Swing	4 sets X 10 reps					
Runner	1 set X 40 reps, 2 sets X 30 reps, 1 set X 20 reps					
DB Incline	4 sets X 8 reps					
BB Snatch	3 X 140	3 X 160	3 X 175	3 X 190	3 X 190	3 X 195
Box Jump	5 sets X 3 reps					
Get Up Sit Up	4 sets X 20 reps					
FRI						
Parallel Squat	5 X 305	3 X 340	2 X 405	1 X 440	4 X ME set	444 X 455
Board Press	3 X 275	3 X 315	3 X 340	3 X 370	3 X 370	3 X 380
Push Jerk	3 X 185	3 X 210	3 X 230	3 X 245	3 X 245	3 X 255
Pistol Squat	4 sets X 8 reps					
SKB SLDL	4 sets X 8 reps					
BB RDL	8 X 240	8 X 240	8 X 240	8 X 240		
Pull Circuit	4 sets X 10 reps					
Turkish Get Up	4 sets X 5 reps					

OFF SEASON WINTER: Week 4

1 rep max/exercise	Set 1 RP x WT	Set 2 RP x WT	Set 3 RP x WT	Set 4 RP x WT	Set 5 RP x WT	Set 6 RP x WT
Power Clean	5 X 195	4 X 220	3 X 260	3 X ME set	333 X 280	
Dynamic Bench Press	2 X 245	2 X 245	2 X 245	2 X 245	222 X 255	
BB Step-up	5 X 220	5 X 220	5 X 230	5 X 230	5 X 235	
Front Squat	3 X 255	3 X 295	3 X 320	3 X 320	3 X 345	
Push Press	55 X 160	55 X 165	5 X 175			
BB RDL	8 X 240	8 X 240	8 X 240	8 X 240		
Abdominals	200 reps					

MON

	Set 1	Set 2	Set 3	Set 4	Set 5	Set 6
Bench Press	3 X 240	3 X 265	2 X 315	1 X 340	3 X ME set	333 X 355
Block Clean	2 X 255	2 X 255	2 X 255	2 X 255	2 X 255	222 X 265
Horizontal Jumps	5 sets X 3 reps					
DBL KB LCY Swing	4 sets X 10 reps					
Runner	1 set X 40 reps, 2 sets X 30 reps, 1 set X 20 reps					
DB Incline	4 sets X 8 reps					
BB Snatch	3 X 140	3 X 160	3 X 175	3 X 190	3 X 190	3 X 195
Box Jump	5 sets X 3 reps					
Get Up Sit Up	4 sets X 20 reps					

WED

	Set 1	Set 2	Set 3	Set 4	Set 5	Set 6
Parallel Squat	5 X 310	3 X 340	2 X 410	1 X 440	4 X ME set	444 X 460
Board Press	3 X 275	3 X 315	3 X 345	3 X 370	3 X 370	3 X 385
Push Jerk	3 X 185	3 X 210	3 X 230	3 X 245	3 X 245	3 X 255
Pistol Squat	4 sets X 8 reps					
SKB SLDL	4 sets X 8 reps					
BB RDL	8 X 240	8 X 240	8 X 240	8 X 240		
Pull Circuit	4 sets X 10 reps					
Turkish Get Up	4 sets X 5 reps					

FRI

OFF SEASON WINTER: Week 5

1 rep max/exercise	Set 1 RP x WT	Set 2 RP x WT	Set 3 RP x WT	Set 4 RP x WT	Set 5 RP x WT	Set 6 RP x WT
MON						
Power Clean	5 X 200	4 X 220	3 X 265	3 x ME set	333 X 295	
Dynamic Bench Press	2 X 245	2 X 245	2 X 245	2 X 245	222 X 255	
BB Step-up	5 X 220	5 X 220	5 X 230	5 X 230	5 X 240	
Front Squat	3 X 260	3 X 300	3 X 325	3 X 325	3 X 350	
Push Press	55 X 160	55 X 170	5 X 175			
BB RDL	8 X 240	8 X 240	8 X 240	8 X 240		
Abdominals	200 reps					
WED						
Bench Press	3 X 240	3 X 265	2 X 320	1 X 345	3 X ME set	333 X 360
Block Clean	2 X 260	2 X 260	2 X 260	2 X 260	2 X 260	222 X 270
Horizontal Jumps	5 sets X 3 reps					
DBL KB LCY Swing	4 sets X 10 reps					
Runner	1 set X 40 reps, 2 sets X 30 reps, 1 set X 20 reps					
DB Incline	4 sets X 8 reps					
BB Snatch	3 X 140	3 X 160	3 X 175	3 X 190	3 X 190	3 X 195
Box Jump	5 sets X 3 reps					
Get Up Sit Up	4 sets X 20 reps					
FRI						
Parallel Squat	3 X 345	2 X 410	1 X 445	1 X 465	3 X ME set	333 X 480
Board Press	3 X 280	3 X 320	3 X 345	3 X 375	3 X 375	3 X 390
Push Jerk	3 X 185	3 X 210	3 X 230	3 X 245	3 X 245	3 X 255
Pistol Squat	4 sets X 8 reps					
SKB SLDL	4 sets X 8 reps					
BB RDL	8 X 240	8 X 240	8 X 240	8 X 240		
Pull Circuit	4 sets X 10 reps					
Turkish Get Up	4 sets X 5 reps					

OFF SEASON WINTER: Week 6

1 rep max/exercise	Set 1 RP x WT	Set 2 RP x WT	Set 3 RP x WT	Set 4 RP x WT	Set 5 RP x WT	Set 6 RP x WT
MON						
Power Clean	5 X 200	4 X 225	3 X 265	3 x ME set	333 X 300	
Dynamic Bench Press	2 X 245	2 X 245	2 X 245	2 X 245	222 X 255	
BB Step-up	5 X 225	5 X 225	5 X 235	5 X 235	5 X 240	
Front Squat	3 X 290	3 X 330	3 X 360	3 X 360	3 X 390	
Push Press	55 X 160	55 X 170	5 X 180			
BB RDL	8 X 240	8 X 240	8 X 240	8 X 240		
Abdominals	200 reps					
WED						
Bench Press	3 X 240	3 X 270	2 X 320	1 X 350	3 X ME set	333 X 375
Block Clean	2 X 260	2 X 260	2 X 260	2 X 260	2 X 260	222 X 270
Horizontal Jumps	5 sets X 3 reps					
DBL KB LCY Swing	4 sets X 10 reps					
Runner	1 set X 40 reps, 2 sets X 30 reps, 1 set X 20 reps					
DB Incline	4 sets X 8 reps					
BB Snatch	3 X 140	3 X 160	3 X 175	3 X 190	3 X 190	3 X 195
Box Jump	5 sets X 3 reps					
Get Up Sit Up	4 sets X 20 reps					
FRI						
Parallel Squat	3 X 350	2 X 415	1 X 450	1 X 465	3 X ME set	333 X 485
Board Press	3 X 310	3 X 355	3 X 385	3 X 415	3 X 415	3 X 430
Push Jerk	3 X 200	3 X 230	3 X 250	3 X 270	3 X 270	3 X 280
Pistol Squat	4 sets X 8 reps					
SKB SLDL	4 sets X 8 reps					
BB RDL	8 X 240	8 X 240	8 X 240	8 X 240		
Pull Circuit	4 sets X 10 reps					
Turkish Get Up	4 sets X 5 reps					

KETTLEBELL WORKOUT: Level 1 Basic Programs

BASIC PIRATE

Single KB Dead Swing	x 5 reps each arm
Single KB Long Cycle Swing	x 10 reps each arm
Single KB Dead Clean	x 5 reps each arm
Single KB Long Cycle Clean	x 5 reps each arm
Single KB Dead Clean + Rack Squat	x 5 reps each arm
Single KB Long Cycle Clean + Rack Squat	x 5 reps each arm
Single KB Rack Squat	x 5 reps each arm
Single KB Dead Snatch	x 5 reps each arm
Single KB Long Cycle Snatch	x 5 reps each arm
Single KB Press	x 5 reps each arm
Single KB Dead Clean + Press	x 5 reps each arm
Single KB Dead Clean + Press + Rack Squat	x 5 reps each arm

* Thirty seconds rest between sets

FINISHER

Turkish Get-Up	x 5 reps each arm
Windmill	x 5 reps each arm

CUTLASS

Single KB Rack Squat	x 5 each arm	
Double KB Sumo Deadlift	x 10	30 seconds rest interval
Single KB Dead Clean	x 5 each arm	
Double KB Rack Squat	x 10	30 seconds rest interval
Single KB Dead Snatch	x 5 each arm	
Double KB Long Cycle Clean	x 10	30 seconds rest interval
Single KB High Pull	x 5 each arm	
Double KB Long Cycle Snatch	x 10	30 seconds rest interval
Single KB Press	x 5 each arm	
Double KB Long Cycle Dead Clean + Press	x 10	30 seconds rest interval

* Each superset is repeated 3 times with no rest
* Rest :30 seconds, Move to next exercise

DAGGER

Double KB Rack Squat	x 30 seconds	
Renegade Row	x 30 seconds	60 seconds rest interval
Double KB Sumo Dead Lift	x 30 seconds	
Low Plank	x 30 seconds	60 seconds rest interval
Double KB Dead Clean	x 30 seconds	
Super Plank	x 30 seconds	60 seconds rest interval
Double KB Long Cycle Snatch	x 30 seconds	
Reverse Crunch	x 30 seconds	60 seconds rest interval
Double KB Press	x 30 seconds	
Pike	x 30 seconds	60 seconds rest interval
Pry squat	x 30 seconds	
Single KB Swing	x 30 seconds	

* Every exercise is coupled with another exercise
* This is a superset - no rest
* Rest :60 seconds after each superset
* Execute the entire sequence - rest 2:00 and repeat

KETTLEBELL WORKOUT: Level 1 Anaerobic Emphasis

T-N-T		
Single Arm KB Dead Swing	5 reps each arm	
Single Arm KB Long Cycle Swing	5 reps each arm	60 seconds rest interval
Double KB Dead Clean	5 reps	
Single Arm KB Long Cycle Clean	5 reps each arm	60 seconds rest interval
Single Arm KB Dead Clean + Press	5 reps each arm	
Double KB Long Cycle Clean + Press	5 reps	60 seconds rest interval
Single Arm DB Vintage Sweep	5 reps each arm	60 seconds rest interval
Single Arm KB Clean + Squat	3 reps each arm	
Double KB Long Cycle Clean + Press	3 reps	60 seconds rest interval
Figure 8 to Hold	x 10 reps	
Box Jump	x 5 reps	

* Each round is a superset
* Complete then rest 2 minutes and repeat twice from top

HEARTBEATS		
A.	KB Cossack Stretch	30 seconds
	Double DB Dead Clean	30 seconds
	Bike	60 seconds
	30 seconds in between	
B.	Single Arm KB Squat + Press	30 seconds each arm
	Single Arm KB Dead Swing	30 seconds each arm
	6 to 90	60 seconds
	30 seconds in between	
C.	2 Handed Swing	30 seconds
	KB Sumo Deadlift	30 seconds
	Russian Twist	30 seconds
	30 seconds in between	
D.	Med Ball Pike	30 seconds
	L Plank	30 seconds
	Cross Pike	30 seconds each arm
	30 seconds in between	
E.	Floor Dip	30 seconds
	Renegade Row	30 seconds
	Reverse Crunch	30 seconds
	30 seconds in between	
F.	Figure 8 to Hold	30 seconds
	Single Leg KB Deadlift	30 seconds each arm
	L Crunch	30 seconds

* Rest 2 Minutes and repeat from top twice

KETTLEBELL WORKOUT: Level 1 Heavy Resistance

21 AND DONE

Double KB Dead Clean + Squat + Press

* Must complete 21 reps in 12 minutes. Rest between sets is optional. Just Finish in 12 Minutes

THE RAGE BEGINS

Double KB Jerk	5 x 3	2:30 rest interval
Double KB Dead Clean	5 x 3	2:30 rest interval
Double KB Long Cycle Swing	5 x 8	2:30 rest interval
Double KB Rack Squat	5 x 3	2:30 rest interval
Single KB Deadlift	5 x 5 each leg	

BIG BOY

Vintage DB Clean	75lbs	x 5 reps each
DBL KB Rack Squat	32Kg	5 x 5 reps
Single KB Swing	40Kg	5 x 10 reps
Single KB Jerk	32Kg	5 x 5 reps each
DBL KB Sumo Deadlift	40Kg	5 x 10 reps
KB Crush		5 x 10 reps
Rope	Slams / Twisting Slams	

*All 5 sets on the minute

All level 1 training is directed towards execution of perfect technique. Resistance should be light to moderate

KETTLEBELL WORKOUT: Level 2 Basic Programs

SEA DOG

Turkish Get-Up	x 5 reps each arm 30 seconds rest intveral
Single KB Long Cycle Swing	x 15 reps each arm 30 seconds rest intveral
Windmill	x 5 reps each arm 30 seconds rest intveral
Single KB Get-Up Sit-Up	x 5 reps each arm 30 seconds rest intveral
Renegade Row	x 20 reps 2 minute rest interval
Double KB Dead Clean + Squat + Press	x 5 reps
Rest 2 minutes and repeat 1-2 times	

FINISHER

Turkish Get-Up	x 5 reps each arm
Windmill	x 5 reps each arm

DOUBLE TROUBLE

Double KB Rack Squat	5 x 5 60 seconds rest interval
Double KB Dead Clean	5 x 3 60 seconds rest interval
Double KB Long Cycle Clean + Press	5 x 3 60 seconds rest interval
Double KB Single Leg Deadlift	5 x 5 each leg 60 seconds rest interval
KB See Saw Press	5 x 5 each arm 60 seconds rest interval
Double KB Sumo Deadlift	5 x 5 60 seconds rest interval
Double KB Dead Clean + Squat + Press	5 x 3
Each exercise is executed for 5 sets	
Rest 60 seconds then move to next exercise	

WALK THE PLANK

Vintage DB Sweep	5 x 5 each arm 60 seconds rest interval
Double KB Dead Clean	5 x 5 60 seconds rest interval
Single Vintage DB Clean	5 x 5 each arm 60 seconds rest interval
Double KB Dead High Pull	5 x 5 60 seconds rest interval
Single KB Deadlift	5 x 5 each leg

60 seconds rest through the entire workout

BEDROCK

- KB Dead Swing	x 5 reps
- KB Sumo Deadlift	x 5 reps
- Double KB Long Cycle Swing	x 10 reps
30 seconds rest interval	
- Single Arm KB Get-Up Sit-Up	x 5 reps each arm
- Chest Pass 1/2 Get-Up	x 10 reps
- Russian Twist	x 20 reps
30 seconds rest interval	
- Single Arm KB Dead Clean + Press	
1. 1 Right - 1 Left	
2. 2 Right - 2 Left	
3. 3 Right - 3 Left	
30 seconds rest interval	
- Wave Squat	x 5 reps
- Single KB Pry Squat	x 5 reps
- Single Leg KB Deadlift	x 5 reps each leg
Level 2 should be executed with moderate resistance.	

KETTLEBELL WORKOUT: Level 2 Anaerobic Emphasis

NASCAR		
Single KB Long Cycle Swing	x 10 reps	
Jump Rope	30 seconds	30 seconds rest interval
Figure 8	x 10 reps	
Jump Rope	30 seconds	30 seconds rest interval
Single KB Dead Clean + Press	x 5 reps each arm	
Jump Rope	30 seconds	30 seconds rest interval
Double KB Rack Squat	x 10 reps	
Jump Rope	30 seconds	30 seconds rest interval
Single KB Long Cycle Snatch	x 5 reps each arm	
Jump Rope	30 seconds	30 seconds rest interval
See Saw Press	x 10 reps	
Jump Rope	30 seconds	

* *Perform 3 sets of each sequence then rest*
* *After 30 seconds rest move to next sequence*

COUNTY FAIR
Double KB Row
Double KB Rack Squat
Double KB Long Cycle Dead Clean
Double KB Sumo Deadlift
Lat Pulldown
Seated Low Row
Double KB Press
Barbell Biceps Curl
Pull-Up
Double KB Dead Clean + Rack Squat

30 seconds on 30 seconds off - Perform 3 Rounds

Level 2 should be executed with moderate resistance.

KETTLEBELL WORKOUT: Level 2 Heavy Resistance

DIRTY DOZEN

Turkish Get-Up	x 5 reps each arm	2:00 rest interval
Barbell Get-Up Sit-Up	x 12 reps	2:00 rest interval
Renegade Row	x 8 reps each arm	2:00 rest interval
Seated See Saw Press	x 10 reps	2:00 rest interval
Med Ball Pike	x 30 reps	2:00 rest interval
Overhead Barbell Squat	x 10 reps	2:00 rest interval
Double KB Hold	x 45 seconds	2:00 rest interval
Super Plank + Floor Dip	x 15 reps	2:00 rest interval
Outlaw Swing	x 15 reps	2:00 rest interval
Russian Twist	x 50 reps	2:00 rest interval
Landmine	x 20 reps	2:00 rest interval
Cossack	x 30 reps	

Repeat twice

HIGH SEAS

Single Arm KB Long Cycle Snatch	x 5 reps each arm	2:00 rest interval
Double KB Jerk	x 5 reps	2:00 rest interval
Double KB Hold	x 45 seconds	2:00 rest interval
Turkish Get-Up	x 5 reps each arm	2:00 rest interval
Windmill	x 5 reps each arm	2:00 rest interval
Double KB Get-Up Sit-Up	x 12 reps	2:00 rest interval
Double KB Long Cycle Snatch Hold	5 x 5 seconds each arm	

TOP DOWN GET DOWN (Total Super Set)

Double KB Press	x 5 reps
+	
Double KB Swing	x 5 reps
+	
Double KB Clean	x 5 reps
+	
Double KB Rack Squat	x 5 reps

* 2:30 rest interval between rounds. Execute 5 rounds

Level 2 should be executed with moderate resistance.

WAR DAY

Groups

Offense	Defense
A	F
B	G
C	H
D	I
E	J

1. Sled Pull	Line	Round 1	AF
Speed Obs.	Skill	Round 2	EG
		Round 3	DH
		Round 4	CI
		Round 5	BJ

2. Sumo Wrestle	Line	Round 1	BG
Free Tag	Skill	Round 2	AH
		Round 3	EI
		Round 4	DJ
		Round 5	CF

3. Board	Line	Round 1	CH
Sumo Wrestle	Skill	Round 2	BI
		Round 3	AJ
		Round 4	EF
		Round 5	DG

4. Escape	Line	Round 1	DI
Str. Obst.	Skill	Round 2	CJ
		Round 3	BF
		Round 4	AG
		Round 5	EH

5. Obstacle	Line	Round 1	EJ
Tug of War	Skill	Round 2	DF
		Round 3	CG
		Round 4	BH
		Round 5	AI

LINE COMBO FIELD

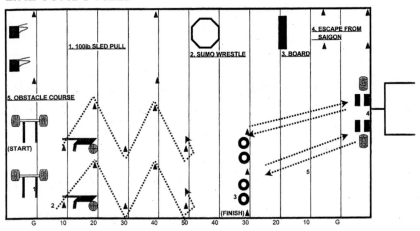

OBSTACLE COURSE
1.(START) Push Press, (155 lbs) 5 Reps, lockout each rep!
2. Wheel Barrow run (250LBS), zig zag around each cone, and return to original start, then run to Pinch grip.
3. Pinch grip plates (45lbs) to goal post.
4. Throw two sand bags and one keg over the goal post
5. Pinch grip plates back to their starting spot. (FINISH LINE)

SKILL FIELD

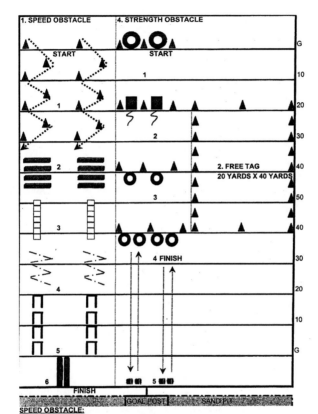

SPEED OBSTACLE:
1.(START LINE) Sprint through cones (zig zag), then sprint to bags
2. Run through the bags, then run to the ladder.
3. Run through the ladder (one foot in each hole), then head to the barb wire.
4. Crawl under the suspended rope, then head to the hurdles.
5. Hop over the hurdles, then sprint to the gauntlet.
6. Run through the dummies, **(FINISH LINE).**

STRENGTH OBSTACLE:
1.(START LINE) Tire flip to cones, then go to the sleds.
2. Drag the sled backwards to the next set of cones.
3. After the sled drag, push the plate (45 lb) by bear crawling to the next set of cones.
4. Pinch grip the plates (45 lb) to the moveable goal post.
5. Toss 2 medicine balls (20 lb each) over the goal post.
6. Pinch grip plates back to their starting spot. **(FINISH LINE).**
* NOTE, BOTH OBSTACLE COURSES ARE APPROX. 7-10 YARDS IN WIDTH AND 100 YARDS

GRIDIRON GRIND 2010
Team Points – 1st – 4, 2nd – 3, 3rd – 2, 4th – 1

1. 60-yard Dash (Walk-on Linemen) - Each team designates one walk-on lineman to race.

2. Mile Relay (Track) - Each designates four men to run 400 meters and successfully pass a baton to a teammate.

3. 800 Meter Run - Each team designates one man to run 800 meters

4. 300 Yard Shuttle - Each team designates one skill, one combo and one line player to run two 300-yard shuttles in 25-yard increments back to back. All of the skill players run the qualifier in 62 seconds. After a 30-second rest, they race to determine the winners.

   The qualifier for the combo is 67 seconds and for the line it is 72 seconds. Any player who does not make the qualifying time is disqualified. Any player who fails to touch the line with their foot on either rep is disqualified.

5. Sled Race - Each participant must pull a sled with a 35-pound plate and pinch grip two red plates 80 yards. The winners will be the first to get the sled and plates over the line. Each team designates one participant.

6. Bear Crawl with Soccer Ball - Each team designates one participant to bear crawl and push a soccer ball with his head or face eighty yard through a chute of cones into a basket. At no time can the player use his hands.

7. Junk Relay - Each team designates four players to carry all junk from Point A to Point B to Point C to Point D. Each man is responsible for his segment of the relay. All junk across Point D wins.

8. 300 Yard Race - Each team designates one skill, one combo and one line player. They run a qualifier rep followed by the race. There is a 30-second rest between reps. The qualifier times are 52 for skill, 57 for combo and 62 for line. The first four players place.

9. PVC Pipe Relay - Each team designates four players to deliver a 10-foot PVC pipe filled with water to the next man. Each man travels 50 yards and passes it off to his teammate.

10. Human Relay - Each team designates three athletes (two racers and a dead guy). One man piggy backs another 30 yards. They pick up the dead guy and carry him back. The opposite man piggy backs the partner back through the finish (the original location of the dead guy).

FINISH

Tug of War - Each team designates six players. There are quarterfinals, semifinals and finals to determine the winner.

CHAPTER TEN

PREPARED TO COACH

There are some very specific requirements and vital categories of physical, mental and spiritual investment necessary to maximize one's total potential. You must possess knowledge and foresight in several important educational domains and also provide yourself the latitude to adjust on the run in order to achieve what we might refer to as deliberate coaching. Remember from the research from Anders Erickson that you have the power to provide your athletes with the proper protocol for them to overcome what was once a limiting falsehood of genetic perspective. It is your responsibility to educate yourself at the highest level and conjointly acquire the communication skills to establish rapport and respect from those you hope to push toward excellence.

In looking specifically at the collegiate football player, the first consideration must be the total time available for developmental training. That time would be further broken down to developmental mandatory training. We would then consider periods that might be referred to as maintenance. We used to refer to breaks in the schedule or periods following a training cycle as active rest. Never assume that any non-mandatory period is "active". Active, in my vocabulary, is when the athlete is being coached. Without a deliberate, master coach, the athlete will exist in a disadvantageous state.

If you don't believe that a coach can take an athlete places that they will never go alone, you probably don't believe in yourself as a coach. You should also keep in mind that most people seek pleasure and avoid discomfort. That's why they must be supervised. Military organizations have this thing called boot camp. The objective is to provide a level of training and tempo that would be totally unimaginable to someone who would attempt it without supervision. If you are not coaching at that level, then you are probably not coaching. I'm not advocating that you have to be a drill sergeant. I am advocating that your style of conveying professional knowledge must be effective and time efficient. Coaching loud doesn't necessarily mean you are coaching smart. I've witnessed my share of clamorous stupidity in the profession. Save the impassioned instruction for the right moments. It will be more effective.

The first aspect we want to look at is the actual developmental training time. There are basically two training phases each year that might be classified as developmental. One is the winter from mid-January until the week before spring break, and the other is the summer training session starting nine weeks out from reporting date. Redshirts, of course, are in a developmental phase throughout the entire in-season. It is important that every athlete is made aware of the small number of opportunities available to optimize performance. Development should start from a solid foundation and take a steady vertical progression so that it is a true building process. At no time do we want to slip into a state of regression. Sometimes it is inevitable due to injury, but it should never occur as a result of excessive lag time or lack of effort. Discretionary time is challenging enough.

Essentially, the collegiate player within a semester system has six-and-one-half significant developmental periods leading up to the final season of their collegiate career. If they redshirt, they gain a training cycle during the in-season phase which extends to somewhere between 12 and 14 weeks. This is a great time to teach technique and establish a level of foundational strength in large muscle groups. It also provides an opportunity to establish sprint posture, balance of strength in the joint areas and core integrity. This will be their one and only extended training cycle without interruption. It is obvious that most strength and conditioning coaches would favor every athlete redshirting to take advantage of that developmental phase.

One of the most important characteristics of the strength and conditioning program is congruity across the board with coaching points. Every coach in the room has to be coaching the same primary teaching cues and using the same progression in conveying that information. It's amazing to me to see how many different ways an exercise might be taught. Over the last thirty years I've attended countless clinics and conferences, and many of these gatherings included methods of teaching the basic dynamic multi-joint free form movements. When you lead a program, you need to make a commitment to an exercise menu and a teaching process to accompany every exercise in that menu. If you ever lifted heavy weights somewhere in your life for any extended period and had success gaining strength ("clean"), you probably have insight. Remember, collegiate athletes are "clean". They are tested frequently.

I don't give a whole lot of credence to the ways and means of individuals who try to sell methods of training that are effective in a totally different environment with totally different rules. They have no time restrictions, no phase duration restrictions, no consideration toward training groups of thirty people and no clue about training people who might not enjoy lifting weights. They are also usually selling a product. I've listened to fitness gurus, kettlebell hot shots, powerlifting phenomenons, Olympic lifting wizards, body building virtuosos, crossfit crackerjacks and headstrong hit advocates. I respect any of them who trained large groups of athletes and squatted at least 450 lbs somewhere in their career. Outside of that, I will probably limit myself to my own wisdom and take my chances. The bottom line here is that strength and conditioning coaches still struggle with recognizing each other without the underlying belief that their own method is better. I can live with that, as long as I have that same option.

Looking at developing strength for the collegiate football player, my experiences have been sifted down to basic beliefs that are the result of the direct observation of working with more than 3,000 players over my career, all trained at least a three-year minimum. Even at this point, I am always looking to learn. We all know that it's a dynamic profession. For example, that's why I recently changed our back squat to focus on posterior chain development and involve more total muscle activation. I chose to coach and test the power clean over a hang clean because I like anything that forces an athlete to bend and I like to eliminate the momentum from a previous repetition. I also believe that coaching points are more easily defined regarding body position because the athlete is forced to reset. I like the hang clean as a component movement option but not as a test. I still prefer a block clean on the alternative day in a four-day split. This is an exercise where we use a tendo unit to measure bar speed or wattage produced. Our program has been defined to the point where I favor double chain on the alternative bench day and box squat with band tension measuring bar speed or heavy barbell step ups on the alternate squat day. We also believe in overhead pressing movements. We have fewer shoulder injuries when we execute push press, push jerk and various forms of kettlebell presses. Some people might not want to hear that, but I believe it to be true.

To me, strength training progression is like when I decided to raise three acres of tobacco as a share cropper. Once the process started, I had to be relentless in my commitment and consistent in my approach. It was never easy, and I had to keep showing up. Once I started down a row I had to continue to work until I got through all three acres. After I initially pulled all of those plants out of the plant bed and headed for the field, there was no turning back. I was inexperienced and one day when I tried to drive the tractor I almost flipped it and killed myself. I had to be coached to be technically sound.

Farmer Spence called me every day at 4 a.m. to tell me it was a great day to work and to bring my sleepy ass to the field. I had to be on time and willing to work. If I neglected to do what was scheduled to be done, my field of tobacco would regress. If I didn't top it and sucker it, it would not respond and reach its potential. I had to stay at it. If I stopped at any time in the process, the yield would be quickly depleted. I had to cut it, spear it, hang it and grade it. Nothing could be excluded. After many hours, weeks and months of intense, unforgiving labor I produced impressive results. It was about sowing and reaping, a very simple concept.

I really don't care what your lifting program looks like; your athletes must show up and must work as hard as they can possibly work to produce results. They must be coached through every rep, every set, every day. I honestly don't think it's difficult to outwork people in 2013. There's an abundance of soft thinking everywhere you turn. Some teams will beat you with exceptional talent no matter what you do—talent and superior coaching can trump hard training. I hate to even think that, but I believe it to be true. On the other hand, an opponent with a moderate advantage in those areas can be taken down. If you learn to coach hard every day, all day, the same way for each athlete and each group, you will gain an edge. Someone told me that I was only as good as the staff I hire. That's not exactly true. It's my program and I'm on the floor to supervise it. The staff must coach it the way I want it coached. I don't expect anyone to coach my program with the passion I bring to it. That's not to say that anyone is not a good coach. It's just a fact. If you place your program on consignment and sit at the computer, you won't be there long. You will be passing out resumes. If you want a strong team, you better be in touch with the weight on that bar for each individual every day. They have to work and you have to work.

You can talk to other coaches and share information on methods of developing strength in large muscle groups. The methods are seldom the same. It's always been interesting to me that volume and intensity can be manipulated so many different ways and terminology can take on so many different meanings. I finally decided to write my own total program, or what some people these days refer to as a template. I refer to it as selective advancement. This means that we will advance our athletes selectively in every aspect of development.

Selective advancement is defined as a multi-track method of integrated training dependent upon frequent assessment of specific characteristics related to performance. Advancement is based upon proficiency specific to motor learning capacity, drill mastery, demonstration of strength and power, level of mobility and levels of conditioning. We are now beyond the realm of just football and moving into common components of multi-sport training. These would include the following categories:

1. Initial assessment and corrective strategies
2. Foundational strength
3. Hip rotary power
4. Methods of developing strength and power
5. Linear speed development
6. Multiple joint sequences
7. Mobility

8. Kettlebell training
9. Conditioning
10. ADR (acceleration, deceleration, re-acceleration)
11. Re-entry following injury

The system is built upon the premise that most of the athletes we train are similar in that they need total body power, mobility and the ability to run. I look at sports such as golf and swimming as special. There is a different type of specificity to be considered there. My recent certification by the Titleist Performance Institute was a wake-up call to the intricacies of training golfers.

I have also developed a category of special auxiliary programming. This would include such things as shoulder rehabilitation and rotary torso training specific to such activities such as baseball. Neck strengthening for football might also be included in this category.

The selective advancement program is also based upon the central peripheral model as discussed by Frans Bosch and Ronald Klomp. I strongly believe that specificity and overload are separated. When the overload is high, the specificity is low and when specificity is high, overload is low. Sports specificity, in my opinion, is related to movement and specific skills and has limited variance within the strength training component. Developing total body strength is necessary to every sport, and as such it is similarly prescribed. There is a continuum from overload to specificity whereby all training methods might be located. The position-specific movements for football would be found very close to sport specificity. On the other hand, the back squat is a necessary component in optimizing performance, but has little connection within sport specificity. It is a foundational tool considered to be overload.

Within the system of selective advancement are a number of levels of development and or mastery. For example, in the category of lower body strength, we progress from Body Squat as a choice in Level 1 to Box Squat with Bands in Level 4. In the category of explosive hip rotary power, Jump Shrug would be listed in Level 1 and Double Kettlebell High Pull to Snatch Combo would be listed in Level 4.

Also within the system is a category named methods of Strength and Power Development as applied to the primary lifts. Listed in the Level 1 is a basic three week mini-cycle. Level 3 would include a max-effort rotating mesocycle. The linear speed template includes three technical levels and four power levels. Hopefully, you are beginning to get the picture. The other areas of selective advancement in the program are the multi-jump sequences, Mobility 1,2 and 3, three categories of kettlebell training with associated levels and conditioning categories and associated levels. This total program is what makes the most sense to me after close to thirty years of study.

Not every athlete has the same level of motor learning capacity, but those who are slower to pick up on the program might have exceptional explosive attributes. Willie Parker couldn't perform a drill to save his life, but he could put holes in the ground when he ran. Many of our football players might not graduate from Mobility 1 but might still excel at football-specific movement. The goal is to progress every athlete in each category with the intention of reaching his optimal potential. It is the closest you can get to comprehensive programming coupled with individualization. It is also another method of discovering weakness and strengths.

As to the process, upon reporting the freshmen are screened through what we refer to as a corrective strategies assessment. Through this process we determine if an individual is deficient in upper and lower body strength, shoulder stability and mobility, hip mobility, running mechanics, core strength and conditioning. This is about a three-day process. We then have a multi-track system through the second session of summer school whereby we aggressively target weaknesses and begin to make some degree of progress through corrective strategies. Most importantly, the athletes get a clue and an awareness toward the plan they must follow to eventually develop at the optimum level. That being said, let's not forget that every athlete must develop strength as a prerequisite to optimizing power and the correct optimization of power to maximize speed. This summer, I had some freshmen who couldn't rack a clean, couldn't overhead squat, couldn't hold a glute bridge or plank and couldn't run without casting the foreleg. There needs to be a strategy of correction for all of those issues.

One of the possibilities here could be referred to as needs-based programming. For example, the winter training program might include several groups with specific objectives. Group one would be the general group with primary objectives and no athletes with specific issues. Group two objectives would be body fat reduction, anaerobic fitness and core strength. Group three objectives would be to maximize lean mass. Group four objectives would be to optimize speed. Group five objectives would be to optimize flexibility. This dictates that within each training group you have multiple sub groups. If you have sound organization skills, you can make it happen. It's a ton of pre-planning and coaching, but I've found it to be worth the effort. Any time you can design and implement programs that address individual issues it reflects a deeper knowledge of your athletes and a commitment to enhancing performance. For all you coaches who sign those "five stars" with genetic perfection as they walk through the door, I hope you don't find this chapter to be too humdrum.

The next consideration in the total program, which is always my number one consideration, is speed. Enough has been said to provide a perspective of methodology, or you might even say a 'template'. (I like that word). I think that it is important to closely consider what you are doing to run strong. Do your players look like sprinters? Do they have noticeable size and development in the glutes and hamstrings? As previously mentioned we changed our back squat to target posterior chain. We included the adductors and hip flexors in our strength training formula and we frequently utilize exercises that are movement-oriented to specifically target certain muscle groups. Posture and elastic response are superior training elements in the total package. We are also drill conscious in our approach, because we can avoid high force levels and high tempo on days where we look to refine technique. When we want an overload directed at a coordinated pattern, we utilize resistance. Drill work also serves to link strength with coordination. Over-speed or supra-maximal training in our program serves one primary purpose that I feel is particularly necessary for football players. We can eliminate anterior pelvic tilt and as a result eliminate swing leg block and other related issues. Football players do not "open up". Obviously, you must be smart about how you implement this type of training, since the jury is still out on its effectiveness. It forces proper hip position, and that's significant in my world.

Other major components of our speed program that have been effective are bounding and blending, contrast bounding with contrast sprinting and the utilization of the sand pit to develop joint strength. Tempo training options are an effective means of conditioning and also provide the link between loco-motor skills and conditioning.

Another area of emphasis in our program is improving the elastic response in the system. Anything you can incorporate into the program to enhance the stretch reflex is going to contribute to the overall explosive characteristics of your athletes. We frequently perform Olympic movements and component Olympic movements in our program to enhance the stretch reflex in the hip complex and emphasize triple extension. The results are undeniable. That has been my experience. The Olympic lifts improve rate of force, the ability to absorb force and kinesthetic awareness. The power clean is a tremendous tool for converting strength to power. You cannot load jumps incrementally, and that's why Olympic lifts are effective and necessary.

Adding band tension to the bar and performing what has been referred to as "dynamic training" with a low level of resistance and low repetitions has been used as a substitute for Olympic lifts. There's one major problem here. Deceleration occurs as a result of inhibitory mechanisms, because we stay connected with the object we are attempting to move fast. I am anxiously awaiting any research that might indicate to me that band tension eliminates deceleration.

A collegiate football team will have a number of individuals who struggle to perform a power clean properly. I'm all about an alternative for those less athletic individuals, who might develop wrist issues for example, because they can't rack a clean. The best alternative for those individuals who can't rack a clean is a snatch. Experience thus far is some form of a snatch. The box squat with band tension is my favorite alternative lift to a back squat because of increased eccentric load from the top and accommodating resistance.

Our multi-jump approach includes horizontal sequences, box jump variations, lower leg hopping and freeze jumps. For the sake of time and practicality we will use multi-jump training in a complex fashion. For example, we have utilized a block clean ladder together with depth jumps measuring wattage. We start with 90K on the bar and add 10K as each unit in the ladder progresses. The athlete executes two repetitions of block clean and supersets two depth jumps. If the athlete achieves a 1000W minimum, he moves to the next bar. We perform eight to twelve sets. When you train groups of athletes, you need to provide feedback whenever possible. Becoming more explosive requires training explosively. The scenario I just described provides feedback from the tendo unit and the height of the box achieved. It always provides a competitive scenario. If you want your athletes to move weight and jump with the intent to be fast as humanly possible, don't forget about effort. You need to believe that they are giving you 100 percent if you're going to have a chance to improve.

Kettlebell training is another means of explosive training, because all essential movement is generated with the hips. You can also use a variety of single or double kettlebell movements to improve anaerobic conditioning and systemic work capacity. This type of training also provides some very favorable options in your menu for injured athletes. The kettlebell swing teaches the hip hinge, which is an important component of many exercises.

My personal opinion of a total approach to training athletes is that you need to acquire as much knowledge of the activity as possible in order to optimize your training program. The specificity is in the movement patterns and energy systems and the combination of the two. Because of that factor, the training prescription reflecting specificity must include detailed movement patterns as instructed by the sport coach. A strength and conditioning staff with collegiate football playing experience is going to have a distinct advantage because of each individual's knowledge of basic fundamentals. If each coach has a background of playing different positions, the diverse knowledge will serve as an additional benefit. General movement pattern concepts such as a come-to-balance reactive sequence can have application to multiple sports such as basketball, tennis, soccer and football. Although the concept is general, there is a specific application to each activity.

Obviously, you need a sound program that is comprehensive, since you are considering every aspect of performance enhancement in your approach. The challenge is to effectively individualize within training groups. When you train collegiate football players, the challenges go beyond defining weaknesses and effective programming.

Let's look at some real-life scenarios and attempt to define some possible strategies:

1. Athlete A has been given a workout time and a weekly schedule. He reports to his first workout five minutes late. All twenty-four of the remaining members of the group witness his late entrance. What are you going to do?

    A. It's only five minutes. You tell him to be on time next time and don't do it again. It's only his first offense.

    B. You administer a physical punishment to the culprit in front of the groups such as push ups, up downs or bear crawls.

    C. You punish the whole group.

    D. You throw him out of the facility.

    There's not necessarily a correct answer. My preference would be to punish the entire group. Since physical punishment is not advised in any situation, you might just change the nature of the workout from traditional to military. P.T. style or possibly high-tempo kettlebell training. The workout needs to be a justifiable option. Any activity that involves an elevated heart rate is deterrent.

2. Same scenario as previous except the athlete has sickle cell.
    Quick answer:
    Don't punish anyone with sickle cell. Ever. End of story.
    Send them to the position coach to deal with the issue.

3. During the workout, you notice that someone is cheating you out of reps. What do you do?

    A. Accuse the athlete of cheating you out of reps and start the exercise over.

    B. Ask one of your assistants to secretly record his reps every set.

    C. Add sets to the workout for everyone.

    D. Count the reps for the entire group and add sets.

I prefer answer D, and I don't even mention that I caught someone skipping reps. My favorite exercise for a group rep count is barbell step ups. It is great for strength development and requires a high level of oxygen. There is no place to hide.

4. You have an athlete who refuses to give you effort during conditioning. Your head coach doesn't seem to be extremely concerned. What do you do?
    A. Look for a job. You're working for the wrong guy.
    B. Call the player in and explain the reasons he needs to be in shape.
    C Scream at him for giving no effort.
    D. Keep him out of the lift and make him run extra while the others lift.

I have invoked all of these responses many times. Unfortunately, your best answer is going to be A. Your life will be a lot easier with 100 percent support from the head coach.

5. The summer is voluntary. Someone doesn't show up. You are not permitted to report attendance to the coaching staff or physically punish the offender. What do you do?
    A. Keep coaching. Overlook it and don't make a big deal.
    B. Lower your standards so everyone shows up.
    C. Secretly call the head coach, who is on the beach in Key Largo.
    D. Tell the athlete he is not permitted to train unless he talks to a coach and you hear back from that coach.

This is a tough one. You are in a very bad place here. No one cares about this scenario but you. Should you throw your hands in the air and lower your standard? No, because you have integrity. The head coach is somewhere with an umbrella drink and the aroma of cocoa butter. You are the last guy he wants to hear from.

Your best option is D. Put it on the athlete. Don't contact anybody. That's against the rules.

6. You are discussing the winter conditioning in the football staff meeting. Your team has good chemistry and has a high level of team discipline. The challenge is that they are not particularly strong. What do you do when you are asked to provide input?
   A. You suggest Bobby Bowden's "mat drills," because you want to appear to be traditional.
   B. You suggest the old 12 station County Fair Circuit scenario.
   C. You suggest winter conditioning to be conducted in the afternoon so you win favor with the coaches who hate to get up early.
   D. You present an argument for investing as much time as possible for developing strength.

Most strength coaches would give you answer D. Why? Because right smack in the middle of an 8-9 week maximum training cycle, the staff is going to pound its team for an hour at 5:30 a.m. for whatever number of days they determine appropriate. The whole staff comes off the recruiting road and is all present and coaching during this process. Whatever number of hours you dedicate will be subtracted from the eight hours you are allotted each week. If you have four one-hour sessions each week, giving you a grand total of four hours that week to get strong. Some programs have also gone to afternoon sessions.

At Carolina, we did something a little different each year. One year, Brad Lawing suggested we do the old Florida State mat drill format that he had experienced during his time at South Carolina. (They borrowed it from Bobby Bowden). This involved three twenty-minute stations, one of which was the wrestling mat agility drill sequence. That sequence is highly regimented and coached hard. Any mistake requires a repeat. It is one hour of continuous high-tempo activity. It is meant to be challenging to one's level of conditioning and mental toughness.

Now let's think back to what we said about neural fatigue and try to envision the thoughts of the strength coach who is well read and trying to optimize the results of the off-season program. After all, some football coaches are going to want to see some significant strength numbers. When you start talking to them about neural fatigue, they're going to look at you like you have a third eye in the middle of your forehead. Another component of the "mat drill" approach is the daily evaluation of each player. The great-effort guys are recognized with a different colored shirt and the poor-effort guys are recognized the same way. We had a magnetic board where we changed the flex lines every day. We would put the best-effort guys in the front and the least-effort guys in the back. There was no question about who needed to be coached harder and who was a self-starter. There are a number of schools that still subscribe to this type of tradition.

The toughest program that I've been part of was at ECU when we had the County Fair Circuit. This was 10-12 stations with a duration of four minutes, each followed by four sets of 15-25 up-downs on a gym floor. Immediately after that early morning session, I had a lifting group of thirty players. No one complained. It was part of the process.

My personal opinion of what has become known as winter conditioning is that number one, you have to be smart. There have been deaths that have occurred during this process. Whatever the reasons, it just can't happen. From that standpoint, I think that continuing with what you do in your strength and conditioning program as opposed to "mat drills" makes sense. Remember, there are only two mandatory training phases.

If a team is undisciplined and has accountability and chemistry issues, I would suppose that any type of rigorous, regimented, high-tempo experience with the position coaches in their faces could be beneficial. One year at Carolina, we were conducting an afternoon ten-station circuit when a player went down. It was a frightening experience because he stayed down for a significant period of time until he was diagnosed and treated. It's a delicate issue. I've never seen anyone go down doing speed work. There isn't an easy answer to this question. We should be smart with whatever we decide.

7. You realize the implications of the strength and conditioning profession that impact your survival and longevity as a collegiate strength coach. What is your plan?

   A. Affiliate yourself with the head football coach and football staff. Be communicative. Be flexible. Be cooperative. If you hear and see things you consider to be totally uninformed regarding what you do, keep smiling and try not to be argumentative.

   B. Go out and meet some boosters. A lot of them are great people. They just don't like to lose. They don't realize how devastating it is for you to lose, but that's ok. It is almost impossible for them to really understand your daily experience with today's athlete.

   C. Pursue an administrative title. It provides you with no real level of security but it sounds good. We all know the only security is a multi-year contract and your only strategy there is to get a job, have one foot out the door and then negotiate. Sad but true.

   D. Try to outwork everybody you see and continue to educate yourself every chance you get. Delegate as little as possible to others around you.

Obviously, the answer is all of the above here. It's a tough profession, based upon winning and losing. Work hard, stay humble and treat people right. That's your best shot. Stay out of all the petty ego battles.

I have a rule where boosters are concerned. In fact, I have a general rule. If I'm out to lunch or dinner with someone who makes more money than me, I always pick up the check. Football coaches are rumored to be some of the cheapest people on earth. I'm not sure where it originated. I suppose they are hoarding their resources with the anticipation of being fired. I just don't want to be classified in that category. There are exceptions to everything; Ruffin McNeill would give you his last dollar. I don't want to make hasty generalizations; it's just hearsay.

8. You have just accepted a position as the director of strength and conditioning at a major university. You will oversee all of the strength and conditioning programs for every sport. What are the first three things you do?
   A. 1. Formulate and share your mission statement
      2. Meet with all coaches
      3. Review data on all athletes
   B. 1. Evaluate the current staff
      2. Evaluate the facility
      3. Evaluate last year's budget
   C. 1. Fire all current staff
      2. Hire your own people
      3. Test and evaluate all athletes
   D. 1. Discuss your methodology with the athletic director.
      2. Share your vision of the future growth of the facility.
      3. Meet with the compliance director to review all NCAA rules that apply to strength and conditioning professionals.

Although there are a lot of important things listed in every category, I would probably choose A.

First, I believe that everyone deserves an opportunity to maintain a livelihood. Give the current staff an opportunity to conform, if need be, to your style and approach. Make them feel comfortable so they can operate and adapt, free from anxiety. Most likely, just because coaches struggle with change, those individuals will search for other opportunities. I don't think anyone works productively in a state of fear and intimidation. I've seen coaches who walk around talking about firing people every day, and I don't find that to be motivational.

Hopefully, somewhere in the interview process, you have already discussed your methodology and vision for the facility with the athletic director. Those things should be part of the selection process. You should have also looked closely at the current staff, facility and last year's budget before accepting the position.

Every effective leader needs a mission statement. You need to know where you want to go and what you need to get there. You should lay it out in the first few days to the staff. That will also help the leftovers plan their destiny, especially if your mission is too lofty for their work habits.

If you are in charge of all sports, it will be very important for you to meet with all of the head coaches early in the process. They can provide the insight necessary to resolve concerns and define future aspirations for that particular sport. They need to know that every athlete is equally important in the total scheme of the program. You should give them some degree of input where the specificity of the training is concerned.

The most important information you will need is the data concerning the physical attributes of your teams. If there is no data, you will need to generate some form of initial assessment.

This will be necessary at some point in the early stages, whatever the situation. The validity and reliability of any testing beyond your own is often questionable. You need to know your athletes.

9. You are a young strength coach just starting in the business. You have a fresh degree in exercise physiology and completed an internship at the local wellness center. You landed a graduate assistant position at the local university. What is your future plan?

A. Attach yourself to the head strength and conditioning coach and learn the system of training currently employed. Ask frequent questions regarding any aspect of training in which you might lack a full understanding of the underlying rationale. Major in a few sports as you also gain an understanding of the full methodology.

B. Take a close look at every major category of training and find the very best sources of further education in each category. Put relentless effort into your weak areas. Be persistent in introducing yourself to the best resources, and don't ever take no for an answer. Stay in someone's face until they recognize your passion.

C. Start a journal and notebook. Sit down every day and write your thoughts and record what you learned. Keep any and all information about training processes that appear to be effective. You need a recipe menu in every category of training. Note any trial and error processes that you think had effectiveness. Observe interactions and communication styles. List coaching cues and always look for the "why".

D. Pursue multiple certifications and target the educational enrichment processes as specific to your personal deficiencies. I'm still seeking information at this point in my career because our profession is dynamic in nature. Training means and methods have endless combinations and there are always new ideas and developments. There are incredibly intelligent people in the profession.

E. All of the above. Bingo.

10. You have a player who has become a problem in your program. He is a locker room lawyer, doesn't show up for study hall and has to be personally coached through every workout to give any type of effort. You decide to meet with the head coach concerning this individual. His response is that e recognizes this behavior but he is in a bind because of the A.P.R. What can you do?

A. Drink alcohol.

B. Go on a long drive.

C. Seek professional counseling.

D. Come to the realization that here is yet another challenge to stack on top of the other factors that enable the athlete to exist in a submaximal state of training accountability. Learn all you can about the A.P.R.

Surprisingly, the answer is D. I get this. I really do. We want to graduate people and we want to closely track their process. I have a Masters Degree in Education from Bucknell University. I love education.

The NCAA manual explains the APR formula like this: "Teams that don't make the 925 academic progress rate (APR) threshold are subject to sanctions. Each student athlete receiving athletically related financial aid earns one retention point for staying in school and one eligibility point for being academically eligible. The team's total points are divided by the points possible and then multiplied by one thousand to equal the team's academic progress rate score.

"Example: A Division I Football Bowl subdivision team awards the full complement of 85 grants-in-aid. If 80 student athletes remain in school and academically eligible, three remain in school but are academically ineligible and two drop out academically ineligible, the team earns 163 of 170 possible points for that team. Divide 163 by 170 and multiply by 1000, to determine that the team's academic progress rate for that term is 959."

If you have a number of players hanging by a string academically and your program is on the precipice of sanctions, (which is not going to make your AD happy), you might have to "smooth over some discipline issues to keep bad boys in the boat." I never imagined the possible complexity in maintaining the discipline of a program when Bill Stewart was kicking my ass for that cafeteria incident in 1977. It was pretty simple then. Oh, well.

One of the ways we can capture the minds of our players so they learn discipline and remain eligible is to utilize everyone. Coach Davis didn't leave any stones unturned here, and he expected you to put some time into your comments about each player. The following list represents the areas coaches and other staff were required to address in detailed annual reports about each player:

Position Coach
1. Production on the Field
2. Football Specifics
    A. Knowledge of position
    B. Technique
    C. Ability to learn and retain
3. Football Attitude
    A. Practice habits

    B. Meetings (on time, take notes, ask questions)

    C. In early, stay late. Studies notes and videos.

    D. Video prep/ does extra

    E. Meets extra with position coach

    F. Helps other players (including freshmen)

    G. Positive/ negative influence

    H. Coachable

4. Contribution to special teams
5. Adds to the chemistry of the team

    A. Attitude (positive or negative)

    B. Enthusiastic/ upbeat/ eager/ self starter

    C. Selfish or team oriented

    D. Willing to help on scout team

    E. Positive influence outside of football

6. Areas needed improvement

Medical

1. Treatment and rehabilitation/attitude
2. Treatment and rehabilitation work ethic
3. Treatment and rehabilitation off season goals and responsibilities
4. Surgeries performed or needed

Strength and Conditioning

1. Work ethic (does minimum, does more than asked)
2. Attitude
3. Trust
4. Tough
5. Nutrition, diet and health
6. Leader
7. Commitment
8. Offseason objectives (flexibility, strength, weight reduction/gain)

Academics

1. Class attendance
2. Tutoring/ mentoring attendance
3. Areas of concern

If you can rely on accurate information coming from the trainer, academic advisor, strength and conditioning coach and position coach, you should be able to draw an accurate assessment of each athlete from this information. When you look at the number of ways you can fall short on game day, you need a very detailed, intelligent exigent strategy. I've never seen anyone more detailed than Butch Davis. He knew how to activate resources.

Being totally prepared to coach is going to require that you have a sound program and knowledge of your athletes. You need great communication skills and the ability to make thoughtful decisions. You also need thick skin and some degree of restraint.

One of the developments in the realm of social media that has totally astounded me over the last decade is the message board. I grew up in an area of the country and in a community climate where you didn't say negative things about anyone unless you were man enough to say it to their face. That was non-negotiable. If you wanted to talk about someone, you were going to have to be ready to defend yourself or be pretty sure that you were going to come out on the winning end of that deal. Even weak people had enough pride to fight you if you didn't respect them. You just learned to respect other people, plain and simple. It bewilders me that someone can anonymously post comments about people and have full-blown discussions directed toward the purposeful degradation of someone's character and reputation.

The most astonishing factor in the whole process is that the message board posters are usually erroneous in their contentions.

They twist information to inflict damage with no sense of restraint. The rationale for the behavior is that the object of attack is a public figure and is therefore fair game. To me, this is an explanation that just reinforces the theory that these people are envious because they've never been able to accomplish anything eventful in their own lives. Let's face it—you have to be leading a mundane existence to actually sit down and type anonymous shots at other people. Seriously, what type of person does that? The best thing you can say about them is that they are cowards. At least politicians don't hide their identity when they sling mud. Like I said, you will need some degree of restraint.

Let's talk about daily operations. As previously mentioned, you will at some point have a staff that was either already intact or you will have an opportunity to bring your own people. Whatever the situation, your leadership ability will be crucial to your success. Providing autonomy to a qualified staff is necessary, but you will also need to communicate some expectations so you can keep everyone moving in the same direction. Also, similar to your football team, you must recognize strengths and weaknesses and place people in an environment with responsibilities where they have a chance to excel. I use the following fifteen points to clarify staff expectations. I feel that these points serve to provide my staff with unity of purpose and to further define my style of leadership:

Employee Expectations:

1. Working hours are 6 a.m. to 6 p.m. These are the hours when athletes are scheduled to train. As a department, we have unique hours, because we have chosen a unique profession. If you choose to work out during these hours, limit your training to 75 minutes. If you need to leave the building for personal reasons

like lunch or errands, limit your total time to one hour. Inform another staff member where you can be found or how you can be contacted.

2. Work hours will change. Adapt.

3. Do not carry cell phones to training areas or the field unless you have some type of serious situation requiring you to be contacted. Athletes want to be coached.

4. Be on time and ready to coach your group or team. That means you should be in your area, ready to go at least five minutes before the whistle.

5. Obviously, social media is part of life. Please use your computer for work purposes. I understand that you will communicate with your family and friends. I also understand that we can all be more productive if we have daily goals to make us better coaches.

6. If you have a TV in your office, I'm assuming you need it for video related work purposes. I don't expect us to spend time in an entertainment mode during work hours. If you want to watch a soap opera, go to lunch somewhere where there is a TV.

7. If you are sick or need to sleep, take a vacation day. There are plenty available. Show up with energy and enthusiasm and be ready to work.

8. Find ways to help your team win. If they are not winning, brainstorm and try to find a way that you can help. Be a part of the solution.

9. Take care of your family. If you have an emergency, I will personally cover for you. If you need time, take time. Please make sure that everyone is aware of the time you need, so we can plan accordingly.

10. Be smart. This is a department that has a high visibility to everyone in the athletic department. We want the perception to be a workplace with high standards of organization, a clean work environment, and a serious approach. Be professional with your coaching demeanor. Encourage, interact and advise, but separate yourself from the athletes.

11. Be positive whenever possible. Think about lifting somebody up every day. You can find at least one person to encourage.

12. Adapt with your coaches so that they have some degree of input, but remain strong in your professional opinions that reflect the department. You are the professional.

13. I need to be aware of anything you do with a team that is outside our central methodology. There is a detailed system that we should be able to follow. Read it and use it.

14. Please inform me if you are considering another job or you have an interest in another job. I will be happy to help you either obtain the job or help you in matching the job offer. No surprises.

15. Loyalty is number one. Both ways, all the time. If I hired you, you can trust me. I will stand on the table for you. Remember the tongue is likened to the rudder of a ship. Use discretion when you speak.

Probably the most important aspect of a training program is your ability to put your name on it. For that to happen, you need to be like the individuals in Chapter six. One of those individuals is our current head football coach at East Carolina University. Ruffin McNeill has a tremendous commitment and allegiance to his alma mater. He has been determined to put all of the right components of a program together to accomplish a journey of long-term success. Coach McNeill is extremely approachable and cordial. He will no doubt be one of the most effective recruiters in the country, given the right circumstances. He brings future continuity to the table because of his passion for the university and the unique heart-to-heart style he brings to his interaction with people. He knows how to show everyone and anyone in the community that they are all important and respected.

There is a lot to be said for a steady stream of warm heartedness coming from a Division I head football coach. I don't see that as a common characteristic among most of the ones I've known. Most head coaches are reluctant to open up. I believe that faith should provide the level of confidence that leads to trust, and Coach McNeill has that faith. He was also a player who was more than happy to knock opponents in the dirt. That's just a wonderful combination of characteristics. Football is all about knocking someone on his ass and helping him up. Coach McNeill has shared some experiences with me that take me back to my own. His dad was also a coach. Like me, he had no choice in learning to be disciplined and competitive. Hearing his story really takes me back in time.

It was about 1966, and Wild Billy had finished his collegiate career and begun coaching at the high school level. One day when I was in about the fourth or fifth grade, my dad puts me in the car and we ride to the high school. The school is empty. We go to the gym. It smells freshly waxed to prepare for the school year. It's extremely quiet. You can hear the echo of every step taken. We approach the connecting rooms and my dad opens one with a key. It's full of boxes of reconditioned shoulder pads. We start opening them and begin to count and categorize each pair by size. Somewhere in the process I get distracted. I put down the pads and start walking through the locker room. I move down the empty rows and visualize one of those lockers as my own. I'm thinking about dressing for practice. I can see myself heading for the doorway to the field. All of a sudden, right in the middle of my vision, I hear, "Hey, hey, Jeffrey, we need to count these game pants." Ok, back to reality. "I'm coming."

After a few hours of uniform organization, we go to the field. That very distinct smell of freshly cut grass hits you, even in the memory. It's late July and you are dreaming football. It's one of the sweetest bouquets of life. Something you unconsciously savor. I remember my first year out of college, when I walked across some grass in August and literally felt physically ill because I knew it was over. It's like you lost a beautiful woman who you loved intensely and looked forward to seeing every day. All the energy you saved for her presence has to be spent otherwise. Some people really have a tough time with that. It's hard to explain how running and smashing into people calms your life.

That day at the high school, we walked around the field and checked equipment. Back then, tires were very popular for conditioning. It seemed like my dad always had a double line of about thirty tires. He also used bags and ropes and sleds and any other type of equipment that might serve as a conditioning station. He was gearing up for three-a-days.

After a day of squaring away the high school facility for the upcoming season, we began our typical journey home. In Western Pennsylvania, people socialized in taverns, and every road was lined with them—many positioned no more than five miles apart. Those places were a comfort zone for my dad. He enjoyed interacting with the blue-collar type people and talking with them about whatever was on their mind. Most of them knew him as Coach Connors, and so they would talk football. If he sensed that they needed anything, he was quick to help. A lot of them needed another drink, and he was always willing to buy someone a cold beer and listen to their comments, concerns or problems.

I was unaware at the time that through my dad's example I was learning to respect people and realize that there were diversities in the world. Wild Billy would find something good to say about everyone sitting at the bar, unless they were allowing that alcohol to cause them to be loud and opinionated. I always hoped that someone did not go that direction because I knew the result. Those types of people were the ones who made Billy wild. Once you got into a difference of opinion with the man, the conversation was inevitably going to escalate, and you were either going to submit to his way of thinking or get ready to throw hands. That was a scenario that I witnessed at least on a weekly basis for many years. Most people eventually submitted. Sometimes it got ugly.

One time when I was in seventh grade I was at a bar called Joe's and Josie's Tavern with my dad. Two bikers were arm wrestling, and I could sense that it was starting to annoy my dad, who was quietly enjoying a cold beer at the end of the bar. I could feel the storm brewing as I slammed down another orange "pop". (I've never heard of soda). He said to me, "When I hit the guy on the left, you run and hit the other guy low and take him down". I looked at those two dudes and was thinking to myself that the guy had to outweigh me by about 150 lbs. I was thirteen years old and wrestling in the 126-pound class at the time. I had all kinds of crazy thoughts going through my head. I was definitely considering that orange pop bottle as a weapon. I'm not sure what happened, but over the next fifteen minutes the two guys started talking to Billy and ended up buying him a drink. I think my father might have been testing me, but I will never know.

Another time, when I was in ninth grade, we were sitting at the Blue Diamond Grill with a guy who started talking to Billy about athletics. It was the middle of wrestling season, and the guy told us that he wrestled in high school before he went to Vietnam. I think at that time I was in the 138-pound class, and the Vietnam vet was about 165 pounds. As he got louder, my stomach began to churn, because I knew it was going to be game day. The next thing I know, my dad said, "My son will wrestle you". The guy answered, "OK, it's on." I was thinking this guy was going to have some flashback to the jungle and try to rip out my eyeball. At this point we were already walking back to the polka dance hall, which had a wooden floor. Of course we started on our feet, and I didn't know what to think. After about the third time the guy slapped me in the head, I decide to do something, so I swept his leg. We were still standing, but he was only on one leg. I hit him with a cradle while we were still on our feet, and I took him straight to the back of his head. The wooden floor resounded and the small crowd erupted. Billy was smiling.

I quietly shook the guy's hand, hoping that it was over. No such luck. The vet wasn't going to let it go because his pride was a little damaged, so eventually I had to arm wrestle him. His old man strength got me. Carrying that rifle through the jungle no doubt gave him grip strength. His honor was restored, and we proceeded to foster a great friendship for the next three hours. I think I almost overdosed on ginger ale and barbecued potato chips that day.

Experiences with my dad have caused me to think deeply about the hundreds of young men I've coached who never had one around. I remember one summer when we went fishing every single day. My mother was very generous in supporting all the "man" time I spent with him. She spent a lot of time alone because I was an only child. She knew that I was getting a first-hand education on the inside story of athletics and developing a unique set of people skills. Very unique.

One of the greatest things that ever happened to me was in 2011 when I joined my dad in the Pennsylvania Sports Hall of Fame. It was more about being in that group with my dad than anything else. All the endless hours that I had spent trying to be the kind of influence on others that he was to me became immeasurably worthwhile. Being able to get up in front of a crowd and express gratitude to parents and friends for all the ways they helped me bring something meritorious to the world was an honor.

And so it goes. Everything Wild Billy stood for was a manifestation of the principles I have espoused, the ideas that are fundamental to winning. Some of it was pounded in my brain during practice through my experience as his quarterback. Most of it came from observation. My father was more than a role model and more than a parent. He was animated, unyielding, fiercely competitive, single-minded and demanding. He laughed hard, cried hard, fought hard, and celebrated hard. He taught me what it meant to serve others. All I had to do was watch.

JEFF CONNORS COACHING TREE

JOBS HELD BY MEMBERS OF CONNORS' COACHING STAFFS OVER THE YEARS

POSITIONS HELD	UNIVERSITY/TEAM
1 Jay Butler	
Head Strength & Conditioning Coach	Tampa Bay Buccaneers
Asst. AD of Strength & Conditioning	Rutgers University
Head Strength & Conditioning Coach	Dartmouth University
Asst. Strength & Conditioning Coach	East Carolina University
2 Sonny Sano	
Director of Strength & Conditioning	Ohio University
Asst. Strength & Conditioning Coach	Virginia Tech
3 Jarrett Ferguson	
Director of Football Strength & Conditioning	Virginia Tech
Asst. Football Strength & Conditioning Coach	University of North Carolina
4 Kerry Harbour	
Head Strength & Conditioning Coach	Winston Salem State University
Director of Strength & Conditioning	Delaware State University
Director of Strength & Conditioning	North Carolina A&T State University
Asst. Football Strength & Conditioning Coach	University of North Carolina
5 John Williams	
Asst. AD of Strength & Conditioning	Baylor University
Head Strength & Conditioning Coach	South Carolina State University
Director of Football Strength & Conditioning	University of Kansas
Asst. Strength & Conditioning Coach	Oklahoma State University
Asst. Football Strength & Conditioning Coach	University of North Carolina
6 Aaron Walker	
Head Strength & Conditioning Coach	Elon University
Football Strength & Conditioning Coach	University of North Carolina Central
Asst. Strength & Conditioning Coach	East Carolina University
7 Tanner Kolb	
Asst. Strength & Conditioning Coach	East Carolina University
Asst. Strength & Conditioning Coach	University of West Virginia
Head Strength & Conditioning Coach	Waynesburg University
8 Brannon Simpson	
Head Strength & Conditioning Coach	Middle Georgia Junior College
Asst. Strength & Conditioning Coach	University of North Carolina
9 Tom Howley	
Asst. AD of Strength & Conditioning	Cornell University
Asst. Strength & Conditioning Coach	East Carolina University
10 Brett Gerch	
Head Strength & Conditioning Coach	Unviersity of Cal-Poly
Football Strength & Conditioning Coach	United State Military Academy
Asst. Strength & Conditioning Coach	University of Delaware
11 Tobias Jacobi	
Asst. Strength & Conditioning Coach	Elon University
Coordinator of Strength & Conditioning	Western Carolina University
Head Strength & Conditioning Coach	Kent State University
Director of Strength & Conditioning	Charleston Southern University
Asst. Strength & Conditioning Coach	East Carolina University
12 John Bush	
Head Strength & Conditioning Coach	Morgan State University
Asst. Strength & Conditioning Coach	University of North Carolina
Head Strength & Conditioning Coach	Austin Peay State University

13 Jennifer Jones	
Director of Women's Basketball Player Development	Texas A&M University
Head Women's Strength & Conditioning Coach	University of Arkansas
Asst. Strength & Conditioning Coach	University of Houston
14 Jeremy Cole	
Head Football Strength & Conditioning Coach	Rutgers University
Asst. Football Strength & Conditioning Coach	Rutgers University
Asst. Football Strength & Conditioning Coach	University of North Carolina
Asst. Strength & Conditioning Coach	University of Kansas
15 Blaine Kinsley	
Asst. Strength & Conditioning Coach	East Carolina University
Head Strength & Conditioning Coach	Peoria Chiefs
16 Wes Herlocker	
Head Strength & Conditioning Coach	Wofford University
17 Robert Tate	
Asst. Football Strength & Conditioning Coach	University of North Carolina
Asst. Strength & Conditioning Coach	East Carolina University
18 Andrew Klich	
Asst. Strength & Conditioning Coach	University of Miami
19 Emmanuel McDaniel	
Asst. Strength & Conditioning Coach	East Carolina University
Defensive Backs Coach	University of Akron
20 Charles Colburn	
Asst. Strength & Conditioning Coach	East Carolina University
Lead Strength Coach	MARSCO
21 Jay Andress	
Asst. Strength & Conditioning Coach	Cornell University
22 Steve Gisselmen	
Asst. Strength & Conditioning Coach	University of North Carolina

Special thanks to Tobias Jacobi for putting this Coaching Tree together.

29 - The number of Head Strength Coach positions filled by coaches who have worked under Coach Jeff Connors

31 - The number of Universities that have hired coaches who have worked under Coach Jeff Connors

2 - The number of Master Strength & Conditioning Coaches who have worked under Coach Jeff Connors

11 - The number of Post Season Bowl Games Coach Jeff Connors has coached in to this date

55 - The number of players Coach Jeff Connors has coached that have been elected in the NFL Draft, with 8 being selected in the 1st Round

16 - The number of Pro Bowl appearences earned by former Coach Jeff Connors coached players

15 - The number of Super Bowl rings won by former Coach Jeff Connors coached players

ACKNOWLEDGEMENTS

Many different people assisted with this book and encouraged me throughout the process of putting it together. I am grateful to Natalie Kozlowski and my wife Michele for spending hours typing the pages of the manuscript. Tom McClellan at East Carolina gave photo and editing help and Kevin Best at North Carolina also supplied photos.

Also, Chuck Young, John Lowe and the Rev. Stephen Harrison helped me find the scriptures that I used in the book and Jeff Foster gave his time to take photos for me and read portions of the manuscript.

Jeff Connors took over ECU's top athletic performance position in 2011 after spending the previous 10 seasons on the University of North Carolina staff as strength and conditioning coordinator and assistant athletics director, a title he was elevated to a year after his arrival in 2001.

His current assignment at East Carolina marks his second stint with the Pirate program after an earlier 10-year strength and conditioning leadership tenure with head football coaches Bill Lewis (1991 season) and Steve Logan (1992-2000). Connors' efforts helped produce five bowl appearances, three post-season victories, 15 National Football League draft selections and representation in two final Top 25 polls (9/1991, 23/1995).

The Pirates also gained a reputation as one of the best fourth-quarter teams nationally under Connors' conditioning guidance. In 1996, the ECU defense did not allow a point in the fourth quarter until the seventh game of the season, and in 1999, the Pirates outscored their opponents 102-56 in the final period. In 2000, ECU held a 94-57 advantage in the fourth quarter.

He is also credited for playing an integral role in the design and development of the Pirates' 22,000-square-foot strength and conditioning facility inside the Murphy Center, which opened in 2002 after his departure.

Connors joined his father in the Pennsylvania Sports Hall of Fame in 2011. He has been honored as a Master Strength & Conditioning Coach by the Collegiate Strength and Conditioning Coaches association (CSCCa). The Master Strength & Conditioning Coach certification is the highest honor that can be achieved as a strength and conditioning coach, representing professionalism, knowledge, experience, expertise and longevity in the field.

In addition to helping develop some of the top players in UNC's program, including Julius Peppers, Jason Brown, Ronald Curry, David Thornton, Kentwan Balmer and Hakeem Nicks, 73 of 77 all-time football strength and conditioning records were bettered during Connors' stay in Chapel Hill. Before accepting the East Carolina position prior to the 1991 campaign, Connors was the head strength and conditioning coach at Bucknell from 1987 to 1990.

Connors is a frequently requested speaker asked to present his strength and conditioning program and philosophies to clinics and conferences across the country. He was also a competitive powerlifter who won four state titles in powerlifting and held a ranking as high as fourth nationally by the ADFPA. Connors holds Level I certification in Olympic Weight Lifting by the U.S. Weight Lifting Federation and has had numerous articles published in Wrestling USA, NSCA Journal, Training and Conditioning Magazine and Bigger Faster Stronger Journal. A 1980 graduate of Salem (W.Va.) College, Connors was a starter at both quarterback and cornerback

After college, Connors served as a police officer in Palm Beach County (Fla.) for two years. Prior to becoming a strength coach, he coached high school football and wrestling at The Benjamin School in North Palm Beach, Fla., and coached linebackers at the Tennessee Military Institute in Sweetwater, Tenn. Connors and wife Michele are the parents of two children - daughter Kaitlin and son Beau.

CPSIA information can be obtained at www.ICGtesting.com
Printed in the USA
LVOW06s0925300815

452091LV00022B/1046/P